The
New Six-Point Plan
for Raising Happy,
Healthy Children

Other Books by John Rosemond

Teen-Proofing

Raising a Nonviolent Child

Because I Said So!

*John Rosemond's Six-Point Plan
for Raising Happy, Healthy Children*

*Parent Power! A Common-Sense Approach to
Parenting in the '90s and Beyond*

Ending the Homework Hassle

Making the "Terrible" Twos Terrific!

To Spank or Not to Spank . . .

A Family of Value

John Rosemond's New Parent Power!

Family Building

The
New Six-Point Plan
for Raising Happy,
Healthy Children

John Rosemond

**Andrews McMeel
Publishing, LLC**
Kansas City

09 10 RR4 10 9 8 7 6 5 4

Library of Congress Cataloging-in-Publication Data

Rosemond, John K., 1947–
    The new six-point plan for raising happy, healthy children / John Rosemond.
        p.cm.
    ISBN-13: 978-0-7407-6077-8
    ISBN-10: 0-7407-6077-7
    1. Child rearing. 2. Parent and child. I. Title.

HQ769.R7142 2006
649'.1—dc22

2006045858

www.andrewsmcmeel.com

ATTENTION: SCHOOLS AND BUSINESSES
Andrews McMeel books are available at quantity discounts with bulk purchase for educational, business, or sales promotional use. For information, please write to: Special Sales Department, Andrews McMeel Publishing, LLC, 1130 Walnut Street, Kansas City, Missouri 64106.

To Willie

Contents

Acknowledgments

Thanks to everyone at Andrews McMeel, and especially my editor, Christine Schillig, for all of their invaluable help and support over the years.

Thanks to my family, friends, and fans for their faith in me and for all the great material.

Thank you, Father, for everything, from the beginning, and especially for the gift of your Son. I only wish I'd known then what I know now.

Introduction

These days it seems that the more things change in parenting, the more they keep right on changing. Today's parents are trying to have wonderful relationships with their children. Our foremothers and forefathers did not, realizing that a child required leadership first, and that while the parent/child relationship should by no means be "bad," a parent could not provide proper leadership if the parent's energies were focused primarily on having a "wonderful" relationship with the child. Some things just had to wait.

Today's moms orbit around their children, dedicated to making them happy. Yesterday's moms were at the center of their children's attention, dedicated to teaching them to stand on their own two feet. Today's moms are trying to do as much for their children as they possibly can. Yesterday's moms were consciously trying to do as little for their children as possible, in addition to insisting that their children both do for themselves and do for the family (in the form of chores). Today's moms function as servants to their children for the term of their dependency, which is lengthening. Yesterday's moms functioned as authority figures, as dispensers of responsibility. Today's moms work for their children in perpetuity, believing that the best mom is the mom who serves best. Yesterday's moms had their children working for them by the time the youngsters were three, believing that the best mom was the mom who prepared her child for a life of his own.

Which brings us to today's dads. The new ideal in American fatherhood is that of being the child's best buddy. Yesterday's dad was an authority figure, a mentor. He taught his child magic tricks, how to ride a bike, use a hammer, train a dog, and the like. He and his child had fun together, but he was not his child's friend. He knew that parenting came before friendship, and that when the time came—after the child's emancipation—he could not be a good friend if parenting issues were still begging for resolution.

Yesterday's parents were married to one another. They knew, intuitively, that their relationship had to be stronger than either of their relationships with their children. In today's all-too-typical family, the parent-child relationship is stronger than the husband-wife relationship, which is a clue as to why so many marriages dissolve after the emancipation of the last child.

Yesterday's parents were attuned to the voice of common sense, which was why they did not complain that raising children was the hardest thing they'd ever done. For today's parents, the voice of common sense has been drowned out by a confusion of psychobabble, which is a primary reason why so many parents tell me that raising even one child leaves them emotionally and physically exhausted at the end of many a day.

Yesterday's parents took child rearing, but not their children, seriously. Today's parents are prone to taking both child rearing and their children much too seriously. The former attitude is essential to the healthy parent-child relationship; the latter is a form of self-oppression that drains all humor from the enterprise of child rearing and turns it into drudgery.

Why are today's parents having so many more behavior and school-performance problems with their children than did parents just two generations ago? It's simple, really: You cannot approach child rearing in two entirely different ways and arrive at the same outcome.

You will not encounter psychobabble in this book. It is *not* a book about the supposed psychology of the child. The term *self-esteem* is mentioned but once, in the third paragraph of chapter 1, and the reference is in passing. It is a book about how to strengthen a child for the world, which is where a child will need strength. That job requires that a parent be strong, as strong as the child will eventually need to be.

A father once told me he didn't discipline his child in certain ways and in certain situations because he didn't *like* to. I told him that being a good parent required that one sometimes do exactly what one doesn't like doing. Good parenting isn't about what a parent likes or doesn't like. It's about what a child *needs*, whether the parent likes it or not.

I've written this book to help parents get their feet on solid ground, their priorities in order, and their heads out of the clouds of babble. It's my aim to help restore common sense and a sense of humor to what is at one and the same time the biggest and most rewarding of all responsibilities.

Be forewarned: I'm trying to turn the clock back. As Paul McCartney put it, "I believe in yesterday." I am absolutely, without a shred of doubt, convinced that parenting was stronger fifty years ago than it is today, and that children were stronger as a result. I am also absolutely, without a shred of doubt, convinced that it is possible for today's parents to raise today's children in like manner.

Whenever I say this, it is inevitable that someone will protest, "But times have changed!" Yes, they have, but those changes do not require that the fundamental principles of parenting change. After all, today's world is a far, far different place from the world of 1787, the year the Constitution of the United States was finalized. But the Constitution's principles are as relevant today as they were two hundred years ago. Similarly, the parenting principles that guided yesterday's parents are as relevant today as they were then.

The problem is that many of today's parents have embraced new principles. These new principles have been pushed on our culture by psychologists and other "experts" for two generations now, time enough to see that they don't work. Fifty years ago, when traditional, time-honored parenting principles prevailed, children did their own homework. Today, Mom sits with her child while he does his homework, and she ends up doing much of it for him. Fifty years ago, a child talked back occasionally. Today's child is likely to talk back several times a day. Fifty years ago, children were mischievous—they tried to get away with misbehaving *when adults weren't looking.* Today's children misbehave whether or not adults are looking.

Believe it or not, it is still possible to raise a child who does his own homework, talks back only occasionally, and is nothing more than mischievous.

I wrote this book to help make that possibility a reality—for you.

The
New Six-Point Plan
for Raising Happy, Healthy Children

The Parent-Centered Family

Because I'm regarded as an expert on such matters, parents are forever asking me questions about raising children. These questions run the gamut, but most parents really seem to be searching for the supposed *secret* to raising a happy, successful child.

Quite a number of books have been written on that very subject, and we certainly haven't seen the last of them. But in the course of thirty-eight years of being a husband, thirty-seven years of being a father, and nearly twelve years of being a grandfather, I have come to the conclusion that the secret in question isn't complicated enough to merit a book. I can state it in one sentence: The secret to raising a happy, successful child is to give more attention to your marriage than you give to your child—a lot more, in fact. If you succeed at that, you will have given your child the greatest gift of all.

That's not what most parents expect to hear. They're set up for me to say something poetic about a child's need for unconditional love or something perhaps a tad more practical about building self-esteem. In other words, most parents expect me to say something child-centered. Instead, my answer has more to do with the health of the family as a unit than with any particular person in it. I'm saying that by ordering priorities properly within your family, you give your child or children the greatest possible guarantee of happiness. Don't misunderstand me on this point: I am most definitely *not* saying that you should take *better* care of your marriage than you do your children, or that you should love your spouse *more* than you love your children. I'm simply stating what was once obvious to people: A child's sense of well-being depends fundamentally on knowing that his parents' marriage is in good shape.

"Now just hold on there a darn minute!" someone is exclaiming. "I'm a single parent! Are you saying that I can't take as good care of my kids as someone who's married?"

No, I'm not saying that at all. The fact is, being a married parent and being a single parent are two very different situations. It is impossible to talk about both in one breath or paragraph. Therefore, I'm going to talk about them separately. First, I'm going to address children who are growing up in homes where there are two married parents. Then I will turn my attention to the matter of children who, as was the case with me for most of my first seven years, grow up in single-parent households.

"My Children Come First!"

A number of years ago, I conducted a series of parenting workshops for working mothers at Central Piedmont Community College in Charlotte, North Carolina. I began each series by walking into the room, picking up a piece of chalk, and writing *In my family, my children come first* on the blackboard. Turning around, I then asked for a show of hands from those women who subscribed to that principle. Hands shot up everywhere, and many of the women turned to one another and smiled and nodded as if to say, "Why, of course! We all put our children first and foremost in our lives, don't we?" To me, however, those hands and those unspoken exchanges of consensus reflected the degree to which we, as a culture, have misplaced our family priorities.

In the years since World War II, Americans have become increasingly and neurotically obsessed with the raising of children. Something that used to be a fairly commonsense responsibility has taken on the trappings of science. Along the way, child rearing has become "parenting," with all its high-pressure implications. In the process, children have attained a position of prominence within families that they do not warrant, have certainly not earned, and from which they definitely do not benefit (however much they may *like* it). In the families in question, children sit center stage while parents orbit busily around them. Within these child-centered families, the implicit understandings are (a) children are a family's most important members and (b) the parent–child relationship is the most important relationship within a family. Not surprisingly, the more child-centered the American family has become, the more demandingly self-centered American children have become, and the more frustrating, anxiety-ridden, and exhausting has become the task of raising them.

Countless numbers of parents have told me that the raising of children is the hardest thing they've ever done. Underneath this complaint I sense a paradoxical feeling of pride, as if these parents need the raising of children to be difficult in order to feel that they're doing a right and proper job. They seem to think that the more difficult child rearing is, the more energy they must be putting into it; therefore, the more devoted parents they are! It follows that parents who do not find the raising of children to be disproportionately difficult must not be devoting enough of themselves to the task. Being worn out is the modern badge of parenting courage.

Just two generations ago, however, parents did not feel child rearing was grueling in the least, and those parents seem to have done a fine job. I'm speaking of my parents' generation. I've spoken with many of these people about their parenting experience, and asked them to describe it. Their descriptions are remarkably similar. To a person, they've told me that while the raising of children was certainly a big responsibility, it was also fairly enjoyable. It was not generally marked with stress, frustration, worry, agony, or guilt. And remember, the typical parent of the 1950s was raising more children than is the case today. As one woman, in her nineties, said, "It was just something you did." She was by no means downplaying the significance of raising children. She was simply saying that it was but one of many responsibilities that one assumed as an adult. It did not dominate her life; therefore, it was not associated with stress. Because these parents kept the raising of kids in proper perspective, they were able to go about it in a fairly relaxed manner. They didn't orbit around their kids. Their kids orbited around them. In those not-so-long-ago days, the most important relationship in the family was the marriage. The marriage came first, and these folks wanted their marriages to last. Children were temporary visitors in the household. Yes, they were the most important visitors of all, but they were visitors nonetheless. One's spouse was not a visitor. When the children were grown and gone, the marriage was what remained (hopefully and usually), and to remain in good shape, it needed to come first always.

By putting your children first in your family, by putting your relationships with your kids in front of your relationship with your spouse, you guarantee your children will become manipulative, demanding, and unappreciative of anything and everything you do for them. You guarantee they will grow up believing they can do pretty much as they please, that it's unfair of you to expect them to take on any responsibilities around the home, and that it's your duty to give them everything they want and serve them in every conceivable way. Putting children first in the family further guarantees that you will experience parenthood as the single hardest thing you've ever done—at best, enjoyable in spurts. Worst of all, it guarantees the ultimate unhappiness of your children, because happiness is achieved only by accepting responsibility for oneself, not by believing that someone else is responsible for you.

The Life of a Cell

When I talk about the marriage-centered (or parent-centered) family, I often use the analogy of a cell. A cell is the basic building block of biological life. At the functional center of any particular cell, there is a nucleus that runs the show, so to speak. It is the executive authority within that cell. As such, it regulates the cell's metabolism, reproduction, and other essential functions. It also mediates that cell's relationship to its neighbor cells and determines what role the cell performs within the larger organism of which it is a part. Furthermore, as any biologist knows, if the nucleus of the cell is healthy and performing its role properly, the cell itself will be healthy and capable of making a positive contribution to its host organism. On the other hand, if the nucleus is not healthy, if it has been disturbed by disease or the invasion of foreign matter, it becomes less capable of performing its role, and the cell begins to deteriorate.

In a similar way, the family is the basic unit of social life. It is a social cell within a larger social organism called society. A family has a nucleus, too. In a two-parent family, the nucleus is the marriage. In a single-parent family, the nucleus is the single parent. If the needs of the marriage or the single parent are being met, the family as a system will be healthy, and each individual within it will be healthy as well. In other words, if the marriage is being taken care of, or if the single parent is taking care of her- or himself, the children will, in all likelihood, be fine. They will feel protected. They will feel secure. They will have a clear sense of identity, and they will therefore have a foundation upon which to build the self-assurance that they are competent, capable people who can handle what life is going to throw at them.

This means that in a two-parent family, the marriage must be held in the highest of regards. It must be the most important relationship within the family, even more important than any single individual within the family. The marriage created the family, and the marriage sustains it. The marriage preceded the children and is meant to succeed them. If you don't put your marriage first and keep it there, it's likely to become a mirage.

The preceding paragraph would be mere rhetoric were it not for the fact that one of the highest divorce rates is for people who are relatively new "empty nesters." This cannot be explained in terms of any one single cause, but I've spoken with enough of these unfortunate folks to know that for many of them, the raising of children slowly eclipsed their marriages. After twenty-plus years of "We exist because of our children," they could no longer find a reason to exist for one another. That is nothing short of very, very sad. Sadder still is the very real possibility that the consequences of endemic child-centeredness will be passed down from generation to generation.

Passing It On

A journalist once asked me, "When they become adults, what will be the biggest problem facing today's kids?"

I answered: "That many if not most of them, even those growing up in two-parent homes, are not developing a functional sense of what is truly meant by 'marriage' and, therefore, 'family.'"

Today's all-too-typical child is prevented from learning what marriage is all about by well-intentioned parents who rarely act from within the roles of husband and wife; rather, they act almost exclusively from within the roles of mother and father. This is, after all, the new American ideal, based in large part on the nefarious modern notion that the more attention you pay to, the more involved you are with, and the more you do for your children, the better parent you are.

I am a member of the last generation of American children to grow up in families where the marriage, irrespective of its imperfections, occupied center stage. Your mother was a house*wife*, not a stay-at-home *mom* who was in perpetual orbit around her kids. Even if she worked outside the home, as mine often did, the fifties mother did not arrive home from work bearing a load of guilt that she attempted to discharge by dancing as fast as she could in her children's lives throughout the evening until they finally consented to go to bed. She came home ready to relax, and she expected her children to help her relax by staying out from underfoot. When your father came home from work, he had no intention of romping with his children all evening, "rebonding" with them. He came home looking forward to spending a quiet evening with his wife, his intended partner for life. After dinner, Mom and Dad retired to coffee and conversation in the living room, and the kids, well, they found things of their own to do including their homework, which they also did on their own. They did not slink off into the Land of Unwanted Children. There were exceptions to this general rule, of course, but there are two living generations (mine and my parents') who remember that once upon a time in America, the husband-wife relationship was stronger than the parent-child relationship, as it should be.

"Come on now, John," someone is saying. "You don't actually mean *stronger*. You mean *as strong as*."

No, I most definitely mean stronger. Unlike today's mom, the mom of the 1950s and before was not married to her child; she was married to her husband. And unlike today's dad, the dad of bygone days was a husband first, and a father second, and he was most definitely not his child's best buddy. Under no other circumstances can children learn what marriage truly means and involves; and that learning is far more important than being an honor student or a star athlete, infinitely more important, in fact.

If you want more proof of why the husband-wife relationship should trump that of parent-child, consider this unarguable proposition: Nothing makes a child feel more insecure than the feeling that his parents' relationship is not on solid ground, that it might come undone at any moment. It follows that nothing makes a child feel more secure than knowing his parents' relationship, while not perfect, is strong enough to endure any hardship, any disagreement.

The primacy of the husband-wife relationship gives a child full permission to begin preparing for his emancipation. Most people think emancipation is an event that occurs when a child is in his early adulthood. Not true. Emancipation is a *process* that begins when a child is a toddler. It is the slow moving away from a state of dependency toward and into a state of self-sufficiency. The act of emancipation is nothing but the culmination of the process. The fact that the child is not essential to his parents' well-being—that their well-being is contained within their marriage—gives him full, unfettered permission to leave and venture out into a life of his own. A child's leaving home should be a cause for celebration, exciting and full of promise for all concerned. When the parent-child relationship is foremost, however, emancipation is difficult

8

for all concerned. Sometimes, the child is able to leave physically but not emotionally. At other times, emancipation takes the form of a painful "divorce" from which it is difficult for any of the parties involved to ever fully recover.

The greatest gift one can give a child upon his emancipation is not the keys to a new car or condominium, but the security of knowing that in the truest sense, he can always come home again—not to live, but to visit. I have spoken to many young emancipated adults who tell me that the greatest pain in their lives involves the turmoil they go through when trying to decide how to split up "visiting time" between Mom's house and Dad's house.

Sometimes, our own children tell my wife, Willie, and me how "lucky" they are that we are still together, and they know that we always will be. It's actually a slip of the tongue, because they both know that luck has nothing to do with it. It is a matter of keeping the natural order of things in their natural order.

Attention Deficit Disruption

By the time a child is three years old, he has come to one of two conclusions concerning his parents:

CONCLUSION NUMBER ONE:

"It's my job to pay attention to my parents."

CONCLUSION NUMBER TWO:

"It's my parents' job to pay attention to me."

A child who reaches Conclusion Number One can be successfully disciplined. Furthermore, his discipline will be relatively easy. A child who reaches Conclusion Number Two cannot be successfully or easily disciplined. This is so because the discipline of a child rests primarily on whether or not he is paying attention to his parents, and it is a fact that *a child will not pay sufficient attention to parents who are acting like it is their job to pay as much attention as they can to him.* Another way of saying the same thing: *The more attention you pay to your child, the less attention he will pay to you.*

The three-year old child who reaches Conclusion Number Two has acquired an attention deficit. Not attention deficit *disorder*—there's nothing at all wrong with him. Nonetheless, there will definitely be disorder in the house. His parents will say things like, "He doesn't listen to us," "We have to yell to get his attention," and "We have to tell him at least three times and get right up in his face, before he does what we tell him to do." Yep, he has an attention deficit, all right, but not one caused by a chemical imbalance or some malfunction in his brain. This attention deficit was caused by well-meaning parents who think good parents pay as much attention as they can to their kids—that the more attention one pays to the child, the better a parent one is. That is the prevailing attitude, and it has prevailed since the late 1960s, when the newly emerging professional parenting class—people like me, with capital letters after their names—let it be known that a child's psychological health was a function of how much positive attention he received from his parents and other significant adults. I know this to be the case because I beat this drum myself during the first six or seven years of my career as a psychologist. During two of those years, I was one of several psychologists who staffed a hotline service that parents could call to receive parenting advice from a real live expert. As you might imagine, the typical caller was a mother at the end of her rope about something. The child in question was pummeling a younger sibling, biting the dog, or doing something equally vexing. Meanwhile, Mom was climbing the walls. It was our job to calm her down and give her advice on how to solve the problem. It slowly dawned on me that every single person on staff was saying the same thing: The problem, whatever it was, was the child's way of communicating that he wasn't getting enough attention. The prescription was also the same: The parent needed to find more ways to give the child positive attention, to "catch him being good."

I also realized that the same parents kept calling over and over and over again. They'd assure us they were doing what we told them, but the problems just kept getting worse. Not considering for a moment that *we* might not be giving good advice (unthinkable!), we'd say, "You're not being consistent enough," or "You're giving more positive attention, but you're still giving negative attention, and the negative is canceling the positive," or something equally trendy and insipid. In any case, the assumption was that any discipline problem was the result of too little positive parental attention. The problem was the child's way of "crying for help." Discipline, especially punitive discipline, would probably make the problem worse. Praise and other "warm fuzzies" would make it better. I am discomfited to admit I once believed this malarkey.

I slowly came to the conclusion that too much attention creates as many problems as too little. I came to the further, admittedly radical conclusion that beyond infancy, children do not need much attention at all. They need *supervision* from parents who know where they are, what they're doing, and whom they're with, but giving supervision and giving individual attention are two different things. Children do need a certain amount of direct, one-on-one attention, but where the giving of attention to a child is concerned, one quickly reaches the point of diminishing returns. Let me help you digest this hard-to-swallow tidbit by discussing children and food.

Children need *food*. But they don't need a lot of it. If you persist in giving a child more *food* than he needs, that child will become dependent upon receiving excessive amounts of *food*. If you continue to feed that dependency, it will grow into an obsession that will function as a powerful, driving force in that child's life. The child's sense of well-being will increasingly be based on the idea that, in order to feel secure, he must always have ready access to *food*. Eventually, the child will become a *food* addict, and that addiction will hang like a stone around his neck, encumbering him in every conceivable way.

Now go back and reread the previous paragraph, substituting the word *attention* wherever you see the word *food*. Go ahead, I'll wait.

Quite revealing, isn't it? It is as absurd to say that children need a lot of attention as it is to say that children need a lot of food. Too much attention is every bit as damaging as too much food. No one would argue that it is part of our job as parents to set limits on how much food a child may consume. It follows, therefore, that it's also part of our job to set limits on how much attention a child is allowed to consume within the family. Many parents fail to set adequate limits on the amount of attention their children can expect to receive. So in many families, the children constantly interrupt conversations, want in on the action when parents are being affectionate toward each other, talk incessantly and loudly, and act silly. They behave as if all of life is a performance, and given the choice, they would rather be inside with a group of adults than outside playing with a group of other children.

I'm describing an addict, and the child who develops an addiction to attention stands a better-than-average chance of someday transferring that dependency to drugs, alcohol, or some other form of self-destructive behavior. At the very least, the attention-addicted child may never really grow up, may never truly attain emotional emancipation.

The Life of a Solar System

Earlier, I compared a family to a cell. A family can also be compared to a solar system—which is like a galactic cell. At the center of a solar system, there is a source of energy that nurtures and stabilizes it—its sun. A number of planets in various stages of maturity revolve around this central core of energy.

A family also needs a powerful, stabilizing, and nurturing source of energy at the center. The only people who are qualified to sit in that position of power and responsibility are parents. Their job is to define, organize, lead, nurture, and sustain the family.

Children are the "planets" in this system. When they are very young, they orbit close to the parent sun because they need lots of nurturing and guidance. As they grow, their orbits steadily widen. By their late teens or early twenties, they should be capable of escaping the pull of their parents' gravity and embarking on lives of their own. Our children's ultimate task is to move away from us, and our task is to help them. Allowing a child to bask in the spotlight of attention, however, encumbers his ability to establish greater and greater degrees of independence. A child cannot be the center of attention in a family and move away from that center at the same time. It's either one or the other.

If you put a child in the family spotlight, you create the illusion that he is the most important person in the family. That center stage position is cozy, warm, and comfortable, and the child who sits there will naturally want to stay, basking in the warm glow as long as possible.

That this has become a national problem is attested to by the fact that since the late 1960s, the average age of full economic emancipation has increased by nearly seven years, from twenty to nearly twenty-seven. Over the past thirty years, the percentage of twenty-two-year-olds still living with their parents has more than doubled, while the U.S. economy has been growing rather steadily. Furthermore, we now have something called "boomerang kids"— kids who leave home, fail to manage their lives responsibly (lose jobs, ring up massive debt, become evicted, and so on), and wind up coming back home to live with their parents. All of this tells us that today's children are having serious problems when it comes to something previous generations of children had no great difficulty with at all—emancipating themselves. It also tells us that the problem is not "out there," in the world. The problem is at home, in the way these kids are being brought up. Either we are clinging to them or they are clinging to us—or both.

One Is a Whole Number

Now we can turn our attention to the question of how all of this applies to a single parent.

Although I've never been a single parent, I am as qualified as anyone to speak on the subject of how to best serve the needs of a child within that context because I was such a child. My mother was a single parent for most of the first seven years of my life. During that time, she was a very interesting person in my eyes— one of the most interesting people I've ever known, in fact. She worked outside the home. She went to college and eventually obtained a Ph.D. in biology. She had a seemingly endless variety of friends. When she did her homework, she often took the time to explain to me things like the differences between animals with backbones and animals without. Sometimes she took me with her to the library, where I sat in awe of how quiet and still grown-ups could be. Sometimes I'd go with her and her friends to the beach or the movies. She did not include me in everything she did, but she included me enough.

Because she was *interesting*, I paid attention to her. I was fascinated by her. She did not orbit around me; rather, I orbited around her, and she made sure that my orbit was ever expanding. Through her independence, she encouraged mine. More than once she told me it was her job to make sure I could stand on my own two feet, which required that she not let me stand on hers. I do not remember her ever getting down on the floor and playing with me, but she encouraged me to finger paint and make armies of soldiers out of clothespins and castles out of empty oatmeal cartons. She also read to me at least once a day—usually at bedtime, in my *own* bed, in my *own* room—from children's classics like *The Wind in the Willows*. She was affectionate, loving, and I always knew I could rely on her, but it was perfectly clear that she had a rich life beyond being John Rosemond's mother.

When Mom was home, she was often studying, and when she was absorbed in her work, I did not have permission to hang around her. If I did loiter, she would look at me sternly and say something like, "You're underfoot. You need to find something to do, or I'll have to find it for you." I felt loved, but I also knew I had permission to be independent. Mom was always there when I needed her, but she was also quick to tell me when my need was not need at all, but simply unnecessary want.

In retrospect, I now realize that shooing me out from underfoot was simply Mom's way of letting me know she had a life of her own separate from being my mother, and that I had a life of my own as well. By not allowing me to become overly dependent on her presence and attention, Mom gave me permission to grow up and away from her.

That's exactly what the job of parent is all about. It's about helping our children get out of our lives. When I say that to an audience, some people laugh and some look shocked, as if I've just said something sacrilegious or obscene. But it's no joke, and I don't say it for shock value. It's the truth. When you strip away all the intellectual rhetoric and the flowery sentiment, you realize that the purpose of raising children is simply to help them out of our lives and into successful lives of their own.

It's significant to note that my mother never, ever gave me the impression that having no father in my life was an excuse for misbehavior, not doing my best in school, poor manners, self-pity, cruelty to animals or smaller children, or anger. I was responsible, fully accountable. When I misbehaved and tried to explain it away, my mother would look at me sternly and say, "There are no excuses; no ifs, ands, or buts." By virtue of not being allowed to wrap myself in a "my father doesn't care about me" soap opera, I was given permission to have a truly happy childhood.

Unfortunately, our culture no longer gives single mothers permission to be that kind of mom. Today's single mom is expected to feel guilty, not independent. She is expected to compensate for the supposed psychological trauma her divorce has imposed upon her children by orbiting around them, making them her life, which ensures that she will not have one of her own. She thinks she can validate that she is a good mom only by doing things for her children; therefore, she rarely does anything for herself, and even more rarely does she spend free time without her kids. She does not feel she has permission to discipline, because she thinks her children misbehave only because they are "angry" about the divorce at the same time they (supposedly) feel responsible for it, which (supposedly) makes them even more angry. As a consequence of the box into which our culture squeezes the single mom—a box with walls constructed of psychobabble—single mom–hood in America is not what it was for my mother. Instead of a state of relatively satisfying independence, it is confining, exhausting, and guilt ridden for all too many single moms.

When my mom came home after a day at work or of college classes, she did not come home feeling guilty. She came home feeling that she had accomplished what she needed to do in order to be the best single mom she could possibly be—put a roof over my head, shoes on my feet, and food on my plate. Today's mom, because she feels that every minute spent away from her child creates a psychological deficit, comes home feeling not that she has discharged her obligations, but that she is obligated. She comes home not feeling content, but feeling guilty. She comes home facing not an evening of relative peace and quiet, helped by a child who understands that it's his job to entertain himself, but an evening of parenting frenzy, at the center of which is a child who feels he is entitled to a mother who entertains him.

The single-parent trap is more likely to snare single mothers than single fathers. For a number of reasons, mothers are more likely than fathers to neglect their own needs in the course of meeting their children's. Mothers also have more difficulty making the distinction between what their children need and what they simply want. When single mothers have primary custody of their children, they usually feel that they need to compensate for the absence of a father in the home. In the process, they fall into the trap of overindulging and overprotecting the children and wind up stretching their emotional resources to the breaking point.

Look at it this way: You can't supply anyone else's warehouse unless your own is fully stocked. Instead of taking care of themselves well enough to keep their emotional warehouses full, today's single mothers often feel compelled to forgo their own needs in favor of their children's. They give and give—both emotionally and materially—to children who begin to take their giving for granted and appreciate it less and less. In no time at all, the children are likely to begin acting like demanding, ungrateful brats. Eventually and inevitably, the single mother's ability to go on giving collapses, and she vents her frustration on her children. Then guilt sets in.

"I shouldn't have gotten so mad at the kids," she says. "It's not their fault there's only one parent in the home."

At this point, our single mother feels compelled to do something special for her children in order to make up for having lost her temper with them. Then, it's back to business as usual.

In this continuing soap opera, the children are victims of circumstance and Mom does penance through self-sacrifice. Every time she gets angry at her kids, she ends up feeling like a bad parent. "If I could only control my temper," she thinks, "everything would be okay." But her temper is not the problem; rather it's her lack of *tempering*. To solve the problem, she has to learn to temper her own needs with those of her children. She must temper her giving to her children and begin getting for herself.

Compensations never work. Instead of solving problems, they eventually become part of them. A single mom must establish an identity that has nothing to do with her kids. She must allow the adult woman in herself to separate from her role as mom and get her needs met—social, vocational, and recreational. For her children's sake as well as her own, she must give herself permission to be creatively selfish. Only then will she have inventory enough to share freely with her kids.

As my mother used to say, "John Rosemond, you don't need a mother right now, and I'm not going to be one."

A single mom recently told me that because she had always wanted to learn to paint, she was thinking of enrolling her four-year-old daughter in art lessons. I suggested that she forgo doing something for her daughter and enroll *herself* in art lessons. Then perhaps she could turn around and teach her daughter to paint. She looked at me quizzically for a few moments, then smiled and said, "I get it."

I hope she's enjoying her art lessons.

The Real Meaning of Quality Time

The concept of quality time was coined in the early 1970s to address the anxieties of mothers who feared they were harming their children by entering the workplace.

"Not so!" announced the purveyors of quality time. "It isn't necessary to spend a *lot* of time with your children, as long as the time you spend is of good quality."

True enough, but your average American working mom takes that to mean she's obliged to spend every free moment giving her children large compensatory doses of positive attention. So after picking up the children from the day-care center, she goes home and flogs herself with the quality-time whip until the children go to bed, by which point she's too burned out to put anything of quality into the marriage. If Dad joined in the fun, he's burned out, too. If he didn't, he's either too numb from watching television or too stressed out from working on stuff he brought home from the office to be much of a husband.

I'm thinking about a young couple whom I once saw concerned about their four-year-old daughter's apparent need always to be the center of attention. These parents were besieged by a steady stream of disruptions and interruptions, all of which were variations on the theme of "Look at me!" If they didn't immediately attend to their daughter's demands, she began whining. If that didn't bring results, she'd begin jumping up and down, flapping her hands, and crying—an absolutely ludicrous sight, to be sure, but one that can be frightening, especially for inexperienced parents.

These parents, both of whom worked, felt trapped between a rock and a hard place. On the one hand, even though their daughter was in one of the best preschool programs in the city, they felt their dual careers were depriving her of much-needed time and attention. Her constant demands for attention, they theorized, were expressions of insecurity. Unfortunately, these dual careers were not a luxury. At this point in their lives, they were an economic necessity. "What can we do?" they asked.

"First," I said, "tell me what you're already doing."

"Well," said the wife, "when we get home, we more or less devote ourselves to our daughter. We play with her, read to her, and take her for walks—that sort of stuff. After being away from us all day, we feel she deserves to have us all to herself."

"Stop right there," I said. "I think we've located the problem."

I proceeded to tell this young couple about some friends of mine, both of whom have careers. They also have two school-age children. After school, the kids are transported to a day-care center, where they stay until shortly after five o'clock, when their father picks them up and brings them home.

Several years ago, my friends created a rather unusual rule: For thirty minutes after everyone gets home, the children are not allowed in the den, kitchen, or any other room where their parents happen to be. They can play in their rooms or, weather permitting, go outside. The parents take this time to unwind and talk as they prepare the evening meal.

Until they created the thirty-minute rule, my friends had felt obliged to devote themselves to their children throughout the entire evening. The more attention they gave the children, however, the more demanding, self-centered, disrespectful, and disobedient the children became. Eventually, my friends realized that the kids had taken over the family. In pursuit of good parenting, they'd created monsters!

Realizing that their relationship with each other was more important than their relationship with their children, they moved their marriage back to center stage in the family. The thirty-minute rule was one of many major policy changes. After everyone had arrived home in the evening, my friends set the stove timer for thirty minutes and directed the children to find things to do. When the children tested the new rule, the parents refused their requests and sent them packing, firmly but gently. For the first few weeks, as soon as the kids heard the timer go off, they'd race into the kitchen, eager to get some parental attention. As time passed, the interval between the buzzer and the children's appearance began to lengthen. Eventually, setting the timer became unnecessary. The children came home and found things to do until supper. After the meal, they'd return to their play until nearly bedtime, when they'd ask for a story and a proper tucking-in.

I would describe these children as independent, secure, outgoing, happy, mature, playful, obedient, and polite. Their parents cured them of their addiction to attention by putting the marriage first. In so doing, they defied a whole set of "shoulds" that operate in many if not most two-career families.

The little girl's parents were sufficiently impressed by my story to try my friends' technique. I lost touch with them for about six months and then happened to run into them in a shopping center. They apologized for not having gotten back in touch with me but said there hadn't been a need. As we exchanged pleasantries, I could tell that things were different in their family. For one thing, the little girl stood quietly next to her parents without interrupting our conversation.

"We tried the thirty-minute rule," they said, "and it worked! These days, after we all get home, Julie takes responsibility for entertaining herself. We talk during dinner, but afterward she finds things to do until it's time for bed. At that point, we spend about thirty minutes reading and talking until lights out. We're all a lot happier these days." Looking down at her daughter, this young mother asked, "Aren't we, Julie?" Julie looked up, first at her mother, then at me. Smiling, she nodded and gave me a great big hug.

I love happy endings, don't you?

More Quality Time

Here are several more ways of making quality time for the marriage as well as helping children understand that Mom and Dad's relationship is Numero Uno. Single parents, these apply to you, too!

• Don't allow children to interrupt your conversations. Make them wait their turn, preferably in another room. Say, "We'll let you know when we're finished talking." A child who simply "can't wait" probably needs five minutes of cool-down time in his room.

• Create a weekly "Parents' Night Out" and don't let anything except acts of God interfere with the commitment. Every now and then, go off for a weekend without the kids. They need to realize that the marriage is a separate and autonomous entity in the family with a life and needs of its own.

• Put the children to bed early. Remember that your children's bedtime is for your benefit. In other words, determine how much downtime you need in the evening during which you have no child-rearing responsibilities and set bedtimes accordingly. Instead of putting children to bed when they're ready, put them to bed when you're ready. Then hang up your roles as mom and dad and just be husband and wife. I've always felt that eight is late enough for preschoolers; eight-thirty for children of grade-school age. I recommend that older children be in their rooms no later than nine, particularly on school nights. If children are willing to "make themselves invisible," it's all right if they read or work on hobbies until a slightly later lights-out.

• Once the kids are in bed, reduce distractions that interfere with communication and intimacy. Agree not to do either housework or office work after the kids' bedtime. Spend this time getting back in touch with the feelings that led to your original commitment. In this regard, the worst possible, and least creative, thing you can do is get in the habit of spending your time together in the evenings staring at the television set.

Watching Television Alone

Since the early 1950s, the divorce rate in the United States has climbed steadily. Interestingly enough, it was in the early fifties that television invaded the home and began dominating family life, especially in the evening. In the average family, the television is on six hours a day, or forty-two hours a week. In a recent poll, couples married for one year were asked to identify their most prized household possession. Most named their TV sets. These couples were also asked what single aspect of their marriage needed the greatest amount of improvement. Ironically and sadly, the majority answered, "Communication."

A study found that the average American couple engages in less than thirty minutes of meaningful one-to-one conversation in a week's time. Each of those two people, however, is likely to spend more than twenty hours a week in front of a TV set.

The language of television-watching conceals its reality. People talk about watching television "together," but the two things—watching television and togetherness—are mutually exclusive. When a family gathers in front of a TV, each individual becomes isolated in a private audiovisual tunnel. You may as well be twenty miles away from the person sitting next to you if you're both staring at the boob tube. You can't watch television and truly communicate or be intimate at the same time. It's either one or the other. Ask your-selves: What's more important?

Questions?

Q: **I'm a single mother with two children, ages six and four. Their father and I have been divorced for over a year, and I've been involved in a serious relationship for the last six months. Unfortunately, the children don't seem to like my boyfriend. He has bent over backward to win them over, but the harder he tries, the less they seem to care. On more than one occasion, they've made it clear that they don't want him over. The four-year-old has even told him, "It's time for you to go home now." I couldn't believe it! We're talking about marriage, but the children's attitude toward him gives me doubts. How should I handle this? Also, when is it all right to begin showing affection to each other around them?**

A: Actually, although "It's time for you to go home now" was a fairly outrageous statement, it's typical of the things kids say under circumstances such as these. Not having learned the art of social diplomacy, young children can be rudely candid when things don't suit them.

Keep in mind that their dislike of your boyfriend isn't really personal. In their eyes, Dad has a continuing interest in the family. Your boyfriend's presence, therefore, evokes a strong protective response from the kids.

Consider, also, that from Dad's leaving to the time your boy-friend arrived on the scene, the children enjoyed your undivided attention. They're probably having difficulty accepting the fact that some of those goodies are now going to someone else. This doesn't mean that you should give them more attention. It means they need to adjust to getting less.

Talk to them about their feelings. Acknowledge that what they're experiencing is normal, and help them understand that it's the situation, and not really your boyfriend, they don't like. Ask for their cooperation in extending hospitality and courtesy to any and all of your guests. An open discussion of this sort, in which you give the children an opportunity to express themselves and are accepting of their feelings, may or may not solve the problem. If it doesn't, you'll have to get more assertive.

Confront any further displays of rudeness on the spot. Tell the children that they do not have permission to be rude. Then banish them to their rooms until they decide to apologize. If you're consistent with this policy, the problem should disappear from view in fairly short order.

To help the kids adjust to seeing you and your boyfriend be affectionate toward each other, take things one step at a time. First, let them see you holding hands. If they try to break you apart, put them in their place and go on holding. When they seem to accept hand-holding, you can go public with hugging and kissing.

It would also help if your boyfriend made gestures of affection toward the children. He might, for instance, offer to read to them. If you're on an outing and one of them gets tired, he might offer to carry the youngster. Eventually, he can help you put the kids to bed. Again, don't rush it. Be sensitive to the children's comfort zone. If your boyfriend extends an invitation to the kids and they turn him down, he shouldn't take it personally. He should just step back, regroup, and try again later. Patience is the most important factor here.

If you and your boyfriend are hugging and the kids try to get in on the act, let them know it's not their turn. This says that your relationship with your boyfriend is, at times, exclusive. If you eventually decide to get married, this precedent will help you put the marriage at the center of the family.

Q: **I'm a married working woman with a six-week-old baby girl. Before she was born, I had planned to return to work after three months. Now that she's here, I'm beginning to feel I should be with her more than my job will allow. Is it psychologically damaging for a baby to be separated from her mother for long periods of time? When is the ideal time for a mother to return to work if her job isn't financially necessary?**

A: In a perfect world, parents would take primary care of their children for the first three years. Realistically, that's not always possible. If economic necessity dictates, or you truly feel your own mental health is at stake, stay home for at least six weeks and then go back to work. Having said that, I need to point out that research has consistently found negative effects associated with early day care. These include heightened aggression, short attention span, and an increase in disobedience. Research findings, however, do not predict individual outcomes. I am convinced that although it is generally better for children to be taken care of by an in-home parent for the first three years, day care does not ruin a child.

Obviously, it's important that you choose quality care. For example, a day-care center's child-to-staff ratio should be low enough to ensure each child adequate individual attention. For infants, the ratio should be no greater than five babies to one staff person.

Some of the questions parents should ask when shopping for child care are: Does the center require prior formal training and certification of key staff persons or are they hired off the street? Does the center have enough play materials to go around and are they of sufficient variety? Does it have a safe, interesting outdoor play area? What are its discipline policies?

Most states have an office within their Department of Human Services that oversees the delivery of child-care services. They will be glad to provide parents with information and referrals concerning child-care resources.

Q: **My husband and I were married in our mid-thirties and now, five years later, have a two-year-old boy. We've tentatively decided not to have any more children. To be perfectly frank, we just don't have the energy for another baby at this stage of the game. We'd like to know whether you have any particular concerns or recommendations regarding only children.**

A: There are several caution flags I raise with parents of only children.

First, because all the parents' eggs, so to speak, are in one basket, the only child tends to receive more attention and more things than does the child in a family of two or more children. If the attention is excessive, it can be a problem for all concerned, but particularly for the child. As I pointed out earlier, too much attention is addictive and detrimental to the growth of independence and self-esteem. Overindulgence also leads to behaviors typically associated with the "spoiled" child: making unreasonable demands, acting starved for attention, throwing tantrums, being disrespectful and disobedient.

We have seen that the prevailing child-rearing myth of the sixties and seventies was that children need a lot of attention from parents. Except for the first few years of life, this simply isn't true. Children need attention, but too much can create a dependency that stifles emotional growth and development.

Second, I've often heard from parents of only children: "It was just easier to take Bobby with us everywhere we went." On the surface of things, this degree of parent–child closeness may look desirable, but in the final analysis it is not. As a result of being included in so many adult activities, Bobby begins to perceive the marriage as a threesome, centered on him. This family dynamic makes it difficult for Bobby to outgrow his infantile self-centeredness. Also, when the only child is treated and regards himself as an equal to his parents, Mom and Dad will have a difficult time establishing themselves as authority figures. Furthermore, because the boundary between the child and the marriage is blurred, the child may fail to develop a clear sense of his own identity.

Third, the only-child syndrome breeds its share of behavior problems. They typically include interrupting adult conversations, demanding to be a part of adult activities, having problems with separation, wanting to be included any time parents show affection toward each other, showing disobedience and disrespect, and wanting constantly to be the center of attention.

Fourth, despite the bickering that often characterizes sibling relationships, siblings help one another learn to share and resolve conflict. Only children sometimes have problems in both these areas. With other children, they tend to be possessive of their belongings and want everything to go their way. These potential problems are made worse by the fact that, by virtue of being included in so many adult activities, the only child is often better socialized to adults than to peers. Consequently, the only child is often perceived by peers as having a superior, know-it-all attitude.

A little foresight can prevent the aforementioned problems from ever developing:

- Center the family around the marriage, not the child.
- Limit the child's inclusion in adult activities.
- Enroll the child in day care—a facility that emphasizes creative play as opposed to academics—around age three.
- Avoid indulging the child with either too much attention or too many things.

Q: **What suggestions do you have for the parents of a five-year-old only child who is addicted to attention, television, and toys? Our son is very demanding and easily bored. Instead of playing with other children in the neighborhood, he either wants us to play with him or wants to watch television. If we go somewhere, he either goes with us or stays with his grandparents. We want to undo the damage we've done, but we aren't sure where to begin, what to do, and how quickly to go about doing it.**

A: To begin with, you haven't done any permanent damage. You've simply set certain precedents that aren't working to anyone's advantage. You need to dismantle and replace them with more workable ones. Making major changes of this sort demands a well-organized and strategic approach. If you're ready, here are some tips on getting started:

First, limit your son's TV watching to no more than thirty minutes a day. The more time children spend occupied with television, the less able they are to find creative ways of occupying themselves. By turning the TV set off, you force him to find other ways of using his time.

Second, you'll find he'll want you to occupy his time for him, so you must limit the time you spend playing with him to two 15-minute periods a day, once in the morning and once in the afternoon. When he asks you to play with him, set the kitchen timer for fifteen minutes. When it rings, excuse yourself and go back to what you were doing. This doesn't mean you're at his beck and call twice daily. If he asks you at an inconvenient time, tell him he's going to have to wait. If he pesters or whines, send him to his room for fifteen minutes.

Third, stop taking him with you everywhere you go. When you go out, leave him with babysitters instead of with relatives. Hire a teenager who relates well to children to come into your home one night a week while you and your husband go out to dinner or a movie. The understanding that he isn't a member of the marriage will help your son develop independence and a clear sense of personal identity. In the long run, it is also a prerequisite to successful emancipation.

Fourth, reduce his toy inventory. A child of five should have very few store-bought toys, and those should consist primarily of flexible toy sets such as Lincoln Logs, Tinkertoy, and LEGO. Where toys are concerned, I often tell parents that if the toy wasn't in production before 1955, it's probably not worth buying. The right toys encourage initiative, resourcefulness, and creativity.

Prepare him for all this by sitting him down one evening and telling him in a gentle but straightforward manner about the changes you're about to make. If he asks why, just say, "This is what happens when children are five years old." A more involved explanation will only confuse him or make him feel there's something wrong with him.

Later, if he balks at some new way of doing things, you can simply say, "Remember the talk we had? This is one of the changes we were talking about."

By the way, it's really not necessary that you do this one step at a time. In fact, your son will adjust more quickly to the changes if you implement them all at once.

Q: I am black and my husband is white. We have weekend visitation with his sons, ten and eight. The weekends are torturous because in our home, the children do not have access to video games, hundreds of toys, and as much TV as they want. They have a "Disneyland mom and step-dad" in their primary home. They also have a very low opinion of black people, and thus they do not pay any attention to me when I try to correct their behavior. My husband is somewhat hamstrung by his ex-wife in that she once accused him of being "abusive" because he spanked the boys on several occasions (not harshly at all, but that made no difference to her). As a consequence, he second-guesses any attempt at discipline, even mild reprimands, on his part. We want to have more harmony in our home during these weekends, and we want to teach these kids to behave. What can we do, short of forgoing visitation, to improve our family life?

A: Is this ever a double bind! Unfortunately, it's all too common. If I've heard it once, I've heard the story a thousand times: The ex-wife levels spurious charges of abuse at the ex-husband, often resulting in termination or restriction of visitation. At the very least, these accusations effectively put Dad in check when it comes to discipline and make visits a living hell for the new wife. Believe me, the boys may have been brainwashed into harboring racist attitudes, but your skin color is not the issue when it comes to their disregard for you. I suggest that they would not listen to you or respect you if you were the whitest white person on the planet.

Experience tells me you have inherited a situation that is probably not going to change until the boys are old enough to think critically for themselves. That's a good six years away, at best, and probably more. In the meantime, the ball is squarely in your husband's court. He will have to decide whether his marriage is more important than his children. That's a difficult decision, but I hope he would choose his marriage over his children, who are being well taken care of otherwise and will someday have lives of their own. The second decision he needs to confront is whether or not he's willing to pay a price for laying down the law with these young tyrants.

The most promising approach involves a firm policy of taking the boys back to their mother immediately at the first instance of disrespect or disobedience while in your home. No threats, no second chances, no negotiations. If this meets with your husband's approval, plan a fairly nice weekend with the boys. In advance, he should let them know what's planned and what the new policy is: "If one of you disobeys or is disrespectful toward either of us, but especially my wife, then I'm going to take you home immediately. There will be no second chances. I'm not asking you to like us; I'm just telling you I will no longer tolerate displays of disrespect or disobedience. Knowing this, if you'd rather not come this weekend, let me know and [your name] and I will have our own wonderful time."

As I said, your hubby must be willing to pay a price for taking a strong stand of this sort. In that regard, I'd say to him, "You are married not to your children, but to your wife. From this point on, to do what is best for your kids, you have to stand up for your marriage."

Q: I am a single mother with a nine-year-old son. My ex-husband and I divorced when Teddy was three. I've recently decided to get married again. My fiancé, who has been married before but has no children, and I have been seeing each other for almost two years. He and Teddy have a good relationship, which was one of the things I considered before saying yes. What are some of the problems we may face in our new family?

A: You and your husband-to-be are creating what's known as a stepfamily, a family in which one parent is a stepparent. The stepfamily is the most rapidly growing family type in America, representing more than 25 percent of our nation's families. At the millennium, nearly thirty million children were living in stepfamilies, and another million are added every year. At this rate, the stepfamily will eventually replace the traditional family as the dominant American family type.

There are actually two types of stepfamilies, the primary stepfamily and the secondary stepfamily. The primary stepfamily includes the parent who has primary custody of the children. The children visit with but do not reside with the secondary stepfamily. Since most mothers retain custody of their children after divorce, most primary stepfamilies are headed by a mother and stepfather.

The primary stepfamily faces a set of problems that are different from those faced by the traditional family. The two biggest hurdles involve the need to establish the marriage at the center of the family and the need to establish the stepfather as an authority figure.

Unfortunately, in many stepfamily situations, certain precedents were set before the remarriage that interfere with the accomplishment of these goals.

The first of these involves the fact that following a divorce, a mother becomes a single parent. Because she has no spouse, her relationship with her children may become the most important relationship in her life. Increasingly, the single mother devotes herself to the raising of her children, and her children become increasingly dependent on her attention. In effect, an unwritten pact evolves that reads essentially, "You meet my needs, and I'll meet yours."

Enter a boyfriend who quickly perceives the strength of the mother-child relationship and adopts an "if you can't beat 'em, join 'em" attitude. Wittingly or unwittingly, he begins to court not only the mother but her children as well. He tries to become their friend, a good buddy. He correctly realizes that he must obtain the children's approval if he stands a chance of having their mother accept his proposal of marriage.

After the remarriage takes place, everyone continues to cling to old habits that, unfortunately, no longer work. The mother has difficulty moving out of a primary relationship with her children and into a primary relationship with her spouse. As a result, the stepfather begins to feel like a third wheel.

Making matters worse is the fact that the stepfather's need to shift gears from good buddy to parent causes everyone anxiety, confusion, and even anger. He attempts to discipline the children, and they run to their mother, complaining that he's being "mean."

She responds protectively, accusing him of overreacting or taking his "jealousy" out on the kids. Round and round they go, and where they stop, heaven only knows.

All this can be avoided, or at least minimized, if people who plan stepfamilies remember two things:

1. The marriage must be the most important relationship in the family. Stepfamilies are no different from other families in this respect.

2. The stepparent must assume authority equal to that of the natural parent. This means that the natural parent must be willing to share authority equally with his or her new spouse.

An ounce of prevention is always better than a pound of cure. Take the time to discuss just exactly what you're going to do to avoid these problems and how you're going to handle them when and if they do come up.

Q: How should a husband and wife handle arguments when the children are around? We do our best not to argue in front of our two children, ages seven and four, but occasionally we let something slip when they're within earshot. It always seems to bother them, which makes us feel guilty. In fact, the younger one has sometimes told us point-blank: "Stop!" When this happens, which isn't often, we stop and apologize to them. Since neither of us ever heard our parents argue, we don't feel secure in this area of our relationship with our children.

A: First, I suggest that you start letting your children hear some of your arguments. Second, never allow them to interrupt while you're in the midst of one.

Disagreement is a natural and inevitable aspect of human relationships. As intimacy within a relationship increases, so does the likelihood of disagreement. You can't have marriage without disagreement, but you can have marriage without argument, which is the confrontation and working through of disagreement. Unfortunately, when two people don't confront the disagreements they inevitably face once they're married, their relationship stands a good chance of never growing. It's too bad your parents never taught you the facts of being married. Don't make the same mistake.

Your children need to learn that arguments come with marriage. Then they need to learn that arguments don't destroy people. Finally, they need to learn how to engage in constructive disagreement with other people. If they don't learn these things from you, how are they going to learn them?

I said your children should hear some of your arguments. Obviously, there are certain topics children should not overhear their parents discussing, whether they're arguing or not. If you want them to learn that arguments aren't necessarily destructive, you are responsible for conducting your disagreements in a civilized, constructive manner. This doesn't mean you can't raise your voices, but it does mean you should not slander or belittle each other. You show respect for each other's points of view through active listening, making an attempt to consider points of view other than the two you brought to the discussion, and trying to reach a win-win resolution.

There will undoubtedly be times when you will want to save your disagreements for after the children are asleep. At other times, you may want to have your disagreements when they're awake and perhaps even in the same room. If you choose to have an argument in front of them and they attempt to interrupt you, you should say something like, "We are simply disagreeing with each other. If you don't like it, you may leave the room. If you stay, you may not interrupt us or cry. If you do, we'll send you to your rooms until our discussion is over."

If you start arguing and the children suddenly appear in the room with you, it's because they want to make sure everything is going to be all right. Reassure them that you're both alive and well and intend to stay that way and send them from the room.

Q: Our two-year-old son frequently calls my husband by his first name, Frank. He has only addressed me by my first name a few times. We would prefer that our son address his father as "Daddy." We feel this is more respectful, not to mention that my husband wants to enjoy his "Daddy" rights. So far, we have not corrected him. We feel that drawing attention to it may only make it worse. Instead, when he addresses his father by his proper name, one of us will point at his father and ask him, "Who is that?" His response is always correct: "Daddy!" Nonetheless, he continues to call his daddy by his first name. I understand that my clever son is intrigued by discovering and using our names, but how do I make him understand this is not acceptable?

A: You obviously don't know how to think like a two-year-old. Let me help you. When your son calls his father by his first name and you point at your husband (or he points at himself) and say, in a dramatic voice, "Who's that?" your son thinks you're making the first move in a game—the name game. So he proudly replies, "Daddy!" And you gleefully say, "That's right!" And once again, your son has won the game.

If a two-year-old discovers that he can elicit a dramatic response from someone, he will attempt to repeat the sequence at every possible opportunity. This is not willfulness; this is fun! It's a two-year-old's attempt at comedy.

In other words, while this is not "bad," you should correct it. Mommy and Daddy (Mom and Dad) may seem informal, but they are titles. First names are not titles, and it should go without saying that one attaches more respect to a title than to a first name. Therefore, children should address their parents as "Mommy" and "Daddy."

To stop this, you need to stop engaging in what your son interprets as a game and to correct him, clearly and firmly. When he addresses his dad by his first name, his dad needs to say, "I'm not Frank, I'm Daddy. Call me Daddy." For the time being, you should also refer to your husband as Daddy. That should end the game and clear up the confusion.

Q: What do you think about letting children sleep with their parents?

A: Generally speaking, children should sleep in their own rooms, in their own beds, but I would bend this rule under certain circumstances. For example, there's no harm in having infants sleep in the same room with their parents. No harm, either, in letting children come temporarily into their parents' beds during illness or periods of extreme stress, such as might follow a significant death or a house fire. Aside from exceptions such as these, I say, "Children to their own beds at a reasonably early hour!"

Sleeping in his own bed helps establish that the child is an independent, autonomous individual, with a clearly separate identity.

Parents who sleep together, separate from the child, enhance the child's view of the marriage not only as a separate entity within the family but also as the most important relationship within it. A child who sleeps with his parents is in danger of never reaching this understanding, and of feeling wrongly that the marriage is a threesome.

Separate sleeping arrangements also set an important precedent regarding separation. Children who separate from their parents at bedtime are better prepared to be away from them under other circumstances—when sitters come, at day care, the first day of school, for swimming lessons, and so on.

Q: Isn't it true that the custom of having children sleep separate from their parents only began in the early twentieth century? Isn't it also true that before this, and since prehistoric times, children were kept in bed with, or at least in another bed beside, their parents? If so, it would then seem that, whether society condones it or not, letting children sleep with parents is more natural than making children sleep alone.

A: I'm absolutely certain that my position rests on firm clinical and developmental ground, as opposed to simply being an extension of societal expectations and prejudices.

I'm correct in saying that in other cultures and in other times, children have slept with their parents only when there were no other options. For instance, it would have been impractical, perhaps even deadly, for our prehistoric ancestors to hold out for nothing less than a two-bedroom cave. Nor does it make sense for nomadic people to lug two-bedroom tents from site to site, or for

Eskimos to waste valuable time and energy building two-bedroom igloos. In cultures where you find parents and children sleeping together, it's usually out of necessity rather than choice.

Furthermore, the fact that a certain child-rearing practice is or was common to more primitive cultures may qualify it as more natural, but natural and healthy are not necessarily one and the same.

I'm sure that the characteristics of the particular culture dictate how this issue will be handled. In cultures where children usually sleep with their parents, other ways of cutting the cord have no doubt evolved. The adolescent puberty rites of some native cultures would be a prime example. In Western cultures, however, the separation of child and parents at bedtime is crucial to the development of autonomy—the child's and the parents'.

Q: I'm thirty-eight and have been happily married for five years. I'm undecided over whether or not to have children. At times, I think it would be wonderful, especially in our later years. On the other hand, I have no overwhelming desire to spend the next eighteen years raising a child. What questions should my husband and I ask ourselves to help us reach this decision?

A: Your dilemma is becoming increasingly commonplace. More and more people are putting off marriage as well as the decision of whether to have children. Considering that this is an extremely emotional issue, it's admirable that you're taking the time to weigh the pros and cons patiently and rationally.

It's unfortunate that our culture continues to communicate to women that they are in some way incomplete unless they opt for motherhood. Instead of enjoying the process of raising children, many women pressure themselves to excel at it. In order to demonstrate what good and conscientious mothers they are, they wind up devoting themselves body and soul to self-centered children who don't know their limits, never learn to accept no for an answer, and take everything they get for granted.

So just because two married people are capable of having children doesn't mean they should. The beauty of being human is that each of us is gifted with a broad range of capabilities. If you feel inspired to raise children, by all means raise children. If you'd rather raise sheep, raise sheep.

Ask yourselves these questions:

- Are we both in favor of having children or does one of us harbor reservations? (When the decision to have children is made for the sake of one of the two adults involved, instead of being mutually arrived at, the eventual toll on the marriage can be enough to destroy it.)
- Do we want to be just finishing our child-rearing responsibilities around age sixty, or would we rather spend our middle years together, relatively free to come, go, and do as we please?
- Do we feel emotionally up to dealing with the loss of freedom and the long-term obligations that come with raising children?
- Do we enjoy being around other people's children or do they tend to annoy us?
- Did we have happy childhoods? (I find that people tend to enjoy raising children to about the same extent they enjoyed being children. A happy childhood is perhaps the best guarantee of a happy parenthood.)

You should also consider that the potential for certain genetic problems increases with the ages of the parents. Are you willing to take the higher risk of having a handicapped child? If you want more information about these dangers, ask your gynecologist to refer you to a genetic counselor.

Q: My five-year-old son is a real people person. Several times a week he cries because he wants someone to play with him. He really hates playing alone. I set aside thirty to forty-five minutes each day to play one-on-one with him. He plays with his cousin once or twice a week, and he attends preschool three mornings a week. He is truly not starved for playmates. But it is very upsetting to me that he is so sincerely distressed so often. After dinner, my husband plays with him until bedtime. Even on weekends, most of my husband's time is spent playing with him. As you can see, he is not starved for attention either. Is there some way I can teach my son to play on his own without his getting so upset so often?

A: Burton White—child psychologist, researcher, and author of *Raising a Happy, Unspoiled Child* (Fireside, 1995)—has said that the prime indicator of good developmental health in a three-year-old is the ability to entertain himself, without the need for parental attention, for long periods of time. According to this criterion, your son is two years behind the curve.

Indeed, a five-year-old who is getting this much one-on-one time from his parents is not starved for attention; rather, he is *addicted* to his parents' attention. It's high time you and your husband stopped being this capable child's playmate. What you have described is a family situation that is all too typical today; a family in which the children rarely sees the parents in the roles of husband and wife.

By pretending to be a victim, your son has effectively wedged himself into the marriage, in between you and your husband. In effect, and especially from your son's point of view, you are no longer married. You are *his* mom and dad (and I'm putting purposeful emphasis on the possessive nature of the word *his*.) It's obvious that you both are there to perform whatever function he demands, whenever he demands it. Under the circumstances, the two of you are not even functioning as mom and dad. In reality, you've become your son's servant, and your husband is playing the role of his buddy. As a good friend of mine would say, "That just ain't right." When you and your husband are together in the home, the majority of your attention should be on your marriage, not on your son.

You will have to put some limits on the amount of time that either of you will play with him, and this is not going to be easy. If you are determined not to make him upset, then I would suggest that there is no solution to your problem. Just resolve to keep doing whatever you both need to do to keep your son from ever getting upset for the thirteen years between now and his going off to college—that's if when the time comes he decides to give up this state of bliss.

If you decide that your marriage is in fact a twosome, not a threesome, then you and your husband need to sit down with your son and tell him that you're going to help him learn to entertain himself. In that regard, and for the time being, he can have thirty minutes of one-on-one time from each of you every day. Every Monday, the time will be reduced by five minutes until there is no time for more than a book or two at bedtime, or an occasional spontaneous playtime.

Let me assure you that if you let this go on, it will only get worse, until your son is insufferable.

Q: My husband and I are about to take a four-day trip, during which we have planned to leave our eighteen-month-old daughter with my in-laws. Grandma works but is planning to take the time off to be with our daughter during the day. We had arranged for a familiar babysitter, but Grandma will have none of it. She also says that we shouldn't be surprised when we return if our daughter looks at us as if we are complete strangers. This has caused me to have second thoughts about leaving at all. What's your take on this?

A: I think you and your husband are right to go on a little trip together. Our son and daughter-in-law left their first child with Willie and me for four days when he was just six weeks old. We have always encouraged them to do this sort of thing, reminding them that their marriage came first and that it's in the best interests of their children that it remain first.

I also think you are right about the sitter as well. Your daughter will do just fine with a familiar person. She may cry a little when Grandma hands her over in the morning, but this has a 99.9 percent chance of passing within minutes of Grandma walking out the door. In situations of this sort, parents and grandparents must realize that crying does not mean the separation will be difficult—rather, just that the act of separation is difficult. The child gets over the act most quickly if the act is quick.

I also agree with Grandma. If she wants to take time off from her job to stay home with her granddaughter during the day, so be it. She should do exactly what she wants to do, and you should stay out of it. After all, Grandma will feel anxious all day at work. She won't fare nearly as well at work as your daughter will at home with a sitter. So, why not have two calm, secure people instead of just one? Therefore, Grandma stays home, saving you some money.

Now, as my regular readers know, I generally agree with "Grandma," but in this case, I disagree that when you arrive home, your daughter may look at you as if she doesn't know who you are. Why Grandma would be trying to invoke the evil spirit of the attachment-parenting demon is beyond me, but consider that a four-month-old puppy recognizes his "master" after a week's absence and rebonds almost immediately. I think we can safely assume that an eighteen-month-old intelligent human being is going to know who her parents are after a four-day separation. At age six weeks, our grandson Jack went right to his parents when they returned from an extended weekend away.

No, you won't come back to a child who is staring vacantly off into space, unresponsive, limp, refusing to eat, making no sounds. You will return to your daughter. She will know you and greet you with as much enthusiasm as an eighteen-month-old can muster.

But by all means, humor Grandma! Take everything she says with mock seriousness. Don't get into a debate with her over this, because you aren't going to change her mind. Just leave! Go! Have fun!

The Voice of Authority

A fair number of postmodern parenting experts maintain that the only truly healthy family is a "democratic" one, where children enjoy an equal voice in determining rules, chores, privileges, and so on. When parent and child differ on any of those issues, a parent should never "pull rank" on the child. Rather, these authors prescribe compromise, thus maintaining the assumption that in a democratic family no one is more powerful than anyone else. In that regard, they market what is called "the art of active listening," which essentially prohibits parents from telling children what to do. Instead, parents should listen nonjudgmentally to a child's point of view, calmly communicate their opinions, and leave it to the child to assume responsibility for his own actions. Sounds good, eh?

Unfortunately, the democratic family is a fiction. You can, if it makes you feel better, pretend to have a democratic family, but pretense is as far as it will ever go. The illusion of democracy in a family is created and maintained with lots of words, lots of discussions and explanations, and lots of asking the children for their opinions. If, however, you sift through the rhetoric and finally get to the bottom of things, you will discover an incontrovertible truth: In this so-called family, someone always has the final say. That simple fact strips away any and all illusions of democracy. Furthermore, that someone had better be an adult, or everyone in the family is in trouble.

The Real Deal

In the real world, there is no possibility of a truly democratic relationship between parents and children—not as long as the children live at home and rely on parents for emotional, social, and economic protections. Until a child leaves home, there can only be exercises in democracy, and these exercises must be carefully orchestrated by the child's parents, lest they get out of control.

If we're going to draw analogies between families and political systems, the most ideal form of family government—the one that works best for both parents and children—is a benevolent dictatorship. In 1976, when I first began using that term, the reaction I often received told me that people were hearing only the second word. Consequently, they thought I was giving parents permission to be rigidly, even punitively, authoritarian. Not true.

A benevolent dictatorship is a form of family government in which parents act on the recognition that their most fundamental obligation is to provide a balance of love (benevolence) and authority (dictation) to their children. This is hardly tyranny. Benevolent dictators are *authoritative,* not authoritarian. They do not demand unquestioning obedience. Quite the contrary, they encourage discussion (as opposed to argument), but they make the final decisions. The rule in their relationship with their children is "You are free to disagree with me, but you are not free to disobey." The authoritarian parent, because he is fundamentally insecure and does not know how to exercise power responsibly, for the benefit of his "subjects," will not tolerate even the slightest disagreement.

Benevolently dictatorial parents create rules that are fair and enforce them firmly but gently. They do not derive sadistic pleasure from bossing children around. They govern not because they enjoy dominating smaller people, but because they realize children are incapable of properly governing themselves. As such, they recognize that it's a child's right to be governed well, and that it's every parent's responsibility to provide good government.

In a benevolent dictatorship, children experience increasing responsibility and privilege as they grow up. This ensures that by the time they reach their late teens or early twenties, they are ready for self-government. Having experienced the model in their lives, they know how it works. Within the framework of discipline created for them by benevolently dictatorial parents, children learn the value of independence. They learn it is not something to be taken for granted, but something to be worked for and, therefore, worth taking care of.

Benevolently dictatorial parents keep their love for their children and the responsibility of exercising authority over them in a state of balance and harmony. They understand that (a) you cannot effectively communicate your love to a child unless you are also a source of effective authority, and (b) you cannot effectively discipline unless you are also a source of genuine love.

When parental authority is weak, love becomes indulgent and possessive, overly protective. Similarly, without the tempering effect of love, parental authority becomes harsh, severe. Love provides meaning and a sense of belonging to a child. Love gives a child reason to strive. Authority provides direction to the child's strivings. Love and authority are not opposite poles, but two sides of the same coin. The clue to proper parenting is to be both authoritatively loving and lovingly authoritative—I call it "keeping the head and the heart in balance." Not only is achieving that balance essential to a child's sense of well-being, it's also the key to a parent's sense of self-confidence.

Some time ago, I was explaining this concept to a group of physicians, when one of the doctors raised a challenge. "I think you're throwing this idea out in too general a fashion," he said. "Your 'benevolent dictatorship' may work quite well when children are very young, but parents should give older children, especially teenagers, more freedom as well as more opportunity to make their own decisions."

"Yes!" I replied. "What you are saying is absolutely true and dovetails perfectly with my 'benevolent dictatorship.' The key in what you said was your use of the word *give,* and I agree! Parents must be willing to *give* their children greater freedom and more choices as they grow older—even the freedom at selected times to make mistakes. But parents must always retain control of the decision to give. They must never, as long as their children are dependents, hand complete control of their lives over to them."

There is no possibility of a democratic relationship between parents and children as long as children live at home and rely upon parents for legal protection and economic support. Until a child leaves home, there can be only exercises in democracy, which are carefully orchestrated by the parents. Yes, increasing degrees of independence must be given as the child matures, but given from a secure position of authority. You are the boss—for your children's sake.

I received the following e-mail from a person who did not agree with my ideas on family government: "In your constant defense and promotion of authoritarian parenting, you overlook the fact that the United States is a democratic country. You yourself have repeatedly said that parents should raise their children in such a way that they are familiar with and equipped to deal with the real world. If the real world is democratic, then shouldn't American families be democracies?"

This individual makes a common, and somewhat understandable, mistake: He confuses authoritarian and authoritative. Despite the fact that they share all but three letters, they are as different as night and day. The difference is that authoritarian parents exercise power because they enjoy being kowtowed to, whereas authoritative parents exercise power for the purpose of slowly but surely handing over the reins of government to their children. In the vernacular, authoritarian parents are "control freaks."

The idea that the United States would be a "better" democracy if its families were little democracies was first advanced by one of the leading mythologists of nouveau parenting, family counselor and author Dorothy Briggs. In her influential 1971 best seller, *Your Child's Self-Esteem*, Briggs proposed that parents share power with their children, who would have "an equal part in working out limits." Briggs was explicit in arguing that since this is what children *want*, this is what children should *have*. In other words, families should not really be democracies; they should be childocracies.

Briggs defended her position by asserting that "democracy in government has little meaning to a child unless he feels the daily benefits of it at home." This may have a nice ring to it, but Briggs apparently didn't understand that although the political process in the United States is democratic, our society definitely is not. Rather, society is comprised of institutions that are structured hierarchically. Whereas adults who interface with those institutions are guaranteed the freedoms and privileges that come with democratic government, and whereas those institutions cannot abridge those freedoms and privileges, the institutions themselves (e.g., your employer) do not operate democratically. Within them, persons of greater authority—who have been appointed, not elected—are found instructing, directing, and dictating to persons of lesser authority.

Average Joe is free to work for whom he chooses, but once he makes his choice, he must take orders. His employer is not likely to consult him concerning personnel policy, and if Joe disagrees with a certain policy, he'll probably have to choose between abiding by it and taking a professional hike. This is even the case concerning the citizen's relationship with government. Consider that once "We, the People" elect public officials by democratic means, we must abide by the decisions (laws) they make. If we do not like the decisions, we can exercise the future opportunity to elect new officials, but we are not free to break the law in the meantime. For example, I happen to think that many of the powers presently exercised by the federal government were usurped unconstitutionally—according to the Tenth Amendment, they rightfully belong to the states. Nevertheless, I pay my federal taxes. I do not expect the IRS to respect my objections and negotiate my tax bill with me.

Briggs was arguing that the circumstances of a child's upbringing should, as much as possible, reflect realities that exist in general society; I agree wholeheartedly. In effect, Briggs made a perfect case for creating families that are benevolent dictatorships.

People who advance arguments in favor of democratic families are obviously in great need of a refresher course in history. Our democracy has survived many generations of children reared in nondemocratic homes. Notwithstanding their psychologically incorrect upbringings, the overwhelming majority of them, as adults, demonstrated a keen appreciation for the workings of democracy. Did the parents of Thomas Jefferson, Abraham Lincoln, Susan B. Anthony, or Martin Luther King Jr. consult with them concerning disciplinary matters? I think not.

Once Is Not Enough

The mother of a four-year-old girl tells her daughter to dress for school. The child replies, with defiance dripping from every syllable, "I don't want to, and I'm not going to!" The mother tells her that if she doesn't dress, and quick, she will go to school in her pajamas. The child dresses, and that's the end of it. Or is it?

"Did I do the right thing?" the mom inquires.

"Does she defy you about other things?"

"Oh," Mom replies, "all the time."

"Then in this case you achieved a short-term objective—she got dressed," I answer, "—but you made no progress as regards the real problem."

"What's the real problem?" Mom asks.

The real problem is this little girl's recurring defiance of her mother's authority. In this case, Mom won a skirmish, but the war goes on. And it will go on and on and on until Mom wins the battles and puts an end to the war once and for all. The problem is, the longer this war goes on, the worse it's going to get. A four-year-old who has the nerve to tell her mother she's not going to dress for school may well become a thirteen-year-old who tells her mother to go jump in a lake and take a deep breath. This should be stopped—not for Mom's betterment, mind you, but for the child's. Research into parenting outcomes has discovered that the best-behaved children are also the happiest, most well-adjusted children. The research also tells us that these kids have parents who love them unconditionally and discipline them with power and purpose—parents who have their heads and their hearts in balance. The reason children should be well-disciplined and well-behaved is not that it's easier to raise a well-behaved child, although it certainly is. The reason is that it is in the child's best interest to be well-behaved, both in the short and the long term

Before I continue to answer Mom's question, I want to be clear on one thing: She handled the immediate situation in a right and proper fashion. If called for, I would have put the child and her clothes in the backseat of the car and set off for school, telling her that whether she was clothed or not, when we arrived at school, she was going in even if I had to carry her in. When she arrived home from school that afternoon, I would have told her that as a result of her defiance that morning, she would spend the rest of the day in her room and go to bed immediately after dinner.

I would have looked her in the eye and said, "This is the way it's going to be, my love. When you defy me, it will not matter whether you ultimately do what I tell you to do or not. You will be punished."

This little girl needs to know, as do many American children, that obedience is more than simply doing what one is told; it is doing what one is told without even the slightest display of defiance. Some people think this is too much to ask of a child, especially one as young as four. We know, however, that most children born before the 1960s (during which traditional parenting was demonized and replaced with what I call "postmodern psychological parenting") were obedient by age three. Even today, in underdeveloped countries that have not imported our dysfunctional parenting practices, children are obedient by age three. In fact, it is vital to the child's social and emotional health to instill such behavior.

Once Upon a Time, Part One

Once upon a time, I thought discipline was all about punishment. This wrongheadedness had a lot to do with my graduate training in psychology, especially the behavioral aspect of it. When the rat assigned to me in graduate school did something "wrong,"

I gave it the electric equivalent of a spanking, and it straightened right up. I have long since realized that discipline is primarily a matter of communication, not punishment. Now, don't get me wrong. There's a time and a place for punishment, and every parent should have a plan for it so that when the time comes, the parent acts deliberately rather than impulsively. But discipline—the process of turning a child into a disciple, a little person who will follow your lead—is about how one talks. It's about telling children the way it is and the way it's going to be. This telling must be clear, it must be done calmly, it must be said in words the child understands, and it should be concise and to the point. As Jesus told his disciples, "Let your yes be yes, and your no be no." Speak in no uncertain terms so that your child knows exactly where you stand. The preceding formula will prevent, in my very experienced estimate, 80 percent of discipline problems from ever starting, and it will help control most of the remaining occurrences fairly quickly.

Here is a story that illustrates my point. When they were seven and five, respectively, our grandsons Jack and Patrick spent a long weekend with me and Willie. One night, I fixed my celebrated spaghetti sauce and cooked a batch of pasta to a perfect al dente. When I presented Patrick with his meal, he promptly but politely told me he didn't like spaghetti sauce. He said he eats the noodles only with butter on them. I served everyone else and sat down.

"Patrick," I said calmly, "that's your supper."

Again he told me he didn't like spaghetti sauce.

"Did your doctor tell you not to eat spaghetti sauce?" I asked.

He looked at me for a moment, obviously puzzled. "No," he said.

"Then that's your supper," I said. I told him that at our house, we all eat the same meal. No one—absent medical orders—ever gets a different meal. Again, more plaintively, he told me he didn't like spaghetti sauce. I calmly pointed out that it was not polite to tell someone who had fixed food for you that you didn't like it. I added that since God had provided the food for us, it was not polite to God. Some people would say this is an example of "laying on a guilt trip." I maintain it is the truth and that withholding such a truth from a child may cause the child less discomfort immediately but more pain and misfortune eventually. Patrick looked at his grandmother, hoping to be rescued from a fate worse than cod liver oil. Willie gave him a "that's the way it is" look, so he looked back at me and gave it one more try.

"But I really don't like spaghetti sauce," he said, very sweetly and sincerely. "I've never eaten it."

"Patrick," I replied. "I'm not saying you have to eat it. I'm saying that's your supper. You don't have to eat it. But Nommie [Willie's 'grandmother name,' given her by Jack] and I are not going to fix you something else. Furthermore, you need to know that we have planned ice cream for dessert, but dessert is only for people who have finished their supper—all of it." (This does not qualify as a bribe—I was simply giving Patrick information.)

Patrick looked at me for a few more seconds, picked up his spoon, and started eating. He ate everything on his plate, then proudly announced that he liked my spaghetti sauce and would eat it again.

This is a story about the power of speaking with authority. I did not threaten Patrick, nor did I bribe him. I simply told him the way it was, and the way it was going to be. This is also a story about teaching a child good table manners, especially when at someone else's house. It's also a story about helping a child understand that we should give thanks for everything we have, even if it's not exactly what we want. Effective discipline, you see, accomplishes something in the short term and the long term, and it's the long term that truly matters.

Please do not misunderstand me on this point. Effective discipline is not constituted primarily of effective punishment, or *consequences*—the new, less menacing term. As I've explained, it is constituted of effective communication. It's about how a parent *talks,* and by that I am referring not only to the words that emerge from a parent's mouth, but also to his or her tone, facial expression, and body language. Nonetheless, effective talking will not accomplish all of what needs to be accomplished. No matter how effectively one talks, misbehavior will still occur. Effective, authoritative speech—what I call "alpha speech"—will take care of many of those misbehaviors, but it will not take care of all of them. Punishment will sometimes be necessary. When it is required, the object should be to instill a permanent memory in the child, a memory that will deter repetitions of the same misbehavior. Unfortunately, the most popular punishment of the postmodern parenting age, the one most recommended by professionals, is the least effective at instilling such memories. In fact, it has caused more problems than it has solved. I'm talking about time-out.

Once Upon a Time, Part Two

Once, I was a true believer in the power of time-out—having a child sit in a somewhat isolated chair for five minutes or so immediately after he misbehaves. I promoted time-out in my syndicated newspaper column, my books, and my public presentations. I believed it was the ideal response to misbehavior. Used consistently, I said, it should take care of just about any discipline problem. I especially liked the fact that time-out was painless yet still discomforting enough to a young child to give him pause the next time he was inclined to step out of line.

Indeed, I recommended time-out to parents who were dealing with seemingly incorrigible children and I almost invariably received glowing reports. I'm by no means proud of it, but I probably did more to popularize time-out than any other person in America. From sea to shining sea, I carried the good news: Armed with but a chair, a timer, and a short list of misbehaviors, anyone could have a well-behaved child.

I began hearing disturbing reports of children who responded well to time-out for a few weeks and then began backsliding. Not to be undone, I attributed these reports to parents who'd gotten lazy and inconsistent. Then parents began telling me of children who would sit in time-out for the requisite length of time, get up, and immediately misbehave. I started hearing tales of children who would cooperate with the procedure for a few days to a few weeks and would then suddenly begin refusing to cooperate. These were followed by stories of children who sat in time-out and screamed bloody murder, repeatedly slamming their time-out chairs into walls, sliding their chairs from room to room, or a combination thereof.

It occurred to me that it was impossible for parents to apply time-out consistently, and children figured this out quickly. It could not be used if a child misbehaved when the parent needed to exit the house quickly to make an appointment, or the family was in the car or a public place or someone else's home. So, guess when these kids began doling out most of their misbehaviors?

Finally, I figured it out. Time-out works for a short period of time with almost all misbehaving children. Its novelty upends them for a while, but it wears off quickly. In the long run, however, it is nothing more than a minor and only temporarily persuasive inconvenience, especially for a child who is highly disruptive and defiant. I concluded that time-out works with children who are already well behaved—but so does just about anything, including a firm verbal reprimand. With regard to chronically ill-behaved children, however, time-out is insufficiently persuasive. It is like trying to stop a charging elephant with a flyswatter. Dissuading a charging elephant requires something that makes a big boom!

The *Boom* in *Baby Boomer*

I sometimes ask my audiences, "Raise your hand if you think the punishment—in other words, the consequence a child receives for misbehaving—should fit the crime?" Nearly everyone raises a hand, which goes a long way toward explaining why so many of today's parents complain that the consequences they employ don't seem to work, that no matter what they do, their children just keep right on misbehaving in the same exasperating ways.

The old-fashioned parent was unconcerned with the issue of fairness, the perception that there should be equity between the misbehavior and its consequence when it came to discipline. Rather, he or she was intent upon nipping misbehavior in the bud, which was generally accomplished through a lowering of the proverbial boom. The old-fashioned parent realized that the size of a given misbehavior should not dictate the size of the punishment. After all, any misbehavior, no matter how small, can become a major problem if allowed to flourish; ergo, the boom.

Modern parents have been brainwashed into believing that any and all old-fashioned parenting practices should be avoided, since they are supposedly damaging to that psychic attribute I promised not to mention (hint: it begins with the word *self*). In a sense, that is correct. But then, most old-fashioned parents wanted to raise humble, modest children, not children with high you-know-what. Intuitively, before the term came into popular usage, they realized that children with high self-ahem are likely to be obnoxious little brats; ergo, the boom.

As a child, I was boomed on more than a few occasions. So was every kid in my neighborhood. None of us liked it, of course. But when I talk about these experiences with people my age, we all agree that these memorable events eventually proved to be blessings in our lives.

As one fiftysomething fellow recently told me, "I'd have probably been in prison before I was twenty if my parents hadn't been willing to cause me extreme discomfort when I misbehaved." He added, they never, ever spanked him! He meant psychological discomfort; when he got "too big for his britches," they cut him down to his proper size.

Psychologists who promote postmodern psychological parenting want the public to believe that children of my generation were beaten into blind submission. The fact is, most of us baby boomers received few spankings, and I know lots of people my age who were *never* spanked. But spanking or not, when we misbehaved, we were often boomed. The first time one of us violated curfew, he was grounded for a semester; the first time he talked back to his dad, he was made to chop and carry firewood for an entire weekend; the first time he rode his bike where he had been told not to, his bike was taken away for a month; the first time he goofed off in class, he was made to write a letter of apology to the teacher and every classmate. And so on. No, spanking was not the secret to the reasonably well behaved baby boomer. The not-so-secret secret was the boom.

Come to think of it, we postwar kids are not the "boomers." Our parents were.

Bluto Gets Boomed

Here's a true story to illustrate my point. A four-year-old—I'll call him Bluto—has a habit of hitting other children in his preschool program. Bluto's teachers try various approaches, and none of them works. Their latest attempt involved rewarding him with something special on days when he didn't hit others. That didn't work either. Extending rewards to a child who is misbehaving not only sends the wrong message, but may also make matters worse.

At her wit's end, Bluto's mom asks my advice, which I give as follows: When Bluto hits, his teachers should immediately remove him from class, take him to a neutral "holding zone," and call her. As soon as she is able, Mom should retrieve Bluto from school and take him home. There, she should confine him to his room for the remainder of the day and put him to bed immediately after supper. During Bluto's "rehab," his room should be cleared of all toys except two (of his choosing) and all electronic entertainment. Mom says she'll do it and get back to me with a progress report.

Several weeks later, I receive an e-mail from Mom. She reports great improvement. Reminding me that Bluto had been hitting on a daily basis, she tells me she's had to confine him to his room only three times in three weeks, and two of those times were during the first week. She's made a slight change in plan, however, because when she told Bluto's teachers what I had originally recommended, they expressed disapproval, saying they were sure he didn't *mean* to hit other children. His hitting was impulsive, they said, not deliberate, and he should not be punished. So instead of calling Mom when he hits, they inform her of any incidents at pickup time. If Bluto has hit, Mom takes him home, confines him to his sterile room, and puts him to bed immediately after supper. The teachers don't know what Mom is doing because she is convinced that if they knew he was being confined to his room and sent to bed early, they would not give her accurate information.

Actually, I accept the teachers' assertion that most of Bluto's hitting is impulsive. That does not mean, however, that he does not know what he is doing, that he is incapable of preventing it (the outcome of the story is proof of that), or that he should not be held responsible for it. Impulsive may describe Bluto's hitting, but the only way a child learns impulse control is to be punished when his lack of it produces an antisocial behavior. The punishment must be discomforting, because discomfort is motivating. Nothing else will cause the child to exert the effort necessary to master his impulses.

Toddlers are antisocial-behavior factories. They hit, bite, scream, defy authority, and snatch things out of other children's hands. It could be argued that in a toddler this sort of behavior is not deliberate. Imagine what the world would be like if adults failed to punish these antisocial outbursts because toddlers didn't mean it. Come to think of it, the reason many older children today are still behaving like toddlers is that many of today's adults are reluctant to nip antisocial behavior in the bud when it first emerges—during toddlerhood.

Bluto is but one of an epidemic of children who are suffering from extended toddlerhood syndrome (ETS). Instead of supporting his rehabilitation, Bluto's well-intentioned teachers made excuses for him. Had their point of view prevailed, he would have been denied the opportunity to develop self-discipline and improve his social relationships. He might still be hitting five years from now. Good for Bluto's mom that she went ahead and did what is necessary to bring his antisocial outbursts to a halt. She lowered the old-fashioned boom.

Boom! Boom!

Any example of lowering the boom is an example of "psychologically incorrect discipline" (PID), meaning punishment that many mental health professionals would strongly disapprove of. They would claim, without a shred of evidence, that such discipline might stop the misbehavior in question, but cause psychological harm. While I am not suggesting that all examples of PID are justifiable, I am most definitely suggesting that legitimate uses of PID are more powerfully corrective than most examples of the "correct" sort; furthermore, they result in immense psychological benefit.

My next true tale of psychological incorrectness involves a five-year-old girl who was having emotional meltdowns whenever her parents did not cater to one of her frequent whims. The parents had tried numerous correct approaches, including what I call "therapeutic conversation" (the attempt to talk a child into behaving properly), time-out, taking away her privileges for short periods of time, ignoring her tantrums, and rewarding her when she went for a specified time without one. Nothing had worked. They were ready to try PID.

They began by redefining the problem, telling their daughter that only spoiled children threw tantrums; therefore, they must have spoiled her by giving her entirely too many things.

"So," they informed her, "from now on, when you have a tantrum because we will not give you your way, you will have to put one of your toys in a Charity Box we are going to put in the back hall. It must be a good toy, one that you still enjoy playing with. If it doesn't meet with our approval, you'll have to find another one that does. When the box is full, we'll take it to a charity. They'll see to it that children who are not spoiled receive these toys—children who will be grateful for them."

Two weeks, two dozen toys, and one trip to a local ecumenical charity later, the tantrums stopped. The Charity Box still sits in the back hall, and this little girl is constantly reminded of the advisability of keeping her tantrums under wraps. And isn't a child who does not throw tantrums happier than a child who does?

The protagonist in the next story is a nine-year-old boy who was a perennial behavior problem in school. His teachers had thrown up their hands and were now telling the parents they were certain he had attention deficit disorder. They were encouraging the parents to have him tested and put on medication. Actually, the teachers were not interested in the results of these completely unnecessary and expensive tests; they just wanted the boy drugged.

Instead, the parents decided to go with PID. While their son was at school, they stripped his room of everything except furniture and clothing and necessary school materials, turning it into a "military" environment. When he came home and discovered his new circumstances, they told him they were going to ask his teachers for a complete report at the end of every school week. If he had not misbehaved at all, they would give him back an article of *their* choosing, meaning he would be working on his school comportment for a relatively long time before he was able to enjoy his most prized possessions. And a major "at home" misbehavior at any time would cancel even the most glowing report from the teachers.

It should surprise no one that this youngster turned into a model student within two weeks, and his behavior improved remarkably at home as well. Ten weeks later, he was still on track and reclaiming possession of his toys and electronic equipment at the dazzling pace of one item per week.

Good things come to those who wait and work in the meantime.

No Wonder Most Teachers Retire Before They're Forty

A friend of mine happened to be looking in on her son's fourth-grade class one day when he talked back to his teacher. She confined him to their house for a week and made him write a one-page, single-spaced letter of apology. He actually had to write three, because Mom required that the letter sound sincere and contain no spelling or grammatical errors. Now, that's my kind of mom!

The teacher called to thank my friend. In the course of the conversation, she mentioned that the school district prevents teachers from having children write letters of apology to other children they've wronged. It seems that a child might feel punished and humiliated by having to write such an epistle. Furthermore, boys don't like to write, and the feeling is that using writing as a punishment would cause boys to hate it even more. Funny, I'm a writer, and I think of writing as recreation, yet on several occasions when I was a child, I had to write a letter of apology to someone.

In *The Conspiracy of Ignorance: The Failure of American Public Schools* (HarperCollins Publishers, 2000), Martin L. Gross points out that teachers are trained in college, and through later "in-service" seminars that they must attend, in "dubious educational psychology." The above anecdote is a prime example of such brainwashing. Even though "positive discipline"—rewarding good behavior and all but ignoring bad behavior—has proven to be a bankrupt practice, most public schools still embrace it. The problem is not just one of teacher training. Administrators who know positive discipline doesn't work require that it be used to the exclusion of punishment for the simple reason that it keeps parents off their backs and, by extension, lawyers out of their offices. So even teachers who know that misbehavior is best dealt with by punishing the culprit are prohibited from using punishment because of the outraged-parent and litigation factors. In the final analysis, the problem is not teachers, their trainers, or their administrators; the problem is parents who become apoplectic when their very own immaculate children are punished at school for anything at all.

Once upon a not-so-long-ago time, when a child misbehaved in school, he faced the possibility of being punished by four people on four separate occasions: his teacher, the principal, his mother when he arrived home, and finally, the most dreaded disciplinarian of all—his father. In those days, when a teacher called a parent and reported misbehavior, the parent accepted the teacher's version of the story pretty much without question. In many cases, the child was not even allowed to offer up a defense. I'm a member of that generation, and if statistics are any indicator, this was anything but bad for us. Since the mid-1960s, when the parenting tide began to turn away from traditionalism toward psychological correctness, every single indicator of positive mental health in America's children has declined, and significantly so.

As permissiveness took root and blossomed, parents became more concerned about their kids' self-you-know-what than their kids' behavior. Supposedly liberated moms went to work, came home feeling guilty, and began letting their kids walk all over them. Dads let themselves be brainwashed into believing that traditional fatherhood was bad and became sensitive dads who substituted talk for discipline. People—otherwise rational adults—began thinking children had rights. Schools began purveying therapeutic education, which means education that makes a child feel good even if he isn't learning anything of value. In no time at all, as my mother would put it, "everything went to a certain very hot underground place in a handbasket."

Personally, I think it's time every parent in America wrote their child's teacher a note of apology.

Children Don't Grant Adult Wishes

At this point, I want to return to the matter of "alpha speech," which is nothing more than speaking to a child as if you *expect* him to obey.

I'm sure most American parents would say they expect their children to obey. I'm equally sure that most American children are not truly obedient. When told to do something by parents, the typical

American child does not display a willing, cooperative attitude. Instead, he ignores, whines, argues, gets mad, or talks back.

The once-upon-a-time "yes, sir . . . no, sir" obedient child has become a rarity, but this sorry state of affairs is not the fault of children. It's the fault of parents who beat around the bush of obedience, afraid to disturb any of its supposedly delicate leaves lest they damage the child's supposedly fragile psyche. It's the fault of parents who instead of truly expecting children to obey, only go so far as *wishing* they would.

The distinction between expecting and wishing is found in the way parents communicate with children. When parents plead with children, they are wishing for obedience. When they complain to children about their behavior, they are wishing for obedience. When they bargain, bribe, threaten, give second chances, and reason, they are wishing for obedience. These are all relatively passive forms of wishing, but there are more active, less obvious forms as well. For example, the parent who pounds on the table, gets red in the face, and threatens the recalcitrant child with bodily harm, is— appearances aside—actually wishing for obedience. You see, this parent is in a snit precisely because his or her wishes haven't come true.

By far the most common form of wishing takes place when parents argue with children. All arguments with children get started in one of two ways. In the first instance, parents make a decision that the child doesn't like, and the child strains forward, grimaces, and, in a voice that sounds like fingernails being dragged across a chalkboard, screeches, "Why?!!" In the second instance, parents make a decision that the child doesn't like, and the child strains forward, grimaces, and, in a voice that sounds like fingernails being dragged across a chalkboard, screeches, "Why not?!!" Arguments start because parents make the mistake of thinking these are questions.

They aren't! They are invitations to do battle. By accepting the invitation, parents step squarely into quicksand, and the harder they struggle to be understood, the faster and farther they sink.

A question is a request for information. If "Why?!!" and "Why not?!!" (the screeched forms) were truly questions, two things would occur. First, the child would listen to the answer. Second, after having listened, the child would at least occasionally agree. Now think about it. When is the last time your child, after listening to your most eloquent, honest, sincere explanation, looked at you and said, "Well, gosh, Mom! Since you put it that way, I have to agree. Gee, thanks for being my mom!"

What's that? It's never happened? Right! It's never going to happen. Parents *cannot* win an argument with children. Winning an argument with someone means you change the person's way of thinking. As a result of the information or point of view you share, that person adopts a new and probably more mature point of view. Children don't have what it takes to appreciate and participate in this process. To compensate, they adopt an irrational position and hold on to it for dear life. So no matter how eloquent or how correct, parents cannot win because children can see only one point of view—their own.

Discussion requires the participation of two people whose willingness to listen is as great as their desire to be heard. Children want to be heard, but they rarely want to listen. As the parent explains, the child waits for an opportunity to interrupt. Despite the fact that attempting to explain the why or why not of a parental decision serves no purpose except aiding the child's need to argue, parents continue to do it.

This is why I believe in the power of four particular words. As a child, I couldn't stand to hear these four words. They made me mad, and I promised myself I would never say them to my children. When

I became a parent, I kept this promise for several years. Then, having brought myself to the brink of disaster, I woke up to reality and broke it. "Because I said so" became part of my parenting vocabulary.

Some people say that children have a right to know the reasons behind the decisions we make. I agree, but with certain amendments. First, they have a right to know in terms they can understand. Second, they have a right to know only if they are willing to listen. And third, if the truth is "Because I said so," they have a right to know that, too.

Some people argue that "Because I said so" isn't a reason. I disagree. Not only is it a reason, it's often the only reason. Let's face it, most of the decisions parents make are arbitrary. They are matters of personal preference, not universal absolutes. Why, for example, must your son go to bed at eight o'clock when the neighbor's boy is allowed to stay up until nine o'clock? Any and all attempts at explaining this inconsistency simply come down to, "That's the way I want it." Why don't you allow your daughter to ride her bike past the corner, when her best friend can ride three blocks to the convenience store? Again, the explanation boils down to, "That's the way I want it." In other words: "Because I said so."

If those four words stick in your throat, try "Because this decision belongs to me" or "Because I'm the parent, and making decisions of this sort is my job." If you feel you simply must give some manner of "correct" explanation, save your breath by trimming it to twenty-five words or less. Remember that regardless of how carefully you phrase your answer, the child is not likely to agree. In fact, you just might want to preface your answer with, "Okay, I'll pretend you're really asking me a question, and I'll give you an answer. But I don't expect you to agree. On the other hand, don't expect me to change my mind." When the inevitable happens, say, "That's all right. As I said, I didn't expect you to agree. Come to think of it, if I was your age, I wouldn't agree with me right now either."

Then, pull the plug on the power struggle by simply walking away, leaving your child to, as Grandma would have put it, stew in his own juices.

Games Parents Play

Another common form of wishing children would obey is a game called "Please?" (also known as "Okay?") that many of today's parents play with their children.

"Please?" begins when a parent tells a child to do something. It's usually something simple, such as wanting a child who is too big for a car seat to sit in the back. But parents have the darnedest ways of making simple things complicated and even confusing.

To play "Please?" the parent acts indecisive, as though she does not know exactly what she wants the child to do. Therefore, she turns imperative, commanding statements into questions and asks them in a small, imploring voice.

Rather than saying "You're going to sit in the backseat" or "I want you in the backseat," a mother says, "Wouldn't you rather sit in the backseat so Mommy can sit up here and talk to Daddy?" This form and tone tells the child that Mommy needs help in making this difficult decision, help the child is glad to provide.

"No!" he says. "I want to sit in front. You sit in the back."

At this point, it's a jump ball, up for grabs to the quicker player. Often the parent commits a technical foul by changing the rules and becoming angry: "Look, I told you to sit in the backseat, now get back there!" Actually, the parent never told the child anything. More often than not, "Please?" does not come to that abrupt an end. The parent usually negotiates a compromise. For example, the child gets in back, but Mommy sits in back, too.

Parents play "Please?" in the attempt to avoid confrontations, showdowns, and embarrassment, and it works. But what they get in the bargain is no bowl of cherries. Children are quick to learn when their parents are afraid to assert their authority and can be relied upon to give in. When it comes to a question of who's the boss, if parents won't run with the ball, children will.

There should never be any question about who's running the show. It is a child's inalienable right and privilege to be informed early in life that the parent is the boss. As the ancient parenting sage Bobo said, "When parent at loss, child make bad boss." Parents need to tell children what to do and then be prepared to enforce their authority. Don't ask questions if you don't really intend the child to have a choice. Children need to be told what to do by parents who aren't afraid or embarrassed by an occasional showdown. Children feel more secure and comfortable with parents who know where they stand (and where they want to sit).

Count the times you play "Please?" or "Okay?" with your child today. Once is too many.

It's How You Say It!

As I pointed out earlier, many parents communicate instructions in a wishful, wishy-washy manner. They plead, bargain, argue, threaten, and then—when they've finally reached the end of their rope—they get red in the face and yell. This sort of disciplinary style creates and perpetuates an atmosphere of uncertainty and tension within the parent–child relationship.

When giving instructions to children, parents should be commanding, concise, and concrete. These are the three C's of good communication.

1. *Be commanding:* Speak directly to the child and preface instructions with authoritative statements, such as "I want you

to" or "It's time for you to" or "You need to." In other words, don't beat around the bush. If you want a child to do something, you must say so in no uncertain terms. The more uncertain your terms, the more uncertain the outcome.

2. *Be concise:* Don't use fifty words when five will do. Almost all of us were lectured to as children, and we all remember hating it. We should know that as soon as the lecturer gets going, a fuse blows somewhere in the child's brain.

3. *Be concrete:* Speak in terms that are down to earth rather than abstract. Use language that refers to the specific behavior you expect, as opposed to the attitude. "I want you to be good in church this morning" is vague, abstract. "While we're in church, I want you to sit quietly next to me" is clear and concrete. When parents leave doubt in a child's mind as to exactly what they expect, the child can be counted on to appropriate the benefit of that doubt.

Here are some of the more common errors of communication parents commit:

Phrasing instructions as if they were questions. This implies choice, when no choice actually exists.

> *Wrong:* "How about picking up these toys so we can start getting ready for bed?"
> *Right:* "It's almost time for bed. You need to pick up your toys and put them away."

Phrasing expectations in abstract rather than concrete terms. Using words like *good, responsible,* and *nice* leaves the parent's actual meaning open to interpretation.

> *Wrong:* "I want you to be good while we're in the store."
> *Right:* "While we're in the store, I want you to walk next to me and ask permission before touching anything."

Stringing instructions together. The mind of a child younger than five has difficulty holding more than one instruction at a time. With children older than five but younger than twelve, it's best to give no more than two instructions at a time. If it's not convenient to hand out chores in this patient fashion, give the child a list. If he or she can't read yet, use drawings.

> *Wrong:* "Today, I want you to feed the dog, clean your room, take out the garbage, pick up the toys in the den, and help me move these boxes into the attic."
>
> *Right:* "The first thing I want you to do today is feed the dog. When you finish, let me know, and I'll tell you what comes next."

Preceding instructions with "Let's . . . This is another passive, nonauthoritative form of communication. When you expect a child to do a chore on his own, say so. Don't confuse the issue and open the door for resistance by implying that you're willing to pitch in.

> *Wrong:* "Let's set the table, okay?"
>
> *Right:* "It's time for you to set the table."

Following instructions with reasons or explanations. Putting the reason after the instruction attracts the child's attention to the reason rather than to the instruction itself. This makes argument more likely.

> *Wrong:* "It's time to get off the swing so we can go home."
>
> *Right:* "It's time for us to go home now. Get off the swing and come with me."

Making an instruction into a sales pitch. This might work with small children, but a child of four or five is wise to ploys of this sort, and the chance of noncompliance increases.

Wrong: "Hey, Sissy! Guess what? Mom's cooked a really great supper tonight! Let's say good-bye to Sally and come see Mom's surprise!"

Right: "It's time for supper, Sissy. You need to say good-bye to Sally and come inside."

Giving instructions with an open-ended time frame.

Wrong: "Billy, I need you to mow the lawn sometime today, when you get a chance."

Right: "Billy, I want you to mow the lawn today, and I want you to be finished by the time I get home at six o'clock."

Expressing instructions in the form of wishes. This amounts to nothing more than a passive complaint about the child's behavior. Children don't grant wishes, genies do.

Wrong: "I wish you'd stop chewing with your mouth open."

Right: "Stop chewing with your mouth open."

Have a Plan

Expecting children to obey also involves having a plan for what you are going to do if they don't. In fact, the secret to virtually frustration-free discipline is first to have a plan and then to carry it through consistently.

Most parents discipline by the seat of their pants. Consequently, when misbehavior occurs, they respond emotionally rather than with common sense. If businesses were run in this manner, they would all be bankrupt in no time. To make a profit, a business must operate according to a plan. Its managers must anticipate potential problems and develop strategies for dealing with them, if and when they occur. The same goes for parents who value effective discipline. They, too, must anticipate potential problems and be ready to deal authoritatively with them. I call this "striking while the iron is cold." The most effective time for dealing with misbehavior is before it occurs.

Striking while the iron is cold is a three-step process:

1. Anticipate the problem, based on your knowledge either of the child or of children in general.

2. Develop a strategy for dealing with the problem.

3. Talk with the child about the problem, defining it and letting the child in on the strategy (but not asking permission to use it).

By striking while the iron is cold, you put yourself in the most effective position for striking when the iron gets hot. When the heat is on, implement your strategy, following through as promised, and continue to follow through as needed until the problem is solved.

In the language of the business world, striking while the iron is cold is proactive as opposed to reactive. In parenting, as in business, to deal with problems proactively is to control them rather than letting them control you.

Let's see how this strategic process can be applied to a typical behavior problem. Take five-year-old Rodney, who persists in getting out of bed to ask unnecessary questions and make inappropriate requests. To make him stay in bed, Rodney's parents have threatened, bribed, spanked, and screamed—all examples of ineffective (reactive) emotional responses.

Finally, Rodney's parents wisely decide to strike while the iron is cold. They have no trouble anticipating the problem, since it has happened every night for the past two years, so they go straight to the planning stage. They decide Rodney will be allowed out of bed one time, and one time only, to ask a question or make a request. When they tuck him in, they'll give him a ticket, a small rectangle of colored cardboard. Rodney can use this one ticket to purchase the privilege of getting out of bed.

When he gets out of bed, as he surely will, he hands his parents the ticket. In return, they let him ask a question or tell them something. Then they put him back to bed. If for any reason (including "needing" to go to the bathroom), he gets up again, his parents keep him indoors the next day and put him to bed one hour early (again with one ticket).

Having developed their strategy, his parents calmly communicate their decision to Rodney at five o'clock one afternoon. As they're preparing him for bed, they remind him of the new deal. Then they tuck him in, give him his ticket, and turn out the lights.

Does Rodney get out of bed? Of course. Does he get out of bed more than once? Of course. Rodney must test the rule in order to find out if it really exists.

The next day, Rodney's parents deliver his punishment as promised. That night, he gets out of bed twice. The next day, his parents again keep him indoors and put him to bed early. The third night, Rodney gets out of bed ten times. He's trying to find out if his parents will stick to the plan if he acts oblivious to it. The next day, his parents stick to the plan. That night, Rodney gets out of bed one time and no more.

Over the next few weeks, Rodney tests his parents on several more occasions. Each time, he finds out that they are still sticking to the plan. At last, Rodney stops testing. In fact, he eventually stops getting out of bed altogether! And Rodney sleeps easier, knowing his parents mean what they say.

As this example points out, good discipline doesn't have to be complicated. Rather, it must be well organized, easily communicated, and easily dispensed. The simpler, the better.

Keep It Simple, Silly!

Nothing will kill a discipline plan quicker than weighing it down with dozens of if-then considerations. For example: "If you clean your room, you get a star. If you don't, you get a check. At the end of the week, we subtract checks from stars, and that determines your allowance. If there are more checks than stars, then you owe us money, which we take off the top of next week's allowance. If there are no checks, you get a bonus. If you owe us more than the bonus, the bonus is applied to the debt." See what I mean? Einstein couldn't have kept all that straight.

Another way of dooming discipline to failure is to bite off more than you can chew. Let's take a child who is destructive, disobedient, irresponsible, unmotivated, aggressive, disrespectful, bossy, and loud. Instead of tackling all the problems at once, which would be like wrestling with an octopus, you would do better to concentrate your energies on just one of them. Solving one problem puts you in a position to solve another, and then another, and so on.

The parents of two children, ages five and three, were having the usual problems that come with children of those ages—the kids sassed, squabbled, screamed, jumped on furniture, wrote on walls, got into everything, and created general bedlam. These parents spent lots of time and energy racing from one child to the other, from one thing to the next, going bananas in the process. They reminded me of the plate spinners who used to appear on *The Ed Sullivan Show*. The more these parents tried to accomplish, the less successful they were.

"Pick three problems," I told them.

They picked sassing, squabbling, and screaming. Neither child could read, so we drew a picture for each problem. Screaming was represented by a stick child with mouth wide open; squabbling by two children with mouths wide open; sassing by one stick child sticking its tongue out at stick parents.

The pictures were posted on the refrigerator, and the children were told what each one meant. The parents bought a timer and kept it near the children's rooms. When one of the targeted behaviors occurred, the parent closer to the scene would identify the behavior ("That's sassing") and say, "That's on one of your pictures and means you have to go to your room." A squabble sent both children to their respective rooms, regardless of who started it.

At each occurrence, the parent would take the offending child to his room, set the timer (ten minutes for the three-year-old, twenty minutes for the five-year-old, and fifteen minutes when they squabbled), and walk away. When the timer rang, the child was free to leave his room.

Talking with these parents, I stressed the importance of adhering to what I call the "Referee's Rule": no threats, second chances, or deals.

"When you see an infraction," I said, speaking figuratively, "blow the whistle and assess the penalty. In hesitation or indecision, all is lost!"

I saw them again three weeks later. The mother started by telling me she finally found a whistle at a sporting goods store.

"Wait a minute," I said. "You mean you actually went out and bought a real whistle?"

"Sure did!" she said. "It sounded like a good idea to me. When we're home, I wear it around my neck. When I blow the whistle, the kids march to their rooms. I don't even have to tell them to go. Better yet, they set the timer themselves."

I asked how she felt about the plan, and here's what she told me, word for word.

"I feel more confident in my parenting skills and more in control of the kids. Furthermore, the kids are reacting in a way that tells me they're more confident of my authority. They've learned my limits. Before, it seemed we were always in a state of frenzy. Now, the household is calm. It's a very organized feeling, and everyone is happier."

Strike another blow for simplicity.

Rewards and Incentives

"Okay, Junior, I know you don't want to take out the trash, but if you do, I'll give you a dime. How's that sound?" Sounds pretty good, right?

The notion that children need to be rewarded for obedience has become popular, with some unfortunate consequences. Foremost among these is the idea that children perform better when they are promised tangible rewards, such as candy, a toy, or a special treat.

In part, this is true. If you want Junior to do something mundane, such as cleaning up his room, offer him a piece of his favorite candy, a new toy, or a trip to the neighborhood ice-cream parlor. The next time you want him to clean up his room, be prepared to make the same offer. If you're lucky, the child will only expect more of the same. If luck isn't with you that day, he'll want something even better. Yesterday, an ice-cream cone; today, a superdeluxe bicentennial hot-marshmallow-cream commemorative sundae.

Children are impressionable, and nothing impresses them more than stuff for their mouths or hands. It's the "What's in it for me?" syndrome, as much the new American way as Mom's factory-made frozen apple pie.

When Junior learns to expect something in return every time he puts out a little effort for someone besides himself, it's obnoxious, but it's not his fault. The child is the addict, but we big people are the pushers. We adults tend to look for the most expedient way to accomplish things, the shortest distance between two points. When we want cooperation from a child, we know that offering some goody is likely to get the job done fast. In the child's mind, however, cooperation and the performance of certain tasks or chores become hooked to the promise of special rewards.

This can quickly become a revolving-door situation that traps both parent and child. The parent wants the work done without having to deal with the child's excuses; the child wants the handout and has learned that, after enough stalling, the parent will come through with the goods.

Children need certain tools to meet the challenges of adult life. Extremely important among these are the virtues of industry, initiative, and responsibility. All three involve being willing to work, even when the payoff may be intangible or in the uncertain future. Feelings of pride and a sense of accomplishment are the best rewards of all.

"All right, then, I won't ever again offer my child a bribe to get cooperation with one of my requests. And my child won't ever again lift a finger around here to help me! Now whose move is it?"

Well, I'm glad you asked. It's your move, and the sooner you make it, the better. You must play Brer Rabbit and outfox your young Brer Fox.

Begin by listing some privileges your child now enjoys and takes for granted. Any activity that is regularly available but has not been earned can be defined as a privilege. The list might include playing the stereo, having friends over, riding a bicycle, going out to play after supper, and being allowed to stay up later than usual.

Make another list of the chores and responsibilities the child avoids so cleverly. This list might include putting toys away, taking a bath, doing homework, emptying the trash, changing clothes, and walking the dog.

The next step is to look at each item on the lists and ask your-self the question, "When?" On the first list, for example, ask, "When does he like to ride his bike?" For the second list, ask, "When do I want him to take his bath?"

Put the two lists side by side and there you have it! By connecting the items, you can make rules such as "Before you can play your stereo [List 1] in the evening, you must take your bath [List 2]" or "Before you can ride your bicycle after school, you must change your clothes and take the dog out for a walk." Put only one item from the list of privileges into each rule. You can include more than one item from your second list if that seems reasonable. For instance, one rule at our house when our son, Eric, was twelve years old was that he had to take a bath, do his homework, and straighten his room before he worked on his models in the evening. It didn't matter to us exactly when he did the chores or in what order. We didn't remind him, but we checked to see that his chores were done and sometimes applied a little quality control before he was allowed to play. This is also known as the "Godfather Principle," because you are making the child an offer he can't refuse.

Or, can he? Sure he can, and he will. Every child will test every rule you've ever made. Like chemists trying to discover what solu-tion a substance will dissolve in, children will put rules to every conceivable test, but there is one substance in which no rule will dissolve, and that is consistency.

By consistency, I mean enforcing rules under all but the most unusual circumstances. I do not mean that a rule must be enforced in the same way every time. If a rule has many exceptions, if a child discovers that a rule does not withstand stress tests, it is not a rule but simply a wish. Also involved here is the issue of trust. If you establish rules and then fail to enforce them, can you be depended on in other ways?

An approach of this sort may not yield the kind of instant results that bribes do—and they require patience, a rather old-fashioned virtue—but the results are worth the effort.

How Well Is Well-Behaved?

Almost everyone is familiar with the concept of milestones as they relate to a child's developmental health. For example, the average age of walking is twelve months, and a child who is not walking by fifteen months should be brought to the attention of a pediatrician or developmental specialist. Likewise, developmental milestones have been established for talking, mastering the "pincer grasp," and understanding object permanence (something does not cease to exist if it is out of sight), to name but a few.

These days, largely because nearly every child has some approximation of a day-care experience by the time he is three, it has become almost impossible for a child whose development is seriously compromised in a certain physical or perceptual area to escape attention, for long, anyway. So, for example, whereas it was not uncommon in the 1950s to encounter children with pronounced articulation problems in the first grade, most articulation problems today are detected and corrected before children enter elementary school.

What people are not so familiar with is the fact that milestones exist for specific social behaviors as well, and that these behavioral milestones are as crucial to a child's overall adjustment as any developmental milestone. For example, by the time a child is three and a half years of age, tantrums should have stopped completely. This is not to say that the child is at risk if he cries when he is disappointed, but a four-year-old who, when he doesn't get his way, wails at the top of his lungs, spins around, falls on the floor, and acts generally out of control is six months behind the behavioral curve for tantrums. His parents need to act fast to bring these "toddlerish" episodes to a close so that his social adjustment can move forward.

The following is a partial list of additional behavioral milestones and the age at which each should be "passed":

- Uses the toilet independently (but might still require help with wiping behind): twenty-four months.
- Shares toys without adult direction: thirty-six months.
- Obeys most instructions when first given: thirty-six months.
- No longer interrupts conversations: four years.
- Helps without being told (e.g., carrying things): five years.

I did not pull these out of the proverbial hat; rather, I looked across cultures and across history. In most other cultures today, and in America as little as fifty years ago, children usually passed these milestones on time. That this is no longer the case does not indicate a problem with children, but with their parents. Many of today's parents seem to think that social behaviors simply emerge—that just as a child does not need to be taught how to walk, he does not need to be taught how to share. Sharing will just happen, they think, and whenever it happens is when it should happen.

For example, the mother of a five-year-old recently remarked to me that her child was "still bad about interrupting conversations." I thought to myself that the only problem here was parents who were being "bad" about not teaching this child that interrupting conversations is rude, disrespectful, highly annoying, and no longer acceptable at this age. It is to the child's benefit that his parents teach him firmly that interrupting is no longer going to be tolerated, that it must be stopped. People will thank him for his patience, he will (therefore) have something to be proud of, his parents will no longer nag at him for something that is their fault, and his maturity will have been accelerated.

How to stop it? Perhaps the boom might provide the necessary assistance.

The Referee's Rule

Consistency is an integral part of expecting children to obey—it allows for a child to predict the consequences of his behavior. The ability to anticipate consequences and adjust behavior accordingly is essential to the development of self-discipline, which is the ultimate goal of parental discipline. Without consistency, therefore, discipline isn't discipline. It's confusion.

Parents create rules and children test them. After all, testing is a child's only way of discovering whether a rule truly exists. Telling a child "This is a rule" isn't convincing enough. Children are concrete thinkers. They must be shown.

So when a child breaks a rule, parents have an obligation to impose a consequence that gets the child's attention and says, "See, we were telling you the truth." Consistency, therefore, is a demonstration of reliability. The more children feel they can rely on—believe in—their parents, the more secure they feel. If the child breaks a stated rule and instead of enforcing it, parents threaten or talk themselves blue in the face or get excited but don't do anything, the child is forced to test the rule, again and again and again. Testing of this sort spins the child's wheels. It wastes time and energy that the child could otherwise be spending in creative, constructive, growth-producing activities. Because consistency frees children from the burden of having to repeat the testing of rules, it helps children become all they are capable of becoming.

Children who can predict consequences are in the driver's seat of their own discipline. They know what's going to happen if they do this or that, so they quickly learn how to maneuver through traffic. Inconsistency is like a traffic signal that switches unpredictably from red to green, from right turn to left turn. Inconsistency causes children to have disciplinary accidents. Consistency, on the other hand, helps them learn to take responsible control of their own lives.

Children whose parents are inconsistent live in a world of constantly shifting limits, so these children must test their limits just as constantly. This constant testing is what we call disobedience. If the parents' actions are inconsistent with their words, a child learns that parents are unreliable and incapable of controlling the child's world. As a result, in an attempt to reduce insecurity, the child attempts to control the world independently, in the process becoming self-conscious (and self-centered), demanding, disrespectful, and disruptive. This quickly becomes a vicious circle from which a child cannot escape without help. The more inconsistent the parents are toward this misbehavior, the more they demonstrate their lack of control. In turn, the child becomes even more insecure, and the behavior becomes increasingly agitated and inappropriate. As the behavior worsens, so does the parents' inconsistency. Round and round they go, until that child's parents learn the art of benevolent dictation. When previously inconsistent parents finally take control away from a misbehaving child, that child experiences an immense sense of relief and security. The trick to never having to wrestle control away from a misbehaving child is to expect obedience in the first place.

To illustrate the importance of consistency, consider the job of a basketball referee. The referee's job is simply to enforce the rules, consistently and dispassionately. To do so, he simply abides by the universal Referee's Rule: no threats, second chances, or deals. Imagine the chaos that would result if nearly every time a rule was broken, the referee complained, threatened, gave second chances, bargained with the players, and occasionally vented his self-imposed frustrations by launching into a red-faced emotional tirade. Let's join just such a game in progress.

A player on the Red Team takes a pass from one of his teammates and drives toward the basket for a layup. As he nears the hoop, a Blue player sticks out a foot and sends the Red player sprawling unceremoniously across the floor. Immediately, the referee blows his whistle. As play stops, he points an accusing finger at the offender.

"Was that an accident, or did you trip him on purpose?" the referee demands.

Looking sheepish, the Blue player answers, "It was just an accident, honest. I didn't mean to."

"Well, okay," the referee says. "I'll let it go this time, but don't let it happen again."

The next incident occurs as a Blue player sets up to take a shot from the corner. Before he can release the ball, a Red player leaps up from behind and grabs his arm, preventing the shot. Again, the referee blows his whistle, stops play, and confronts the guilty player.

"How many times have I told you not to do that?" he asks, exasperated. "You let me tell you something! I'm about to run out of patience with you! The next time you do something like that, you'll be sorry, believe me!"

Soon, another infraction occurs and another confrontation. "Why did you do that?" the referee pleads.

The player shrugs his shoulders and looks down at the floor. "I don't know," he replies.

"What am I going to do with you?" the referee shrieks, holding his head in his hands.

As the clock ticks on, fouls become more frequent and obvious. With nearly every one, the referee's reaction is the same—reprimand, threat, complaint. Occasionally, he actually follows through with a penalty, but only after putting on a great display of verbal and physical histrionics.

Eventually, the game is in a shambles, a virtual free-for-all. Players push, trip, and even hit one another for control of the ball. All the while, the referee runs around red-faced and sweating, looking increasingly distraught. Finally, as the melee reaches its peak intensity, he suddenly shouts, "I've had it!" and looks pleadingly toward the heavens. We'll leave the referee there, petitioning the powers that be for relief from his terrible burden.

This description may sound familiar, since it typifies the disciplinary tone of many an American family. Children test rules, and parents threaten, berate, plead, and complain, all the while becoming increasingly frustrated. Finally, they melt down in a spasm of exasperation. For a while, all is quiet. Then the children slowly come out of hiding, and once again the snowball begins its downhill descent.

Inconsistency causes children to play at misbehavior in much the same way compulsive gamblers play at games of chance. Compulsive gamblers keep gambling, even when they're losing their shirts, precisely because they can never predict when they're going to win. This randomness fuels the perpetual fantasy that Lady Luck might be just one more throw of the dice away. In the same manner, unpredictable discipline causes children to keep throwing the dice of misbehavior. The only difference between compulsive gamblers and children is that while gamblers eventually run out of money, children never run out of energy.

There is one important question to address: "Is it absolutely necessary that the two parents, Mom and Dad, always agree on how to discipline a child?"

The answer—and it may surprise you—is no. Parents need to agree on the rules and expectations, but they do not have to agree on how those rules are enforced. To the extent that parents feel they must be in agreement, they will have problems. It is unrealistic to expect two fundamentally different people, who come into a marriage with different ideas about children, to agree on a single set of tools with which to regulate a child's behavior.

Each parent's toolbox is different, and each feels familiar and skilled with his or her own methods. Mom is inclined to send Junior to his room when he is disrespectful, while Dad is likely to take away his favorite toy for the rest of the day. So what? There is no conflict here, and there need not be disagreement. That Mom and Dad use different means of enforcing the rule is only superficially relevant.

What counts in maintaining harmony in the family is that Mom and Dad agree on the importance of Junior speaking respectfully to them (and other adults), and that they are equally quick to act when Junior gets out of line. Mom and Dad are acting consistently, even though differently, to reinforce the rule.

Commitment: More Than Just a Try

Not long ago, a young woman asked me about a problem she had with her five-year-old daughter. The problem was not an unusual one, but it had persisted in this family for two years, draining lots of energy and wasting everyone's time.

After I listened to this mother's exasperated descriptions and asked a few questions, I told her what I thought could be done to settle the issue once and for all.

When I finished, she gave a slight shrug and said, "Well, I'll give it a try."

"Well," I replied, "giving it a try won't work."

"What do you mean?" she asked, coming to life again.

"Excuse me for being so frank," I said, "but at best the most watertight of all possible solutions to your problem won't make change happen if all you're going to do is "give it a try"—and I shrugged.

She wasn't alone. Plenty of parents never get past trying. That is why so many of them lose control of their children, and themselves in the process. "I'll give it a try" is another way of saying "I can't." It is a statement of defeat, surrender, and personal ineffectiveness.

When you deal with a problem involving a child, more important than what you do is how you perform the solution.

Parents ask me a lot of questions, and most of them begin with the phrase, "What should I do when . . ." This manner of asking a question reflects the fundamental, widely held misunderstanding that for every specific problem there is one specific best solution. Not so. For every specific problem there are countless effective solutions. It doesn't matter which one you select—you can even invent a new one—because the real solution has nothing to do with technique or method.

The real answer is commitment, or determination, or resolve. It's the sense of purpose you invest in the method of your choice. The difference between method and commitment, the *what* and the *doing,* is the difference between form and substance. Method is nothing more than a vehicle. Without commitment, that vehicle is doomed to stall. Without commitment your method is impotent.

The difference between method and commitment is the difference between saying "I'll give it a try" and "This is the way it's going to be." Commitment is the backbone of whatever you do. Commitment is the energy of change. Believe me, your children will know immediately when you are "giving it a try." They will sense your ambivalence and your lack of determination, and they will not cooperate with you because you will have given them no substantial reason to do so.

When a child tests you, that is precisely what is happening—the child is testing *you*. Not the form, but the substance. And when, in response, you demonstrate your own sense of purpose in what you are doing, you also demonstrate your commitment to the child. Only when children are convinced of your commitment will they cooperate with you.

No question about it.

Decision-Making

Decisions, decisions—raising a child certainly demands its share of decisions. From the moment of birth through eighteen or more years of gradual emancipation, decisions never stop taking up a parent's time. No sooner have you made one than you must make another, and then another, and so on.

To complicate matters, there are not only those decisions you have to make, but also the decisions you must occasionally help your child make: what to wear to school, whom to invite over to spend the night, how to handle conflicts with other children, and so on.

It's enough to drive a parent nuts, and indeed we all veer off in that direction every once in a while. Most of us return from these little side trips with only minor scars, but some of us become lost forever. Some parents drive themselves to distraction simply because they get hung up on the details. Every decision seems momentous, from whether teeth are brushed before or after breakfast to whether or not the child should stay back in the third grade. Believing that any wrong decision has the potential of ruining the child's future, these parents become obsessed with always making the right ones.

This raises an interesting question: "What is a right decision?"

Many parents mistakenly think that for any given child-rearing situation there is only one correct course of action. That's like believing that of the forty or so items on a restaurant menu, only one is perfectly suited to your taste. The way parents make decisions is far more important than the content of the decisions themselves.

The same applies to managing a business. Effective managers are decisive. They don't waste time and energy obsessing over details. They trust their intuition and common sense. More than anything else, good managers realize it's less important to always be right than to always inspire confidence and a sense of purpose in those they manage. Wrong decisions are less harmful to an organization than a faulty decision-making style. To the degree that a manager is obsessive or indecisive, he or she will promote distrust, insecurity, and conflict in the workplace. Indecisive parents create similar problems in the home.

Do you see yourself in the following descriptions?

- You dwell on making decisions rather than trusting your common sense and just snapping them off. Obsessing over every decision wastes time, invites arguments, and is a sign to children that they can probably get their way by pushing harder.
- You include your children in too many decisions. Asking a child's opinion about some things has its place, but when that's the rule rather than the exception, the likelihood of conflict between parent and child increases.
- If your child dislikes a decision you've made, you're almost certain to compromise or give in. Parents give in to avoid conflict. Unfortunately, the more conflict they avoid, the more they ultimately have to deal with.
- You constantly explain yourself to your child. As I've previously said, children don't really want explanations, they want

arguments. Requesting an explanation is nothing more than a means to that end.

If the indecision shoe fits, you need to stop making your life—as well as your child's—so complicated. Start trusting your feelings. Stop worrying that you're going to traumatize your child for life if you make a bad decision. Bad decisions don't do long-term damage. Bad people do.

The Pitfalls of Praise

Beware of truisms. Often enough, truisms turn out to be false-isms, and this is particularly the case within the pseudoscience of parenting.

Most people, for example, think children need a lot of praise and that all praise is good. Both propositions are false. The fact is, children need little praise, and praise can be either constructive or destructive. The turning point is also, as we shall see, the reference point.

A team of researchers once divided twenty 5-year-old children into two groups of ten. Each group was taken separately into a large activity area staffed by several teachers. In the middle of the room stood a table overflowing with art supplies of every sort: colored paper, clay, crayons, paints, scissors. After a brief get-acquainted period, the children were directed to sit down and make something.

With the first group, the teachers moved around the table giving lots of praise, holding each project up for everyone to see, and generally effervescing with enthusiasm for what the children were doing.

These same teachers were considerably more reserved with the children in the second group. Instead of hovering, they stayed back from the table, and were involved in tasks of their own. Occasionally, one of them would ask if anyone needed help or more supplies. If a child showed his project to a teacher, obviously seeking praise, the teacher would respond with a few warm words.

The next day, the teachers brought the groups of children back seperately to the room. This time, they were allowed one hour of free play. The researchers kept track of the time children in each group spent playing with the art material.

Lo and behold, the children in the first group avoided the art table as if it were contaminated, while those children in the second spent little time anywhere else. This tells us that too much praise is negative and causes children to actually avoid the activities, people, and places associated with it.

It's important to distinguish between evaluative and descriptive praise. Evaluative praise is judgmental and personal. For instance, when Johnny brings his teacher a leaf collection, the teacher exclaims, "Oh, Johnny, you're such a hard worker and a joy to teach. If it wasn't for you, this year would have been terribly routine for me."

By implication, evaluative praise takes away the child's right to be imperfect. As a result, Johnny may begin to internalize an unreasonably high standard of excellence and may eventually begin feeling that he can't measure up. The end results of evaluative praise are feelings of inadequacy and discouragement, quite the opposite of what was intended.

Descriptive praise has no such built-in dangers. As the name implies, it is simply a description, an acknowledgment of accomplishment. In the case of Johnny and his leaf collection, the teacher could have said, "You obviously put a lot of time and effort into this collection, Johnny. Thank you for sharing this with the class."

Like sugar, praise can be habit-forming. Children who are praised either excessively or evaluatively often develop a dependence on outside approval. Children so hooked are like tires with a slow leak: Every so often, they must be pumped up, or they'll go flat.

Sometimes, adults praise things that shouldn't be praised, like using the toilet properly. We need not and should not praise children for growing up. A simple acknowledgment will suffice, because growth is its own reward. The adult who praises for an act of self-sufficiency is, in effect, appropriating the inherent pleasure of the event—stealing the child's thunder.

Praise can also backfire, particularly in the case of a child with a poor self-concept. Praise is inconsistent with this child's low opinion of himself, particularly if the praise is evaluative. The mismatch between message and image generates anxiety, which the child may attempt to reduce by misbehaving—setting the record straight.

In other words, praise is not something to be tossed out carelessly. Be conservative and thoughtful about it. Above all else, with praise as with punishment, take aim at the act, not the child.

Questions?

Q: **My daughter and first child is three years, eight months old. She is generally well-behaved except for a bad habit she has of screaming and running away from me when we leave stores, the library, or other public places. She seems to be throwing these fits because she doesn't want to go home. She'll pull away from me and run. Several times, she has run into the street before I could catch up with her. I have spanked her or sent her to her room when we get home. I have even gone so far as to show her a cat that had run into the road. When I punish her, she is sorry for what she did, but the next time we leave a public place, she does**

the same thing again. I recently decided I could no longer pick her up kicking and screaming and carry her to the car. She is just too big. I have been leaving her home as much as I can while I go shopping, but I can't give up my free time forever. What can I do to control this?

A: Before I answer your question, I feel compelled to make it perfectly clear that I do not endorse having small children view flattened house pets as a means of trying to frighten them into not running into the street. This is the sort of desperate thing parents do when they're feeling exasperated.

In situations of this sort, I recommend a method I call the "dry run." In this case, the problem for you is that when you leave the library or a grocery store, your hands are already full. Furthermore, you may be in the middle of a string of errands and can't immediately go home. So, you muddle through the situation as best you can, becoming more and more frustrated, and you end up not sending your daughter a clear, powerful message concerning your expectations.

Take her to her favorite store. Go with no purpose in mind but that of setting a disciplinary precedent. When you get to the store, look around for a while and then buy her something she wants. It is important that when you leave the store, you are not carrying anything except what you bought for your daughter. When it's time to go, and she begins to scream and struggle, you put down what you bought for her—whether or not you've already paid for it, which means it needs to be inexpensive—pick her up, carry her to the car, strap her in, drive home, and confine her in her room for the remainder of the day. Put her to bed early. This is definitely not "too much" for a child this age. Make sure you tell her that this is the way it's going to be from now on. The next day, take her on another dry run. When you get to the store, say, "Remember yesterday? If you scream, I'm going to take you home and put you in your room. When you're in your room, I get a lot done around the house, so scream and try to run if you want." Act nonchalant, like it doesn't matter to you if she screams and tries to bolt or not.

My guess is she won't scream, but if she does, so be it. In any case, three to five dry runs ought to solve the problem. Nonetheless, for the next three months or so, whenever you go to a store, you are going to have to remind her of what "the deal" will be if she loses control of herself.

Q: Inevitably, when we take our four-year-old into a store or restaurant, he begins misbehaving. How do you discipline a child when the eyes of the world are upon you?

A: The sticky problem of controlling a youngster in public places is one parents can unstick by using a simple method I call "Tickets."

Let's just say your four-year-old has difficulty containing his excitement in stores. He darts away from you without warning, wants to handle everything he sees, and interrupts you when you are talking to another adult. In advance of your next perilous trek to a store or shopping center, cut three ticket-sized rectangles out of posterboard and draw a "smiley face" on each. Just before entering the store, review the rules with your son. Tell him to (1) walk with you and stay with you at all times, (2) ask permission before touching something, and (3) not interrupt you when you are talking with someone else. For a child this age, keep it to no more than three rules. Hand over the tickets and say, "These three tickets are going to help you remember the rules. Every time you break one of the rules, I'm going to take a ticket away from you. When we get home, you must have at least one ticket left in order to go outside. If you lose all three tickets in the store, then you will be in the house with no television for the rest of the day."

Having a discipline plan enables you to keep your balance and your cool when a problem occurs. In the past, when he darted away from you in a store or put his fingers on expensive porcelain, you became instantly flustered. Now, however, you simply remind him of the rule and take a ticket. The keys to the success of such an approach are consistency (no threats, second chances, or deals) and a suitable incentive.

The incentive, or "carrot," can be anything your son is looking forward to doing later in the day, but it should be a privilege. Do not offer him a reward for behaving properly in public. Contrary to what most people think, rewards are not effective motivators. The best way to use rewards is to surprise, rather than bribe. For example, if your son is extra good in the store and keeps all or most of his tickets, you can (but are not obligated to) honor the achievement with a surprise ice-cream cone. But beware—don't do this so often that he comes to expect a reward, or you just might undo what you accomplish with the tickets.

"Tickets" is a versatile system that can be used to address a fairly broad range of misbehaviors. Take sassiness, for one example. Your six-year-old daughter has a bad habit of talking back to you and calling you various creative names when you don't do as she commands. Using a magnetic clip, secure three to five (the actual number isn't that important) tickets to the refrigerator at the start of every day. Tell Her Impudence that every time she sasses you, she will lose a ticket. If and when she loses all of the tickets on any given day, she will have to spend the rest of the day in her room and go to bed early. When you are finished with your explanation, she will undoubtedly sass you, giving you an excellent opportunity to demonstrate how the system actually works. Disobedience, teasing the family dog, whining—you name it—"Tickets" can handle it. The number of tickets allotted per day or situation is a judgment call, but the child should be able to beat the system fairly easily at first. Then, you can begin raising the bar by gradually lowering the number of tickets (misbehaviors) allowed per trip to the store, per day, or per whatever, until the problem is eliminated altogether.

Q: I recently left my three-year-old daughter with a sixteen-year-old babysitter for the first time. My daughter was fine for an hour or so and then began refusing to follow the sitter's instructions, running away from her, and screaming when things didn't go her way. When this sort of thing happens with me, I send her to her room until she is ready to obey and/or calms down. I wanted to discipline my daughter when I got home, but it was time for her to go to bed. I don't want to make being with a babysitter a dreaded experience for my daughter, since she is somewhat anxious about me leaving her. On the other hand, I expect her to mind babysitters. What kind of discipline should I tell a sitter to use when my daughter misbehaves?

A: Unless the sitter in question came with lots of experience handling younger siblings or other children along with the confidence of her parents, I wouldn't give a teenage babysitter permission to discipline a toddler. First, this expectation is above and beyond the call of duty. Second, most teens don't know the first thing about disciplining young children. Some high schools and community agencies operate babysitter training programs, and graduates of those programs may be more confident when it comes to disciplinary matters. With that possible exception, I'd relieve sitters of disciplinary responsibilities.

I have two tested ideas for you, the first of which involves making a dry run: Hire a sitter when you actually have an obligation-free evening, but act like you're going out. Make all the necessary preparations, greet the sitter, give her your cell number (or some other number where you can reliably be reached), and tell her to call you at the very first sign of misbehavior. It's important that you stress the need to call before the proverbial snowball begins rolling downhill. Go someplace close to your house and wait for the call, which will almost surely come. When it does, go home, discharge the sitter, and send your daughter immediately to bed. Depending on the nature of the offense the night before, I might carry over some punishment (e.g., no television) to the next day. The next time you hire a sitter, remind your daughter what happened the last time and let her know that you are only a phone call away. You may need to implement more than one dry run to get the point across, but the inconvenience will pay off handsomely in the long run.

My second idea is a variation on my general-purpose "Tickets" method, explained in the preceding Q&A. The next time you hire a sitter, take your daughter and the sitter into the kitchen. Tape two "tickets"—rectangles of colored construction paper—to the refrigerator. Tell your daughter that if she misbehaves, and be specific in that regard, the sitter will pull a ticket off the refrigerator. If the sitter has to pull the second ticket, when you come home, the child will be in trouble. If your daughter is asleep when you arrive home, then carry some punishment over to the next day. At her age, she can readily remember what happened the night before, as long as you are precise in your description.

You can also combine these approaches. Make one or two dry runs, and when you feel the sitter situation is under control, implement the "Tickets" system. In any case, you simply need to get across the point that even when you are absent from the home, your authority is in force.

Q: **My daughter's kindergarten teacher is using a reward system to manage classroom behavior. Children earn smiley faces for good behavior and can trade them in for prizes at the end of the week. On the other hand, nothing of any real consequence happens when a child misbehaves. When our daughter misbehaves at home, we punish her. Won't the teacher's very different approach cause some confusion, and won't it also teach my daughter to expect something whenever she behaves properly?**

A: Indeed, children should be taught that responsible people do the right thing simply because it is the right thing to do, not because it will result in a reward. Behavior modification strategies of the sort your daughter's teacher is using (known in psychological circles as a "token economy" system) undermine that understanding.

Research has failed to confirm the value of what is sometimes called "positive discipline." In the first place, rewards seem to work with children who are already well behaved and who would continue to be well behaved without a reward. In children with serious behavior problems, rewards seem to have no lasting positive effect and may cause behavior to worsen. Studies have also shown that the most well adjusted children tend to come from homes where parents punish misbehavior within the context of a loving, nurturing parent-child relationship.

Unfortunately, most school systems are well behind the research curve when it comes to classroom discipline, because a good number of today's parents will not support the use of punishment by their children's teachers, much less even acknowledge that their children misbehave. When their children are punished at school, these parents complain vociferously. Some even go so far as to threaten legal action. As a consequence, many private and public schools tend to take the "easy way out" on discipline. In the long run, this compromise creates a whole new set of problems, including an increase in the number of children who are referred to outside professionals, diagnosed with "behavior disorders," and put on behavior-controlling medication. The solution is for parents to support the use of effective, punitive discipline methods at their children's schools, with—and this is important—their own children (as opposed to only everyone else's).

Let me assure you that your daughter is in no danger here. The discipline used by her teacher is not going to cause her confusion, nor will it lessen the effectiveness of your discipline. You should ask the teacher to let you know if and when your daughter misbehaves in class, and follow through by punishing her at home.

In the final analysis, a teacher's discipline, no matter how effective, is not as powerful a deterrent as discipline delivered by a parent.

Q: **Life with my sixteen-year-old stepson, who lives with my husband and me because his mother is a mess, has been a battle from day one. School has always been a struggle for him, and he's had a problem with lying since he was a youngster. The really bad problems began a year ago, when he started hanging out with some troublemakers. He dressed like a gang member and began to write rap song**

lyrics involving sex, foul language, and violence. He has flunked almost every class for the past year. Last spring he was caught at school with a switchblade knife. He was arrested and spent seven days in juvenile hall. He's now on probation for two years. We have grounded him for the duration and will not allow him to get a driver's license. He says that we can ground him as much as we want, but we cannot make him care about school or stop dressing like he is a gang member. My husband says grounding is not accomplishing anything and wants to let up on it. I disagree and think his leniency, the result of guilt, has made matters worse. Help!

A: If by "grounding is not accomplishing anything" your husband means it's not causing any bright lights to come on in your stepson's head, I have to agree. Nevertheless, and for that very reason, I'd keep him grounded. First, that's the way the world works. If you aren't responsible, if you behave in an antisocial fashion, privileges are denied you. Call it reality therapy, even though you know it may not have any therapeutic effect at all. From your description, I'd say your stepson is on the road to huge problems as a young adult and that you may have passed the point where your influence matters. This brings me to the second reason why I'd keep him grounded: It will prevent him from getting into further trouble, for the time being at least.

The next time he tells you that grounding him isn't working, say, "Oh, we're not hoping that being grounded will make you a better person. We're doing it to prevent you, while you live here with us, from getting worse. So, you're grounded. When you're eighteen and off probation, you're free to move out and call your own shots. Until then, we have a responsibility to this community to see to it that your ability to cause trouble and create problems for others is minimized."

In other words, grounding this child is not so much for his good as it is for the good of others. Consider it a form of quarantine that will prevent the spread of the behavioral virus that is infecting your stepson. Little does he realize—and any attempt to get this through to him will fall on deaf ears—that if he does not do some serious soul-searching during the next couple of years, he probably is headed for a far longer and bleaker quarantine.

Your husband's intentions are good, but he sounds like a textbook example of the guilty divorced dad who unwittingly becomes an enabler where his children are concerned. Sad but true, too many divorced dads are not stand-up guys where their boys are concerned. Their guilt is largely induced by a culture that believes divorce damages children, when the truth is that it's the aftermath, including the guilty dad, that's damaging. Guilt paralyzes their ability to square their shoulders when their boys test the limits. They cradle, coddle, and cave in when they should be paragons of the virtues of fatherhood.

Stay the course, keep fighting the good fight, not because it will save this child, but because you'll feel better about yourself as a result.

Q: My ten-year-old son recently taught my fiancé's six-year-old daughter to play spin the bottle. When I asked my son where he learned this, he told me he'd seen it in a movie. I told him that he used poor judgment, and that he will pick up lots of things at school and on television that he should not pass on to younger children. He's a well-behaved child, and this is the first real problem in a long time. My fiancé

thinks I should have dealt more strictly with him. What are your thoughts?

A: Please reassure your fiancé that this is the stuff of childhood foolishness, nothing more. Playing spin the bottle at age ten or having it taught to you at age six by a ten-year-old does not presage later sexual promiscuity. It is inappropriate, but it doesn't merit any more of a response from adults than the response you provided. It sounds to me like you said all the right things; furthermore, that you said enough, but not too much. Good for you! Poor judgment, which your son was guilty of, is to be distinguished from a deliberate misdeed, and poor judgment can generally be corrected in an otherwise well-behaved child with a few well-chosen words.

Q: My two sons are seven and four. When their cousins of the same ages come over, they all go down into our basement to play. Invariably, within thirty minutes my youngest will come upstairs crying because his older brother is being mean to him, excluding him from games, and causing the cousins to gang up against him. I find myself going down into the basement every half hour to settle one of these disputes, but I'd like to solve the problem once and for all. What can you suggest?

A: You're absolutely right. Settling one of these conflicts does not solve the problem. As you've discovered, settling 1,358,495 of these disputes will not solve the problem. In fact, your willingness to serve as a mediator is making matters worse. By coming to your youngest son's rescue, you unwittingly cause the other boys to resent him. Therefore, they want to get back at him. When they do, he cries, and you come running again; and again you rescue, and again they resent. It's just a matter of time before another episode occurs.

Some experts might tell you to ignore it, but that's unrealistic. I couldn't ignore it. In fact, I'd be every bit as irritated as you are. Another expert might say, "Let them work it out." Not me. It may take the children years to work this out. Meanwhile, you will slowly become a prime candidate for the funny farm. I say you should help them work it out.

The secret is to transfer the emotional burden of this problem from you back to your sons. Leave the cousins out of this. They are guests in your home.

Here's how you do it: The next time the cousins come over to play, let only one of your sons down into the basement to play with them. Flip a coin to determine who it will be. Say, "Obviously you both cannot go down into the basement with your cousins at the same time without causing a problem. I'm tired of the provoking, and I'm tired of the crying, so only one of you goes down today. This is the way it's going to be for quite some time. Today, I'm going to flip a coin to determine who goes down, who stays up. Next time the cousins come over, the child who stayed upstairs today is allowed downstairs, and the child who was allowed downstairs today will be upstairs. Are you ready? Heads is older, tails is younger. Here goes!"

Bada-bing, bada-boom! The problem is solved. If the weather is nice enough to let them outside, let only the son whose turn it is to be in the basement go outside with the cousins. What this does is cause both boys to become equally highly motivated to solve the problem. And they will. Maintain this policy over the next four times the cousins come over. Then, when each of your sons has experienced forced exclusion twice and the cousins are scheduled to come over, ask the two of them, right before the cousins show up, "Do I need to keep one of you upstairs today?" I don't need to tell you what the answer will be. Let them both play with the cousins until a problem develops, then separate the son who would have been excluded that day.

What this strategy does is force the boys to solve the problem, something you cannot do. Before your boys can solve the problem, it must be *their* problem.

Q: My husband, who is a sports fanatic, has taught our two-year-old son to high-five, which our son does by hauling off and slapping the other person's hand as hard as he can. I think this equates to teaching him to hit, but my husband thinks I'm being silly, even though our son once high-fived another toddler so hard the child cried. This business of teaching male children to slap other people's upraised hands seems to be common. I'm beginning to feel like an old fogy. What do you think?

A: I propose that you and I found the Society of Fogies Opposed to Teaching Young Children to High-Five, because I, too, think this practice is dumb, moderately dangerous, and debasing of a child's respect for adults. Mind you, I have no problem with adults high-fiving one another, although I participate in this uncivilized display of exuberance as little as possible. I don't even have a problem with older children hauling off and slapping one another's open palms. It is, after all, childish.

One of the problems with teaching preschool children to high-five is their general lack of self-restraint, especially when the preschooler in question is male. As you described, preschool boys tend to rear back and *slap* the other person's upraised hand as hard as they can. The few times I've been foolish enough to cooperate in this inanity, my hand has suffered no small amount of stinging pain.

Pain in the palm aside, high-fiving implies a familiarity that simply should not exist between adult and child, even parent and child. In my old-fashioned estimation, this is a practice that should be reserved for mutually consenting peers, age ten and older. To me, high-fiving is the physical equivalent of a child calling an adult by his or her first name. Children should be taught to address adults with formal titles—sir, ma'am, Mr., Mrs., Miss—and shake, not slap, their hands. This high-fiving business is symptomatic of a strong need on the part of contemporary adults to be approved of by children, to be perceived by them as cool. Personally, I have no such need and fail to relate to the inherent insecurity it presents. Which gives me an idea: You can always threaten that if your husband does not stop the high-five lessons, you will take the earliest possible opportunity to teach his son the art of flower arranging.

I can see it now: "Nice bouquet, son. Slap me five!"

Q: I am the at-home mother of four boys—ages three, five, eight, and ten. They are well behaved (other people tell me this often), but lately I feel like all I ever do is discipline them. I'm not talking about yelling, screaming, or having a mommy-meltdown, yet I feel like I must be doing something wrong for discipline to take up so much of my interaction time with my sons. I spend much more time doling out consequences than I do having fun with them. Shouldn't this be getting easier if my boys are so well behaved, or does the fact that I have four kids mean that I

will always be disciplining somebody? My five-year-old recently told me that Daddy is more fun than I am. Is it possible to be a fun mom with respectful, responsible kids? If so, where do I start?

A: It sounds to me like you are micromanaging in the discipline department. A micromanager is always anticipating the worst, and that becomes a self-fulfilling prophecy. By nature, micromanagers are frustrated, but they don't realize they bring it on themselves. Because they hound people, because they nitpick, micromanagers create a predictable set of problems: conflict (in this case between parent and child and/or between one child and another), frequent miscommunication and misunderstandings, deceit, disloyalty (rejection of your values), and just downright, flat-out disobedience. In other words, micromanagers create problems, make existing problems worse, and solve absolutely none.

And to answer your first question: No, the fact that you have four boys does not mean that discipline is going to be a constant hassle. You are having a constant hassle because you are not letting the small stuff go by the boards and picking your battles carefully. Instead, you're picking on every little thing that happens. This is not discipline. This is harassment.

Make a list of the misbehaviors, big and little, that the boys have produced in, say, the last week. When you've finished, put them in order of "badness." For example, the kids' stealing from one another is obviously worse than a sassy tone of voice, so stealing would go above speaking to you with a "saucy" tone. When you've finished, write the top three misbehaviors on an index card, and next to each write the good behavior that needs to replace the bad one. Those three misbehaviors—called target behaviors—constitute your immediate discipline project. Post the index card on the refrigerator.

Now it's time to inform the boys. Tell them what you've done and why (you're nagging too much), and say, "This is what we're all going to begin working on. Your job is to replace the bad with the good. My job is to stop nagging. At the end of every week, I'll review your progress, and you will be free to comment on mine." As for consequences, I'd suggest that on any given day, when any one of them presents a target behavior, his bedtime automatically drops back a half hour. Make it clear, however, that this doesn't mean they have blank checks to misbehave in other ways, but only that you're going to make a conscious effort not to nitpick about every little thing they do.

At present, your approach to discipline is disorganized. That's why you're not seeing any results. An organized approach is almost guaranteed to bring results, but you must be consistent when it comes to enforcing and following through with the consequence. When one of the initial target behaviors disappears, move the top misbehavior from your original list to the index card. Never work on more than three misbehaviors at a time. By taking smaller steps and more time, you'll go a lot farther in the long run.

Q: Yesterday, while I was helping my seven-year-old daughter review for her spelling test, my five-year-old son began kicking the back of the front passenger seat and making obnoxious noises. My daughter asked him nicely to stop, but he didn't, so I pulled over and told him in no uncertain terms to stop. When I pulled back onto the road, however, he started up again, worse than before. I pulled over again and made him get out of the car. I then began pulling away slowly, keeping him in sight in the rearview mirror. He started running to catch up with us, at which point I stopped and let

him back in. I stressed to him the importance of being quiet while I helped his sister with her spelling words, and we didn't have another problem. When I told my sister what I'd done, she basically told me I don't deserve to have children. Do you think what I did was wrong?

A: While I might not go so far as to say you don't deserve to have children, I am in accord with your sister's disapproval of your way of handling your son's misbehavior. A moving automobile is not an appropriate place to conduct a review of a child's spelling words. It obviously didn't occur to you that when you are driving a car and are solely responsible for the safety of two young passengers, you need to be concentrating on the road, not on spelling words. If I were a policeman and I'd seen you doing this, I would have arrested you for driving under the influence of a spelling test (DUIST). If this isn't a misdemeanor in your state, it should be, punishable by having to write "disestablishmentarianism" one thousand times with a quill pen.

Apart from driving while spelling, you shouldn't be helping your daughter review for her spelling test in the first place. Learning her spelling words is her responsibility, not yours. I know, I know, most mothers help their kids review for spelling tests, but the ubiquity of this modern practice is testimony not to widespread good parenting, but to great numbers of parents who have little if any sense of boundaries where their children's academic responsibilities are concerned. A good number of these parents have no sense of boundaries as regards *anything* concerning their children. This does not apply to you, however, as you clearly demonstrated when you put your son out of your car and pretended to drive off.

With respect to your daughter and her spelling tests, buy her an inexpensive cassette player and a tape and instruct her as follows: (1) Put the player on "Record" and pronounce the first spelling word; (2) count silently to thirty; (3) spell the word into the player; (4) do the same with the rest of the spelling words; (5) rewind the tape, push "Play," and take the spelling test.

As for your son's misbehavior in the car, keep in mind that none of this would have happened if you had both sides of your brain focused on the road. There are no circumstances under which putting a child out of a car and pretending to drive off is appropriate. When children misbehave in my car, they simply lose a privilege later in the day. My penchant for boundaries inclines me toward simply sending them to bed early. If that isn't convenient, I make them memorize some spelling words.

Q: **My husband's eight-year-old son lives with his mother. We see him every other weekend and for two weeks in the summer. He has major problems in school, mostly with not finishing his work. He's well behaved when he's with us, but his mother lets him get away with a lot. Also, she doesn't believe she should punish him if he gets in trouble at school. She thinks the teacher should punish him for school problems, and that she should punish him for home problems (but she doesn't). We disagree. We have planned a trip to Disney World and have told Charlie that if he doesn't do his schoolwork between now and then, we will not give him spending money for the trip. He did his work for a week, then stopped. Now we're second-guessing our decision. What do you think?**

A: My general rule is that when divorced parents do not agree on disciplinary matters, the noncustodial parent (NCP) should not discipline for misbehaviors and problems that occur while the child is in the care of the custodial parent (CP). The rationale is practical, not psychological. In a situation of this sort, punishment meted out by the NCP is not likely to have any lasting positive effect and may cause the child to begin resisting visitation. The CP may also seize the opportunity to score points with the child by compensating for and effectively neutralizing the NCP's discipline. Under the circumstances, the original problem may well worsen.

Let's say you follow through with your original plan and give Charlie no spending money at Disney World. When he returns to his mother's, she makes it up to him by taking him on a relatively lavish shopping spree. Ultimately, Charlie is rewarded for not doing well in school. Then, with his mother's subtle (or not so subtle) encouragement, he begins resisting visitation. Suddenly, despite the undeniable fact that you have Charlie's best interests at heart, you are the villain in an unfolding soap opera that has the potential of spiraling quickly downward. In the end, Charlie is the loser.

When you arrive at Disney World, just give Charlie a reasonable amount of money to use as frivolously as he chooses. Don't even say, "We've changed our minds." Just give it to him. Do all you can to create a family experience that will forever stand out in Charlie's memories of his childhood. After all, Disney World is not a place to make an issue of things that have happened in Real World.

Q: So, John, are you saying it's all right for divorced parents who agree on disciplinary matters to be a "tag team" where discipline is concerned?

A: That's exactly what I'm saying, but the tag team approach should be limited to major behavior or school performance problems and only be employed upon request of the parent in whose territory the problem occurs. Needless to say, it is not appropriate for a parent who simply does not want to discipline a child to hand that responsibility off to the other parent. In the previous example, if Charlie's mom had requested her ex to follow through with certain consequences when Charlie fails to do his work in school, it would be appropriate for him to do so. As do all children in all family situations, Charlie needs to hear the same message from every significant adult in his life. But again, I wouldn't deliver the message at Disney World.

Q: My five-year-old son has difficulty making decisions. He starts the day unable to decide what he wants for breakfast. The more things I suggest, the more confused he becomes. During the day, he agonizes over everything from what friend to invite over to what toy to play with. At bedtime, he can't decide what book he wants read to him. Then he can't decide what clothes he wants to wear the following day. Since both my mother and I have problems making decisions, I'm beginning to wonder whether his problem might be genetic. Any ideas?

A: Your son is having problems making decisions because you're giving him too many decisions to make. A problem doesn't have to be genetic in order for it to get handed down from one generation to the next. Indecisive people try to get other people to make decisions for them. When you were a child, your mother probably dealt with her indecisiveness by asking you to make not only too many decisions, but also decisions you weren't capable of making. In so doing, she overloaded your decision-making capacity, and you eventually became indecisive, too. Now that you have a child of your own, you're passing that indecisiveness along by asking him to make too many decisions. And round and round you go, and where you stop—nobody can decide.

The solution is obvious. You must stop expecting your son to make so many decisions. But wait, that means you're going to have to start making more decisions yourself. We need to take a closer look at your own indecisiveness.

Indecisive parents are usually afraid of making mistakes. They think bad ones scar children for life, so they end up making no firm decisions at all, which is one of the biggest mistakes a parent can ever make. In fact, it's better for a parent to make a mistake every day than to be generally indecisive. Bad decisions can either be shrugged off with an "Oh, well" or corrected. A faulty decision-making style, however, can spell long-term trouble.

A child's sense of security is founded upon parental love and authority, and parents' indecisiveness causes children to feel insecure. That insecurity is likely to be expressed in the form of behavior problems. Do you see? The more you try to avoid making mistakes that could cause problems, the more problems you cause.

So, get decisive! Time's a-wastin'!

Tonight, while you're preparing your son for bed, go stand in front of the bookshelf and with your eyes closed pick out a book. Say, "This is the book I'm reading to you tonight." Don't say, "Is this one okay?" That's not decisive! If he says the book you picked isn't the one he wants, say, "Well, it's the one I want to read, so lie down and enjoy."

When you finish the book, pick an outfit, any outfit, for him to wear the next day. Say, "Put these on when you wake up." Don't ask if he approves, and if he questions your selection, say, "Because it's what I've decided." Then tuck him in and say good night.

The next morning, when he gets up, blow his young mind by fixing a breakfast and putting it in front of him with, "Here's your breakfast." If he says it's not what he wants, tell him he doesn't have to eat it. Then go sit down and read the paper. You see how simple this is?

Anytime you see him becoming indecisive, either walk away (if you have the time) or take over (if you don't). If you show him how decisions are made, it shouldn't be long before he begins following your lead and taking better control of his life.

Q: I'm a single mother with custody of my fourteen-year-old son. His father, whom he sees infrequently, has mental problems stemming from battle experiences in Vietnam. My son is obviously harboring a lot of anger concerning his father, but I can't for the life of me get him to talk about it. It comes out in the form of a lot of disrespect and hostility directed toward me. What should I do about this?

A: I assume that by "this" you mean your son's supposed anger toward his father. If I'm right, you're focusing on the wrong issue. The problem is the disrespect and hostility your son directs toward you.

In the first place, when you attribute your son's brutish behavior to his feelings about his father, you're playing amateur psychologist. You're speculating, which is what all psychologists do when they claim to know what causes a person to behave in a certain manner. You may be right. Then again, you may be wrong. If you're wrong, you're giving your son carte blanche to behave as abusively toward you as he pleases, whenever he pleases. If you're right, if your son is angry at his father, the question becomes "So what?"

Since when did less-than-perfect family situations entitle children to misbehave? My parents divorced when I was three. I had no relationship to speak of with my father until I was nine, after which I saw him only once a year for two weeks. In the interim, I missed my dad, was fairly frustrated by not seeing him, and didn't really understand why visits weren't more frequent. Nonetheless, I behaved respectfully toward my mother because she would not have tolerated anything less.

You're doing what today's parents have been trained to do by the media and mental health professionals: You're trying to understand your son's misbehavior. In so doing, you are not acting when he misbehaves. Because you do nothing, your son keeps on disrespecting you. Your intentions can't be faulted, but you have become your own worst enemy.

If I had disrespected my mother, she would not have tried to understand me. She would have punished me. If I'd said, "Mom, I claim immunity due to grieving and anger stemming from unresolved divorce and visitation issues," I'd have earned double punishment for refusing to accept responsibility for my actions. That was discipline before the Age of Psychobabble, and I daresay it was better for children, families, and our culture.

When you stop tolerating your son's disrespect, when you stop regarding him as a victim who is entitled to dump his feelings on you, when you begin acting worthy of respect, your son will begin treating you with respect. Toward that goal, I'd suggest that the next time your son blows up at you or treats you like a doormat, you say something along the following lines: "Well, isn't that interesting! Equally interesting to you, I'm sure, is the fact that you will not go anywhere except school and church for the next two weeks, during which you will receive neither friend nor phone call at this house. And every single time you act disrespectfully toward me during the next two weeks will add yet another week to your grounding."

Your son is in desperate need of learning that women are not dumping grounds for male anger. This is a lesson only a woman can teach him. Are you woman enough for the job?

Q: My parents live relatively close, and we see them fairly often. Spending the night with Grandma and Grandpa is a big thing for our four-year-old, who also happens to be their only grandchild. The problem is that during visits, whether we're there or not, the folks ignore our rules and let Michael do and have just about anything he wants. As a result, Michael is very hard to handle when we get him home, and it sometimes takes several days to get things back on an even keel. How would you suggest we deal with this problem?

A: I'm going to take the grandparents' side in this one. When our children were younger, we had the same problem with Willie's parents, whom we saw fairly often. After much frustration, we finally realized that no matter what we said or did, the folks weren't going to change. We also remembered that our grandparents had treated us pretty much the same way, and we were none the worse because of it. Finally, we admitted to ourselves that when the time came, we were probably going to spoil our grandchildren as well!

This change of attitude enabled us to realize that the control problems we were having with our children after visits with the folks weren't the grandparents' fault. Blaming the children's behavior on them was buck-passing of the first magnitude. If we were willing to let the grandparents spoil the kids, we had to take full responsibility for discipline.

Taking the bull by the horns, we sat down with the kids and told them that visits with Grandma and Grandpa were vacations from a lot of our rules, but when the visits were over, so were the vacations. Immediately after every visit, we held a transitional conversation with the kids, reminding them of our expectations. If they still had difficulty with self-control, we sent them to their rooms with instructions to remain there until they felt settled.

It wasn't long before we were truly enjoying our visits with the folks, and the kids were making the transition without difficulty.

Q: **We realize we've been much too indecisive and inconsistent with our six-year-old son. As a result, he's developed some behavior problems. How is he likely to react if we suddenly transform ourselves from parent wimps to benevolent dictators?**

A: Your child may not welcome the transformation. After all, it's going to require that he give up a significant measure of control within the family. For a time, his behavior problems are likely to escalate as he struggles to return things to the way they were. As they say, "Things get worse before they get better." If you stick to your guns, however, his behavior will improve, as will the overall relationship.

Unresolved disciplinary issues impede communication and expressions of affection between parent and child. Resolving the issues removes those impediments. It's impossible for parent and child to have truly good communication with each other until the child completely trusts and feels he can rely upon the parent's authority. As they say, the horse is your authority, and the cart is an open, loving parent-child relationship.

The same is true of a teacher-student relationship. Good classroom teachers recognize that they can teach only as effectively as they govern. On the first day of school, before doing anything else, they put the horse in front of the cart by going over the rules. Realizing that some children will be testing them, good teachers also explain exactly what's going to happen when a child breaks a rule. When rules are broken, good teachers follow through as promised. In so doing, they demonstrate their reliability to the students. The students, in turn, don't resent this. Quite the contrary, they trust their teachers because of it.

In the long run, the happiest children are obedient children and the happiest parents are benevolent dictators. Obviously, one can't exist without the other. So, for everyone's sake, go for it!

The Roots of Responsibility

Depending on the context in which it is being used, the word *responsibility* can refer either to an assigned duty—a job or a task—or to accountability for one's behavior. The former usage is represented by the statement "Taking the garbage to the curb is my responsibility." The latter usage is represented by the statement "I accept responsibility for having forgotten to take the garbage to the curb today." In this chapter, I explain the why and how behind each of two propositions: first, children should have regular duties around the home, and second, children should be held accountable for their behavior. I'll deal with them in that order.

Responsibility, Part One

Eight months a year I travel the United States, talking to and conducting workshops for various parent and professional audiences. I often ask my audiences to participate in surveys, one of which begins with this question: "How many of you can honestly say that you expect your children to perform a regular routine of chores around the home for which they are not paid, with an allowance or otherwise?" In an audience of, say, five hundred, no more than twenty-five hands will go up.

I then ask, "How many of your parents would have raised their hands to the same question?" Hands go up everywhere, and people begin to laugh.

This is really no laughing matter. It means that in the short span of one generation, we have managed to misplace a very important tenet of child rearing: *Children should be contributing members of their families.* Without question, the most effective way for children to contribute meaningfully to their families is through the performance of work in and around the house on a regular basis. Here are the reasons why chores should be an important part of childhood:

- As I said in chapter 1, the ultimate purpose of raising children is to help them out of our lives and into successful lives of their own. Therefore, we have an obligation to endow them with the skills they will need to lead successful adult lives, and domestic skills are no less important than any others. By eighteen, all children should be practiced at every single aspect of running a home. They should be able to wash and iron their own clothes, prepare basic meals, use a vacuum cleaner, disinfect bathrooms, replace furnace filters, mow grass, and weed garden areas. By their mid-teens, they should be earning a portion of their spending money and be responsible for budgeting it sensibly. This training not only helps prepare children for adulthood, it also helps develop in them an appreciation for the effort their parents put into maintaining a household, an effort the children might otherwise take for granted.

- Chores actualize the child's participation in the family, thus strengthening feelings of acceptance and security. A child who isn't doing chores isn't participating in his family to the fullest extent possible. Then the child's role in the family is a diminished one, much like that of a baseball player who, although a

122

member of the team, rarely gets to play. Participation generates stronger feelings of membership for both the baseball player and the child.

- Chores enable feelings of accomplishment. Knowing that his contribution of time and energy to the family is regarded as important enhances a child's feeling that he is a competent, trustworthy human being.

- Assuming that parents enforce reasonable quality control standards, chores enhance the development of a functional work ethic.

- Chores prepare a child for good citizenship. In his inaugural address, President John F. Kennedy said, "Ask not what your country can do for you; ask what you can do for your country." In other words, a responsible citizen is one who looks more for opportunities to contribute to the system than for opportunities to take from it. This is the core of the service ethic, which is unique to democracies. As Grandma used to say, good citizenship begins in the home. Child-rearing practices should reflect this principle. Parents should teach children that the reward of family membership comes more from what they put into the family than from what they take out of it. When this principle is turned upside down, when children are allowed to take from the family in greater measure than their contribution justifies, their relationship to the family becomes parasitic. Inherent to this condition is a lack of motivation, a feeling of entitlement, perpetual self-centeredness, and the entirely false idea that something can be had for nothing.

- Chores bond a child to his parents' values. They are a child's only means of making a tangible contribution to the family, and any act of contribution is, by its very nature, values oriented. Think about it. When you make a contribution of time, money, or other personal resources to a political, religious, educational, or charitable organization, you acknowledge two things: first, that you share values with that organization, and second, that you want to do something tangible to help support and maintain those values. The same applies to a child's contribution of time and energy to the family. Children who are enabled to contribute to their families on a regular basis come to a clearer understanding of their parents' values. Furthermore, they are much more likely to use those same values in their own adult lives to create success and happiness for themselves and their children.

The proof of what I'm saying can be found in the pudding of our country's history. In what general areas or regions of this country have family values and traditions been handed down most reliably from generation to generation to generation? Answer: In rural America or, more specifically, in farm country. And what single aspect most distinguishes the life of a child raised on a farm from that of a child raised in a city or suburban environment? Chores.

As soon as they are capable, farm children are expected to perform work within their families. If they are too young to do anything but carry a milk pail, they carry a milk pail. If they are old enough to drive a tractor, they drive a tractor. Their parents don't beg, bribe, or bargain for these chores. Typically, no money changes hands, although the child may share in the profit of a certain project. There are no daily arguments over why certain work has to be done or why a certain someone has to do it. There are no temper tantrums, no screams of "It's not fair." Parents don't waste time and energy on repetitious attempts at justification and explanation. Doing these chores is simply expected of these children, and so they get done. For a child raised on a farm, the family and its values take on importance not simply because of parental modeling and enforcement but because the child performs a valuable function. Put another way, the child is given the opportunity to *invest* in the family. When someone invests in something, that investment becomes worthy of protecting and preserving.

Willie and I didn't really begin involving Eric and Amy in housework until they were ten and seven, respectively. Until then, we had required only that they keep their rooms clean and orderly. Their growing reluctance to do anything else around the house finally made us realize the need to increase their day-to-day participation in housework.

We began by making a list of all the chores included in the housekeeping schedule, underlining those we felt certain the children could handle. We discovered there was nothing they couldn't do, and only three things—washing, ironing, and cooking—we preferred they not do, at least for the time being. We listed the materials and steps involved in each chore on separate index cards and divided them into two files, one for each child. The idea was to leave as little as possible to the children's imaginations. Finally, we organized the schedule on two 7-day calendars, which we posted on the refrigerator. We estimated that each child's daily chores would consume about forty-five minutes on weekdays (spread throughout the day), one hour on Saturday, and about twenty minutes on Sunday, for a grand total of approximately five hours a week.

Having put all our ducks in a row, we presented the plan to the children, who believe it or not accepted it without complaint. Well, almost. After we had explained the system, Eric looked at us and said, "What are you guys going to do, watch us work?" Children are so cute.

During the first few weeks, we had to prompt, remind, and even at times apply a little pressure. Our quality control standards were fairly strict. If one of the children failed to do a chore correctly or completely, he or she had to redo it. A forgotten chore resulted in the loss of a privilege, like going outside to play, for a day or two. It didn't take long for the children to discover that conscientious cooperation not only took relatively little time, but also cost less than the alternative. Eventually, it became obvious they were taking considerable pride in the contribution they were making to the family. In addition, they learned firsthand the ins and outs of running a household, a necessary step toward helping them out of our lives.

From that point on, Eric and Amy occasionally complained that they were the only kids they knew who had to do so much housework. Our response was generally a shrug of the shoulders. As young adults right out of college, both of them came to us independently and thanked us for raising them as we had. They each said that although they had sometimes resented the fact they were being raised unlike most of their peers, they now realized how strengthening that upbringing had been.

Good things come to those who wait.

Questions?

Q: At what age should parents begin assigning chores to children?

A: Three is probably the most advantageous age. A child this age has a strong need to identify with parents and expresses that need, in part, by following them around the house, wanting to get involved in the things they're doing, and imitating them if direct involvement is impossible. If Dad's repairing a leaky faucet, the child wants to help. When Mom cooks, the child gets out a few pots and pans and plays on the kitchen floor.

This interest can and should be capitalized upon by starting three-year-olds on a few minor chores. In order to establish a routine, chores should take place at the same time every day. A three-year-old can help make his bed in the morning, help set the table at dinner, and pick up toys every evening before a bedtime story.

Because threes are so eager to please, parents should have little difficulty obtaining their cooperation. Doing a few chores at this age sets the stage for increasing responsibilities as the child grows older. Parents are more apt to encounter resistance if they attempt to assign specific chores before age three. Also, children's "chore readiness" begins to wane if parents wait much later than four to begin acquainting them with this important part of family life.

Q: What can parents do with children younger than three to help prepare them for a responsible role in the family?

A: Parents plant seeds of responsibility by helping younger children learn to do such things as feed themselves, dress themselves, and use the toilet. Each of these accomplishments constitutes a step toward self-sufficiency and enhances not only feelings of competence, but also the child's receptivity to additional responsibilities. As children take these first steps toward independence, it's important that parents be more supportive than directive. In the first place, too much direction communicates the message, "You're not learning this well enough [or fast enough] to suit us." The child's reaction may well be to stop trying altogether. Parental overinvolvement also stifles the child's sense of accomplishment. In order for these successes to be truly meaningful, the child must have full "ownership" of them. The more parents hover—the more anxious they are about mistakes—the more frustrated the child will become, and the longer the learning will take. This policy of supportive noninterference applies equally well to children who are learning to use the toilet, feed themselves, dress themselves, tie their own shoes, make their beds, and even read.

Q: My husband and I disagree over paying children for chores. He feels that just as we get paid for doing our jobs, children should be paid for doing theirs. I say their chores are a family obligation, and that just as I don't get paid for cooking supper, they shouldn't be paid for feeding the dog and so on. Who's right?

A: I agree with you that chores are obligations that should be shared among the members of a family according to age and ability. Applying the word *jobs* to a child's chores leads to the erroneous notion that they are in the same category as an adult's employment outside the home. The difference, of course, is that the parent's job provides for the child's standard of living. This creates an obligation that the child can discharge by performing chores. As such, chores are a service rendered to the family, a child's sole means of contributing to the general welfare. As you pointed out, when the parent is at home, he or she has chores—family obligations—for which he or she is not paid. Under the circumstances, paying a child to do what adults do simply because they must implies that children enjoy a privileged status within the family, free of obligation.

One would think that paying a child for doing chores is motivating. Not so. In fact, it has the opposite effect. Paying a child for doing a chore creates the illusion that if the child doesn't feel the need for money at that point in time, he isn't obligated to do the chore. In this regard, I find that parents who pay for chores have a difficult time getting their children to do them without being hounded.

Paying for chores also obfuscates the fact that they are obligations. A chore that is paid for is no longer a contribution for the sake of the family, but a service rendered for the sake of money. Paying for chores puts money in a child's pocket but no true sense of value in the child's head. It may teach something about business but nothing whatsoever about the responsibility that accompanies family membership.

On the other hand, it's all right for parents to pay children for work above and beyond the standard routine. For instance, when Eric was in high school, I didn't pay him for mowing the lawn once a week during the summer, but I did pay him for occasionally helping me cut down trees and chop them into fireplace logs. By that time, Eric knew that payment didn't mean the tasks were optional.

Although a family is not and should not be a democracy, chores can acquaint a child with the fact that the viability of a democracy such as ours depends on the ready willingness of the citizenry to lay down self-interests and render public service. The service ethic does not arise spontaneously; rather, it is learned.

Unfortunately, all too many of today's parents fail to assign their children to a regular routine of chores as opposed to haphazard, unpredictable assignments. In so failing, they contribute to the notion that the only persons with obligation in the parent-child relationship are the parents. They are teaching their kids that something can be had for nothing.

My standard recommendation is that a child should become acquainted with chores shortly after their third birthday. The chores should become part of the child's daily routine, as predictable as taking a bath before bedtime. Begin with tasks in the child's own sphere, such as picking up toys at a certain time every day. Build on the child's success by slowly expanding the responsibilities into the general sphere. It is not unreasonable to expect a five-year-old to contribute thirty minutes of work per day around the home. To anyone whose eyebrows are suddenly raised, let me point out that thirty minutes represents one-fifth the time the average five-year-old spends in front of a television set on a daily basis. Does the typical child have the time for chores? Of course! Like everything else, this is a simple matter of priorities.

Q: How much housework can parents reasonably expect of a child?

A: At the very least, four- or five-year-old children should be responsible for keeping their bedroom and bathroom orderly. Six-year-olds can be taught to vacuum, starting with their own room. By age seven or eight, children should be responsible for daily upkeep of their bedroom and bathroom as well as several chores around the home. Once a week, children this age should be required to do a major cleaning of bedroom and bath. This should include vacuuming, washing the floor, dusting, changing bath and bed linens, and cleaning the tub, lavatory, and commode.

A nine- to ten-year-old should contribute about forty-five minutes of chore time to the family on a daily basis. It helps to organize the daily routine into three fifteen-minute blocks. The first of these should take place first thing in the morning (straighten room and bath and feed the dog); the second, right after school (unload the dishwasher and put everything away in its proper place); the third, after supper (clear the table, rinse dishes, scrub pots and pans, load the dishwasher, and take out the garbage).

By the way, in this scheme of things, there's no such thing as boy work and girl work. It's all people work. If you are "people," then you work.

Q: Are you against giving a child an allowance?

A: Not as long as the allowance has nothing whatsoever to do with the child's chores. Chores teach responsibility, self-discipline, time management, and a host of other essential values and skills. An allowance helps a child learn to manage money. The two lessons should not be confused. An allowance should not be used to persuade a child to do chores, nor should it be suddenly withdrawn to punish inappropriate behavior. Parents who use money to leverage cooperation from a child are unwittingly teaching that child how to use money as a tool with which to manipulate people.

Q: When there are two children involved, wouldn't it be fair for parents to let the children alternate chores on a weekly or daily basis?

A: As fair as it may sound, an arrangement of this sort never works out. In fact, I find that parental efforts to be fair almost always backfire.

Alternating chores inevitably results in several problems. The children end up arguing over whose turn it is to do what. Because none of the chores belong exclusively to either child, the children take less pride in their work and do just enough to get by. When parents complain that a certain job wasn't done properly, the children point their fingers at each other. Because the chores are alternated, it takes the children longer to learn the routine. As a result, parents must constantly remind and hassle the children to get the chores done. In short, this attempt at fairness leads inevitably to frustration and conflict.

A family is an organization, and everyone in the family should have the equivalent of a job description. Each person's job description helps define his or her role in the family. It follows that the clearer the job description, the clearer the role. In an organization where roles are not clear, people become frustrated and angry, and the organization doesn't run smoothly. I've never heard of a business in which people exchange jobs on a daily or weekly basis. I wouldn't recommend it for a family either.

Q: Our twelve-year-old son and nine-year-old daughter share chores in the evenings. Every night we have to remind them, and they always put up a fight before the jobs get done. The chores in question are definitely not too strenuous for them, and my husband and I feel the responsibility is good for them. What can we do to make sure they do their jobs, preferably without constant reminding and screaming (on their part, not ours)? The kids know their chores need to be done every night, and that they have to do them, yet they mess around until we start nagging, and then they blow up. We are tired of all this. Help!

A: Your children are afflicted with both explosive reaction to parental pestering (ERPP) and attention to chores (ATCHOO) disorders.

Both intensify over time, eventually causing parents to begin wishing they'd never had children.

The treatment plan is very specific: First, stop pestering. Tell the children something along these lines: "You will never, ever again hear us even refer to your chores. You know what they are, and we expect you to start them no later than [say] seven o'clock. If you have not started your chores by seven, we will do them for you. Sound good?" Say no more! To any questions, reply, "That's really all we have to say." Then, just sit back and wait. The next time the kids let the designated start-time pass, just pick yourselves up and start doing their chores. When you have finished, announce that it's time for them to go to bed. Be cheery! When they protest that bedtime is at least two hours away, say, "Oh, didn't we tell you? At seven o'clock, either you are on your way to do your chores, or we will be on our way to do them for you. If we do them, you have to go to bed as soon as we finish. Oh, and by the way, if we do your chores on more than one night, Sunday through Friday, then all weekend privileges for you are cancelled. Any questions?" All of this should be communicated in a matter-of-fact tone of voice, accompanied by dumb looks and many shrugs of your shoulders, as if to say, "Gosh, kids, we're real, real sorry about all this."

This will activate what I call the "Agony Principle": *Parents should not agonize over anything children do or fail to do if those children are perfectly capable of agonizing over it themselves.* The person or persons who become upset over a particular problem will try to solve it. In this case, you are trying to solve a problem—and driving yourselves slowly nuts in the process—that *only* your children can solve. They will solve it when you cause *them* to begin going nuts because of it.

Now, sit back, relax, and let your children learn how the real world deals with people who do not accept their responsibilities.

Q: Our fourteen-year-old son is forever asking us for money. He wants the latest clothes, shoes, and CDs. He wants money for movies, video arcades, fast food, and amusement parks. He wants money just to have money. We're slowly going broke! We give him a $10 per week allowance. Where it goes is anyone's guess. He says it's not enough, but when we give him the chance to earn more money by doing extra chores, he declines. Do you have a solution?

A: I can offer you a plan that worked for all concerned when our children were in their teen years, but let me begin by saying I agree with your son. You aren't giving him enough money. By the same token, you're not expecting enough responsibility of him either. You're making the biggest, and most common, mistake made by parents of teens: You're attempting to micromanage.

As I point out in my book *Teen-Proofing*, parenting a teen is a brand-new ball game, requiring new plays. Unaware of this, or perhaps unwilling to admit it, most parents fail to shift parenting gears when their children enter their early teen years. Instead, they keep right on trying to control them. In fact, because of the heightened anxiety that attends this parenting stage, most parents of teens actually try to control even more than they did when their children were younger. Parental control works with an eight-year-old, in moderation, but it won't work with a teenager. From age thirteen on, the more parents try to control, the less able they are to mentor their children toward a successful emancipation, and mentoring is the secret to winning.

Where money is concerned, your job is to help your son learn to establish good priorities, to budget. This is something he will learn only by trial and error. By giving money with no strings attached, you're making it impossible for him to make errors and learn from them. You can remedy this by giving him more money. Yes, you read me correctly: more money. Here's the plan:

1. For the next month or two, add up all the money you give your son each month for discretionary (as opposed to necessary) expenses: clothes, CDs, fast food, movies, video arcades, and everything else you listed.

2. When you've collected enough data, set up a checking account with all three of your names on it. On the first of every month, deposit into the account 80 percent of the monthly sum arrived at.

3. Give your son the checkbook and tell him that, from now on, he's to use his monthly allowance (changed from weekly) to purchase the aforementioned items and activities for himself. Say, "At your age, it must be demeaning to come to us for money. So you won't have to anymore!"

4. Tell him that, whereas you'll no longer be controlling how or when he spends this allowance, under no circumstances will you ever give him a loan against the next month's money. In other words, if he runs out, he has effectively grounded himself for the rest of the month.

5. Make clear that if he bounces a check, you'll pay both the merchant's and the bank's penalties out of his next month's allowance and deposit only what remains.

Now he'll be able to make mistakes and learn from them. As a consequence, he'll become more responsible and independent! Perhaps best of all, you'll stop going broke.

Responsibility, Part Two

Once upon a time not so long ago, parents expected children to fight their own battles, paddle their own canoes, lie in the beds they made, and stew in their own juices. These old-fashioned parenting aphorisms referred to a then-prevalent notion: Children were responsible for the consequences of their actions. If, for example, a child got in trouble at school, the child was expected to deal with his teacher and the principal and shoulder the punishment on his own. By and large, today's parents fight their children's battles, paddle their children's canoes, lie in the beds their children make, and stew in their children's juices. All too often, the child who goes to school today enjoys having parents who make excuses for him and argue with the teacher and principal over whether the child should even be punished.

I never cease to be amazed at the lengths to which adults will go to protect children from the consequences of misbehavior. They ignore, threaten, bribe, equivocate, run interference, deny, defend, pass the buck, and absorb consequences that rightly belong to their children. In the world of twelve-step programs, this is known as enabling, and it is well known that an enabler, despite his or her generally good intentions, furthers an addict's slide into depravity.

Misbehavior is addicting. It's exciting, it positions the child at the center of adult attention, and it imparts an illusion of power. It supplies the child with a rush that is just as intoxicating as the rush one obtains from an addictive drug. The enabling of misbehavior, then, is every bit as damaging as the enabling of alcoholism.

It is self-evident to anyone who was born before 1950 that a far, far greater proportion of today's children are in thrall to this addiction than was the case forty to fifty years ago. In my youth, children were mischievous. They tried to get away with the forbidden when adults weren't looking, but it was the extremely rare child who belligerently refused to do what an adult had told him to do. I don't need to prove that such behavior is ubiquitous today.

A preschool teacher recently asked my advice concerning one of her pupils. He can't keep his hands to himself unless he is threatened with a misbehavior report. Apparently his parents actually punish him when he comes home with such a report. He cries piteously when he considers this possibility, so the teacher makes a deal with him after he receives a report: If he will keep his hands to himself for thirty minutes, she will tear up the report. The problem, however, is that as soon as she does so, his hands start roving and touching and poking again. She writes another report. He is then good for thirty minutes, so she tears up the report. And round and round they go. Exasperated, the teacher asked me what to do.

I tell her to ask his parents the same question. They obviously know the answer. This teacher, for all of her good intentions, is an enabler of the child's misbehavior. His parents refuse to enable. They hold him accountable when he misbehaves. Naturally, the child prefers being enabled to being held accountable, so he manipulates the enabler, the teacher, so that she protects him from the consequences his parents would impose on him at home. Who does this benefit? No one, and certainly not the child. Actually, the parents in this story are in the minority these days.

All too often, when a child misbehaves, parents shoulder the consequences of the problem. They take on the emotional consequences by feeling angry, frustrated, worried, embarrassed, and guilty. (They stew in the child's juices.) They take on the tangible consequences by absorbing the inconveniences caused by the misbehavior. (They fight the child's battles, paddle his canoe, and lie in the beds he makes.) For example, they may be repeating instructions to the child more than once because the child rarely listens the first time. They may be losing time at work because of the need for frequent conferences with the child's teacher or principal. Perhaps they're repeatedly late to work because the child is never dressed and ready for school on time. They rarely enjoy any privacy in the evening because the child fights bedtime for several hours every night.

Responsibility for a problem is measured in terms of its consequences. When parents absorb the lion's share of the emotional and tangible consequences of a child's misbehavior, they unwittingly accept responsibility for that misbehavior. In effect, the problem now belongs to them, so they will try to solve it. The harder they try, the more frustrated they will become, because the only person who can solve it is its rightful owner—the child.

Situations of this sort call for an enactment of the Agony Principle, referred to briefly in the Q&A section earlier in the previous chapter. The Agony Principle proposes: *Parents should not agonize over anything children do or fail to do if those children are perfectly capable of agonizing over it themselves.* In other words, when a child misbehaves, the child should be assigned both the emotional and tangible consequences of that misbehavior. The child will not be motivated until the agony of it rests squarely on his shoulders. The child will not be motivated to solve the problem until that time.

In order to effect this transfer of responsibility from their shoulders to a child's, parents must draw upon the Godfather Principle. First articulated by a Sicilian philosopher known as Don Vito Corleone, the Godfather Principle simply states that in order to make a child accept responsibility for misbehavior of any sort, the child's parents must *make him an offer he can't refuse.*

A Trip to the Beach

The following true story is an illustration of the Agony and Godfather Principles at work.`

In 1976, shortly after moving to Gastonia, North Carolina, the Rosemond family began taking summer vacations at Myrtle Beach, South Carolina. For the children, the trip was the event of the year, but Willie and I dreaded it. Five hours in a car with two children, ages seven and four, in a state of high excitement might be a useful way of extracting information from POWs, but it's no way to start a vacation.

Two minutes out of the driveway, the children would begin bickering and wouldn't stop until we reached our destination. A typical exchange:

"Make Eric stop looking at me!"

"She has her feet on my side of the seat!"

"I do not! Stop pushing me! Aaaahhh!"

"Oh, be quiet, Amy! I'm not hurting you. You're such a big baby!"

"Stop calling me names! Aaaahhh!"

So it went, from driveway to motel, and nothing would stop it. Not begging, not bribing, not threatening to turn around and go home. Nothing.

After suffering through several of these experiences, and while anticipating yet another, Willie and I devised a way of ending the horror forever. Our salvation came in the form of ten rectangles of colored cardboard and a method we called "Tickets" (for more on this technique, see chapter 2).

When the appointed day arrived, we packed the car and then sat down with the children, colored cardboards in hand.

"Kids," we said, "these are tickets. Each of you gets five of them. Hang on to them, because they're important. They have to do with the rules of riding in the car. Rule One is *Do not bicker.* Rule Two is *Do not make loud noises.* Rule Three is *Do not interrupt when Mom and Dad are talking to each other.*

"Every time you break a rule," we said, "you lose a ticket. If you bicker, you both lose a ticket, no matter who started it. Now, the first thing you want to do when you get to the beach is go in the water, right? That's where the tickets come in, because if you don't have at least one ticket when we get to the motel, you won't be allowed in the water today. Instead, you'll sit on the beach under an umbrella and watch the rest of us play in the surf."

We gave out the tickets, piled in the car, and started down the road. Before we were out of the neighborhood, the kids lost their first tickets for bickering. Soon thereafter, Eric lost one for making a loud noise. Then Amy lost one for interrupting. By the time we were an hour down the road, they'd each lost four of their five tickets.

The next four hours were the quietest we'd ever spent with Eric and Amy, in or out of a car. They said not a word to each other or to us. They clutched those last tickets to their chests and stared out the windows. It was the start of the best family vacation we'd ever had!

Several months after recounting this incident at a speaking engagement, I had a phone call from a woman who had been in the audience. She had tried the technique, but with no success.

"The outbound trip was absolutely horrendous," she said, "so we decided to give your ticket method a try on the way home. We gave each of the children five tickets, just like you said, and promised we would take them out for ice cream if they didn't lose all their tickets by the time we got home."

"Take them out for ice cream?" I asked.

"That's right. They're always asking us to take them out for ice cream. It's one of their favorite things. Well, anyway," she continued, "they were all right for a while, but then the misbehavior started and they proceeded to lose all their tickets in less than fifteen minutes. Then, realizing we had no control over them, they were worse than ever."

No wonder! These parents had unwittingly violated the Godfather Principle by making their children an offer they *could* refuse! The trouble with promising a child ice cream for good behavior and then threatening to take it away for bad behavior is that ice cream—or the lack of it—is of no real consequence to them. Had the children stood to lose something important, such as being able to play with their friends once they got home, the likelihood of success would have increased twentyfold.

In the Q&A at the end of this chapter, we'll look at several other specific examples of how the Agony and Godfather Principles can be used to assign responsibility for a problem to a child.

Running After the Bus

A number of years ago, while I was in Kansas City speaking at a convention of city managers, I found myself on the same bill with Tom Peters and Robert Waterman, the authors of *In Search of Excellence,* the best-selling book about corporate management. Because they were scheduled immediately before me, I had the pleasure of hearing most of their presentation.

At one point during their talk, they flashed the acronym MBWA on the screen. This was not a new graduate degree they'd invented—it stood for a concept they called "Management by Wandering Around." That set off peals of laughter. Peters and Waterman then surprised the audience by announcing that MBWA was perhaps the most efficient and motivating of all management styles. Managers who practice MBWA are skilled at delegating responsibility and equally skilled at staying out of the way of the people to whom they delegate. They are authority figures who make their knowledge and expertise available to the people they supervise, but they do not hover over the people who work for them, watching their every move.

Managers who practice MBWA trust that their staff can and will do their jobs properly, and communicate that trust by not becoming overly involved in their work. They motivate people by giving them responsibility, along with the opportunity to discover the intrinsic rewards of independent achievement. By wandering instead of bustling anxiously around, they create a relaxed work environment, one in which people are free to be as creative and productive as they can be. Instead of being bosses in the traditional sense of the term, managers who wander around are consultants to the people they supervise. Their general policy is one of noninterference, and they break this rule only if absolutely necessary. They are role models, teachers, guidance counselors, gurus.

As I listened to and absorbed what Peters and Waterman were saying about the new manager, it occurred to me that MBWA applied to raising children as well. The most effective parents, I realized, are those who are not constantly busy in their children's lives, but are relaxed. Therefore they create a relaxed environment in which their children can discover their potential. Instead of hovering anxiously, they act as consultants on their children's growth and development.

Parents of this sort are authority figures, but they guide and model more than they order. Their goal is not to make their children subservient or dependent, but to make them independent and responsible. Toward this end, they provide a variety of opportunities for growth but allow their children a great deal of freedom when it comes to choosing or rejecting those opportunities.

Instead of taking credit when their children behave well and feeling guilty when their children behave poorly, they assign their children the responsibility, both positive and negative, for their own behavior. Above all else, they let their children make mistakes, realizing that some of the most valuable lessons in life can only be learned through trial and error. In all these ways, they send messages of trust and personal worth to their children, who are free to discover their capacities for love and creativity. In effect, these parents practice the all but lost art of "Parenting by Wandering Around."

It is unfortunate that more parents are not like these wonderful couples. I am thinking in particular of well-intentioned men and women who insist upon becoming too involved in their children's lives. Because they live through their children, they take their children's successes and failures very seriously and very personally. They overdirect, overprotect, and overindulge. They take on the responsibility that rightfully belongs to their children, thus robbing them of opportunities for growth.

A number of years ago, I came across an article in the *Hartford Courant* written by Nancy Davis, a teacher of journalism at a school in Connecticut. She wrote:

> The advice that children need to try and fail, with supportive parents behind them, is hard for parents to take. We want to spare them the failures, big and small, which we experienced or which we see looming on their horizons. We've been told a hundred times that people learn from their mistakes, but we want our children to never make mistakes because they may be hurt in the process.

Davis's advice to parents was simply, "Don't run after the bus." Those five words capture the essence of good parenting better than any five I've heard in a long time.

The Sound of Face Striking Pavement

A mother asked what she could do to get her six-year-old son to keep his shoelaces tied. "I know this must sound silly," she said, "but every time I look at him, his laces are flopping all over the place. It's driving me nuts!"

"Why do you want him to keep his shoelaces tied?" I asked.

"Well," she answered, "besides looking bad, he's going to trip over them someday."

"And what's the worst thing that could happen if he tripped?"

She thought for a moment. "He might fall and hurt himself."

"Badly?" I asked.

"Probably not," she answered.

"But perhaps badly enough to think twice the next time he leaves his shoelaces untied?" I offered.

After a thoughtful pause, she answered, "Maybe."

"Then I suggest you do nothing at all. Let his shoelaces flop. Let him learn the hard way."

The hard way—my dad used that phrase a lot. "There are certain things I can't teach you," he would say. "You're going to have to learn them the way everyone else does, the hard way."

In retrospect, I realize Dad was right on the mark. Some of the most valuable lessons in my life have been learned courtesy of falling flat on my face.

By and large, today's parents seem to think that letting children fall flat on their faces when the fall could have been intercepted or prevented is not only irresponsible, but downright cruel. The prevailing attitude is that if you see the fall coming and do nothing to prevent it, you are responsible for the results, not the child.

Cedric won't do his homework, so every evening his parents sit down with him and see that it gets done. Whenever Angel has a conflict with another child in the neighborhood, her mother runs interference, calling the other child's parents, making sure everything is set right. To prevent him from falling in with the wrong crowd, Roger's parents censor his choice of friends. Englebert's parents take him to a different after-school activity every day of the week and Saturday morning to make sure he stays "active."

I call this sort of obsessive hovering "Parenting by helicopter," and because of it many of today's children never learn to accept responsibility for their behavior because their parents are doing a fine job of accepting that responsibility for them. But responsibility isn't the only thing at stake.

Almost all learning is accomplished through trial and error. If you prevent the error, you prevent the learning. By making mistakes, one learns what works and what doesn't. Eventually, after a period of failure, the person fine-tunes his or her skills and masters the task at hand.

Standing back and letting failure occur in a supportive but non-interfering way gives a child room to develop initiative, resourcefulness, and numerous problem-solving skills. It also lets the child come to grips with the frustration inherent in learning any skill: social, academic, emotional, and so on. That's how children learn to persevere, and perseverance—as we all know from experience—is the main ingredient in every success story.

It all boils down to this: If we want our children to stand on their own two feet, we must also be willing to let them fail. So let's stop tying their shoelaces.

Making Amends

There is a general tendency among adults to feel that when a child misbehaves, the child should be punished. That's generally true, but it's also true that punishment sometimes misses the point. When a child's misbehavior is hurtful to someone else, for example, it's more important that the child make amends.

A number of years ago, an upset neighbor called to tell us that eight-year-old Amy had been disrespectful toward her. The implication in her outrage was that we must be bad parents for having such a bad child.

When she'd finished venting her anger, I said, "Let me assure you of several things. First, I believe what you're telling me. Second, I agree that what Amy did was completely inappropriate, and there is no excuse for it. Third, I'm grateful to you for letting me know and for being so honest about your feelings. Fourth, Amy will correct the problem she has created. Last, but not least, I want you to feel free to call anytime you see one of our children doing something wrong."

There was a long period of silence on the other end of the line. Finally, in an almost apologetic tone, the neighbor said, "Well, now, you know Amy is usually a very good little girl. This is the only time she's ever given me trouble."

"I'm glad to hear that," I said, "but that doesn't excuse or erase what she's done."

When the conversation ended, I found Amy and confronted her with the neighbor's report. "I'm very unhappy about this," I said. "You do not have permission to be disrespectful to any adult, under any circumstances."

She started to cry. A good sign, I thought, but just feeling bad about what she'd done wasn't going to correct the mistake.

"I've decided that you're going to apologize to our neighbor for your disrespect."

Amy immediately became very agitated. "Oh, please, don't make me do that. Make me stay inside, and don't let me play with my friends, or take my toys away, but don't make me go over there and apologize, please, please!"

"Sorry, kid, but this isn't open for discussion."

"Can I call her on the phone?"

"No, you'll do it face-to-face."

"Will you go with me?"

"No, Amy, I won't. I didn't help you create the problem, and I won't help you solve it. And that is my final word on the subject."

When she realized I wasn't going to budge, she composed herself, walked across the street, rang the doorbell, and apologized. As I watched from the living room window, I saw the neighbor smile, take Amy's hand in hers, and nod as if to say that everything was all right.

Amy came back across the street with tears streaming down her face. There were no more punishments, no more lectures. In fact, we never mentioned the situation again.

Sometimes, when I tell this story or another like it, a listener will remark that it sounds as if I'm in favor of "laying guilt trips" on children. To a certain extent, I am. When children do something wrong, they should feel the wrong of what they've done. The only way to communicate that feeling is through the child's emotional system. In other words, just telling a child she did wrong isn't usually enough. The words you use must come across with enough impact to make the child feel guilty or embarrassed or sorry or all those things.

The term *guilt trip* carries a lot of negative connotations, and guilt can certainly be used in sadistic, hostile ways. At its extremes, guilt is maladaptive. People who are incapable of feeling guilt are called sociopaths. They do what they please without regard for anyone else or remorse for whatever hurt they might cause. On the other hand, people who carry around excessive feelings of guilt are neurotic. They are constantly haunted by the idea that they're doing something wrong. Guilt can also be a very adaptive emotion. Without it, civilization as we know it wouldn't exist. People won't accept responsibility for their own bad behavior unless they feel bad about it. Guilt is a message from inside that says we misbehaved and shouldn't behave that way again. The idea that all guilt is bad came out of the do-your-own-thing philosophy of the sixties and seventies. Well, it's high time we got our heads out of the clouds and planted our parenting attitudes in the soil of common sense.

Our job as parents is to socialize our children. You can't teach a child how to act without also teaching that child how to think and how to feel. Children won't know to feel guilty unless we first teach them that guilt is appropriate to certain situations. That's how a child's conscience develops. Once you've taught children the basics, you can trust them to come to feelings of guilt on their own, when those feelings are appropriate. Even so, there may be times, as was the case with Amy and the neighbor, when parents will need to drive the point home.

Empathy vs. Sympathy

I frequently encourage parents to stop sympathizing with their children's problems and begin empathizing with them instead. They often tell me they didn't know there was a difference, but there is, and it's a big one. Empathy involves understanding and sends the message, "What are you going to do about it?" Sympathy, on the other hand, involves pampering and sends the message, "Oh, you poor thing! You haven't done anything to deserve this!" Sympathy is like custard. The longer you stir it, the thicker and stickier it gets. Eventually, it does more to hinder change than help it.

When a child is having personal problems, a little sympathy can sometimes help open lines of communication, but sympathy has a quickly reached point of diminishing returns. Stir too much into a situation, and you're likely to create more problems than you solve.

Why? Because, like morphine, sympathy in small amounts eases pain, but in large amounts it's addictive. Once addicted, the child stops trying to solve problems and starts trying to get more and more sympathy. Since a problem has to exist in order for the child to get sympathy, problems begin to accumulate as the child settles ever more passively and comfortably into the role of victim.

When Eric entered junior high, he had problems getting along with his peers. At first, he complained of being picked on, then that other kids were trying to get him in trouble, then that he had no friends. Initially, we regarded his complaints with a grain of salt, thinking they were nothing more than temporary problems of adjustment. As time went on, however, things went from bad to worse. We noticed that he rarely received phone calls, that he spent weekend nights at home, and that he was looking and acting increasingly depressed. On occasion, we'd hear him crying in his room. Alarmed, we started asking questions. Out came the most horrendous tale of woe we'd ever heard.

There was a group of kids at school, he said, who were not only making fun of him, but spreading rumors that he was—well, let's just say "different." He was being ostracized by the other boys and ignored by the girls. One particular group of boys had even written an obscene note to a girl and signed Eric's name to it. For that, he was grilled by the principal, who ended up satisfied that Eric had nothing to do with it. Nonetheless, the incident left its mark on the little guy's self-confidence.

We knew junior high kids were capable of sadistic cruelty, but this seemed beyond belief. So we sympathized. We talked; we counseled; we comforted; we even cried with him. We tried building him up by telling him what a really wonderful person he was and said his tormentors wouldn't turn out half as well. We did everything we could think of to let him know how unfair we thought the whole mess was. But things just kept getting worse. He moped constantly, he never went out, and the tales of woe became more and more woeful. Finally, we realized Eric was suffering as much from an overdose of sympathy as he was from anything else.

Our good intentions had whipped a relatively small flame into a forest fire.

Finally, we sat down with him and said, "Look, kid, we feel for you, but we've noticed that you aren't doing anything to solve these problems. So we've decided there are going to be no more conversations about your social problems. We've said all there is to say. Now it's time for you to get in gear and do something for yourself. We're giving you three weeks to find a friend and start doing things with him. If you haven't done anything by then, we'll take matters in hand and begin calling some parents to see if we can arrange some activities. In other words, either you do it or we will."

In two weeks, he had a friend. Within a year, he had more friends than he could keep up with.

That's the difference.

It's Never Too Late

In order for children to become successful at the three R's of reading, 'riting, and 'rithmetic, their parents must first teach them the three R's of respect, responsibility, and resourcefulness.

After I explained this concept to a group of professional educators in Phoenix, a teacher approached me to ask, "Can something still be done for a fourteen-year-old whose parents, until now, have failed to teach your three R's?"

"It may not be too late," I replied, "but in order to reverse a situation with that much history and momentum behind it, the parents will have to do the very thing they've been afraid to do for fourteen years."

"Which is?" she asked.

"Make their child unhappy," I said.

The personality of a child is not, contrary to myth, carved in stone by age six—or by age sixteen, for that matter. It remains flexible and, therefore, malleable, well through adolescence. Even an adult will find that significant events and relationships continue to mold their personality for as long as the individual is receptive to change. In the final analysis, the ability to change is a matter of choice, not chronology. The problem is that teenagers in need of an "attitude adjustment" aren't likely to recognize the need. Since they aren't going to make the decision, someone needs to make it for them.

Once the decision has been made, the first step is that of getting the teenager's attention. The only way to do this is to confront the teen with full responsibility for his behavior. Since responsibility is measured in terms of consequences, this means the parents must stop whatever they're doing to protect the youngster from consequences.

I'm talking about a crash course in reality. This kind of emergency action demands commitment, consistency, and a complete lack of sympathy for the child's sudden plight. In addition, the parents need to let go of guilt for past mistakes—whether real or imagined. Actually, sympathy and guilt go hand in hand. Guilt— the idea that "if I'd been a better parent, my child would be a better person"—drives sympathetic responses. In turn, these responses generate compensatory behavior.

For the confrontation to succeed, parents must stop blaming themselves (dwelling in the past) and charge strategically ahead toward their objectives (focus on the future). It stands to reason that when you confront the irresponsible youth with reality, unhappiness will be the inevitable result.

The fact is that sometimes unhappiness is not only the best form of therapy, it's the only form possible.

Therapeutic Unhappiness

Occasionally, my spirits are lifted by stories of parents who are willing to stand tall, go the distance, fight the good fight—parents who are willing to force reality on children who want no part of it. One such couple discovered that their sixteen-year-old son was using pot. They found the evidence in his room and his car. They informed him of their find. He promised to stop. Several weeks later, they found more evidence. They impounded his car and removed a part that is essential to ignition. To get his car back, he had to stop all association with three accomplices, bring his grades up to their predrug level, and submit to weekly drug testing. If he managed to stay clean for a month, he would get his car back but would still have to submit to random drug tests and maintain good grades. He got his car back. One week later, he came home smelling like pot. The parents said nothing. The next day, they checked with the school counselor and discovered he was again eating lunch with a certain criminal crowd. The parents went immediately to the school, seized his car from the parking lot, drove it to a used car dealer, and sold it.

They told him they would never buy him a car again. If he abided by the rules and passed his drug tests for three months, they would allow him to use one of their cars. If he earned back his driving privileges and subsequently slipped back over the line, then the next time he drove a car would be one that he bought himself, postemancipation. The prodigal is in month two of his new life, and all seems to be going well. Who knows what the future holds? In any case, he has learned that his parents will not fool around with this issue. They will not whine and wring their hands. They will stand tall and continue to do so for as long as it takes.

If there were Congressional Medals of Good Parenting, these folks would certainly receive one.

A Final Word

A fellow who was unhappy with something I'd said in my syndicated column wrote a letter to the *Charlotte Observer*, which closed with "After all, it takes eighteen to twenty years to 'grow a child.'"

Yep, he put his finger right on the problem. These days, after parenting for eighteen to twenty years, many American parents still have children on their hands. To make matters worse, they often continue to enable these children for years to come, thus assuring that their children's transition to adulthood, if it ever truly occurs, will be accompanied by much otherwise unnecessary pain.

In the course of my travels as a public speaker, I have frequent opportunities to talk to managers in the business world. Their uniform lament is that young people are entering the job pool expecting the employer to tolerate what their parents tolerated: sloppy work habits, disrespect toward authority, a casual attitude toward rules, and a reluctance to accept full responsibility for the tasks they are assigned. Not once have I heard a manager or an employer describe the typical young adult employee in glowing terms. Relatively few young people seem to have acquired a traditional work ethic. Instead, they bring to the workplace an entitlement ethic. They believe they deserve to have what they want, and the employer who does not provide it is being "unfair."

The employer's expectations that they show up on time, follow the job description, abide by the policies manual, don't leave early, be courteous to each and every customer—are acceptable only until such time as they become inconvenient to the employee or inconsistent with how he or she *feels* at the moment. After all, these are kids who were told as they were growing up that their feelings trumped all other considerations.

The trend toward delayed adulthood is noticed by college professors who tell me it is no longer unusual for a parent to complain about a grade dispensed to his or her child. One professor at a prestigious eastern university related the story of parents who both flew from California to challenge the semester grade earned by their son, a junior. They were furious, he said, that the grade in question might well prevent their son from becoming accepted by the medical school of his choice. They were unable to grasp that the grade merely reflected their son's unwillingness to do the work required; therefore, if he was refused entry to the medical school, it was not the professor's fault, but the child's. At least a dozen college professors have told me similar tales. One actually told me that a student's parents demanded that he ignore plagiarism and essentially award an outstanding albeit posthumous grade to Henry David Thoreau.

The trend toward delayed adulthood was reflected in the lament of a University of Oklahoma sorority house mother who told me that most of the young ladies under her supervision plan, upon graduation, to go back home and live with their parents until they get married. This has since been echoed by two other sorority house mothers in North Carolina and California. Forty years ago, the typical young adult was fully emancipated, economically and otherwise, by age twenty. The average age of full and final economic emancipation has since climbed above twenty-six, and it continues to climb.

My wife recently remarked that the oversize clothes worn by many of today's young people cause them to look like toddlers. "That fits," I told her, and she laughed at the pun, but this is no laughing matter. The ubiquity of delayed adulthood does not bode well for children, parents, families, schools, American business and industry, the economy, the national defense, or the culture.

Yes, it seems that nouveau American parenting is producing children, not adults. The problem is, these children can vote. We can only be thankful that most of them do not exercise the privilege.

Questions?

Q: We have a very willful four-year-old son who refuses to sleep by himself. Instead, he sleeps with my husband and me. He won't even go into his room by himself during the day. In fact, he won't go anywhere in the house by himself. If he wants something from his room, he makes one of us go in there with him. We've gone over the house security system with him and explained to him that monsters aren't real, but he still refuses to budge. If we try to make him go somewhere in the house on his own, he starts crying and shaking. I know he's not faking it. He is genuinely frightened. It's gotten to the point that he insists on sleeping in between us instead of to one side of the bed or the other. We are at a loss. What should we do?

A: First, you must absolutely stop talking to your son about his fears. It is difficult for parents to understand, but the more one tries to explain, reason, reassure, or cajole a child into not fearing something, the more intense the child's fear will become. Logic has no effect on irrational thinking. Furthermore, I'll bet that you and your husband have said all there is to say about this issue. There is no point in further talk, and from now on you must tell him whenever he brings up the subject, however he brings it up: "We've talked about that, and we're not going to talk about it anymore, ever again."

Second, you must stop cooperating with daytime requests that you fetch things for him from his room. Just say, "Sorry, but I'm not doing that for you anymore, ever, and we're not even going to talk about it." Then turn around and walk away and leave him to his hysterics. By the way, they are "genuine." In his own mind, his fears are real. Nevertheless, they are not based in external reality and for him to discover this, your protection must end.

Third, and about a week after you cold-turkey him off your fetching, you must get him out of your bed. Given the precedent you've set, this cannot be done gradually, nor can it be done easily. The longer you put it off, the more difficult it will be on all concerned.

Since the change from family bed to child's bed may take four or five days of complete resolve, take a Thursday and Friday off and begin your son's bedtime rehabilitation on a Wednesday night. Don't give this a big buildup. Ten minutes before his bedtime on the chosen Wednesday night, sit down with your son and say, "We spoke to your doctor today, and he says you cannot sleep with us anymore. Not one more night. So, you're sleeping in your own bed tonight. He also says that you can keep all your lights on and your door open, but neither of us can be in there with you. He says that if you try to come into our room, we have to lock our door, in which case you can sleep in the hall outside our door. We can't let you in, no matter how much you scream and cry. Do you have any questions?"

Please note that this conversation should not end in "Do you understand?" or "Okay?" Rather, "Do you have any questions?" And remember, answer questions, but do not, under any circumstances, engage in conversation or explanation. Needless to say, you should not linger in his room at bedtime, even if he begins to become hysterical.

Be forewarned: He may scream all night. That's one reason why the night before several days off work is the best time to begin his recovery. In the morning, after the worst night of your lives, come out of your room, look at him, and say, "Well, look at you! You're still alive! We're gonna do this again tonight, you know." Then take his hand and say, "C'mon, let's go get some breakfast and talk about our day."

Q: My thirteen-year-old son waits until the last possible moment to begin doing his homework. He no longer has a set bedtime, but he must be in his bedroom after 9:00 in the evening. It doesn't matter how much homework he has or even whether he has a test the next day, he doesn't crack a book until he's in his room. I've talked myself blue in the face about the importance of making good grades and about how he simply can't be doing his best if he does homework when he's tired, but he says his grades are good enough (mostly B's with an occasional A). Should I let him make this decision? This is driving me nuts! What can I do to get him to do his homework at a decent hour?

A: Nothing, apparently. I can't solve this problem for you. No, make that I *won't* solve this problem for you. I agree with your son. He should be allowed to make this decision. I'd suggest, therefore, that you do yourself a favor and abandon this issue forever. You're obviously causing yourself a lot of unnecessary aggravation and being a certifiable pest in the process.

As I point out in *Teen-Proofing*, the biggest and most frequent mistake made by responsible, well-intentioned parents of teens is the attempt to micromanage. You have to micromanage an infant or a toddler, and you might be able to successfully micromanage a preschool or elementary school–age child, but you cannot micromanage a teen without creating more problems than you solve. In fact, I'll go a step further and say that the attempt to micromanage a teen will solve none of the problems and is likely to create a whole new slew of 'em.

Your obsessive concern about when your son does his homework falls into this perilous category. Do you really think he's going to get better grades if he does his homework when you want him to? It's more likely that if you manage to force him to do his homework under your eagle-eyed supervision in the afternoon or early evening, he will rush through it, in which case his grades will drop. Why? Because you will have given him a good reason to prove you wrong.

Instead of trying to make your son do his homework when you think he should do it, give him permission to learn—the hard way if necessary—how to effectively manage his own time. Your job here is not to manage his time for him, but to demonstrate that choices result in consequences. Good choices result in good consequences (better grades, more freedom), and bad choices result in consequences that are undesirable (bad grades, restrictions on his freedom). For the time being, his grades are not a problem, but when he enters high school and academic demands increase, that may change. This gives you the opportunity to be the agent of reality. In the meantime, take a load off your shoulders and find a more constructive outlet for all that well-intentioned energy.

Q: The punishments I give my fourteen-year-old daughter— mostly for blatant defiance of the rules—seem to make her even more defiant. For example, I recently removed her phone, stereo, most of her favorite clothes, and her video game box from her room, only to have her inform me that I'm not her boss and can't mold her into the person I want her to be. I must not be doing the right thing. Instead of

learning her lesson, the consequences I'm using only seem to make her more rebellious. On the other hand, she and I are very close and she talks to me a lot and listens to my advice about relationships. Discipline is where I feel I'm failing. How do I know if the consequences I choose for misbehavior are making a difference in a positive way, or just adding to the rebellion?

A: You must understand and accept that your daughter is absolutely correct—you cannot make her into the person you want her to be. Furthermore, you cannot make her accept that you are the boss, and as long as she refuses to accept it, then you aren't. It's as simple as that. A child has to *consent* to parental governance in order for that governance to be effective, and your daughter is not ready to give her consent. The good news is she obviously wants a relationship. She wants a mentor. She just refuses to accept that the decisions she makes for herself merit negative consequences.

Like many parents, you are obviously laboring under the misconception that the right consequence will change wrong behavior. So when you deliver a consequence and your daughter's behavior doesn't change or gets worse, you conclude that perhaps the consequence wasn't right. The fact is, the right consequence, consistently applied, will change the behavior of a dog or a rat or a pigeon, but an appropriate consequence may or may not promote a change in human behavior. Unlike dogs, rats, and pigeons, humans have the power to choose, and humans have a reputation for making choices they know will result in punishment.

Another way of saying the same thing: If a consequence fails to produce change in a dog's behavior, the dog's handler needs to change the consequence. But if a consequence fails to alter a child's behavior, it is not necessarily true that the consequence must be changed. Unlike a dog, a child can choose to continue misbehaving in the face of overwhelmingly negative consequences. This doesn't mean there is anything wrong with either the child or the consequences. It just means the child is not a dog.

At this point in her life, it's more important for your daughter to prove that you aren't her boss than for her to enjoy privileges. So be it. If her misbehavior warrants loss of privileges, then you must take away her privileges. The purpose is to simply illustrate to her how the real world works. Explain that to her. Tell her that you don't enjoy punishing her; it is simply your responsibility to demonstrate to her that when someone makes a bad decision, bad things ensue. The fact that she values a relationship with you says to me that someday she is going to "get it" and begin making right choices. She will do this in her time, not yours. Meanwhile, your job is to simply love her and be there for her, and at the same time be an effective agent of reality. Good things come to those who patiently wait.

Q: Our sixteen-year-old son's room is a perpetual pigsty. Clothes, CDs, electronic equipment, magazines, and an assortment of various other personal belongings are strewn everywhere. If his bed is made, it's because I made it. If his clothes are put away, it's because I put them away. When I complain, he comes back with the "It's my room, and I can do with it as I please" bit. He also points out that his door is almost always closed, which is true, but the fact that he no longer functions as a member of the family is another problem. If he's not on his computer playing fantasy video games, he's talking on the phone to his friends. Help!

A: This business of "It's my room, blah, blah, blah" is pure, unadulterated hogwash. The room he occupies is not his by a long shot. It is your property, for which you are responsible, as evidenced by the fact that not only do you pay the share of the mortgage, insurance, and utilities represented by that room, but if a guest were to slip and fall and hurt themselves in that room, you would be liable, not your naive, deluded, and very self-absorbed sixteen-year-old.

The chair he sits in at meals is not "his" chair, to do with as he pleases, is it? He is not free to smash it to smithereens to make a statement of rage at the injustices of the capitalist system that maintains him in the lap of luxury, is he? To borrow from the vernacular of his articulate generation: Not! I could cite numerous other examples, but I'm sure you get my drift.

He is not entitled. Rather, he is obligated, and he can begin expressing his obligation by maintaining "his" room in a manner consistent with the standard of cleanliness you have established in your home. Whether he agrees or not is irrelevant.

You're probably saying, "But, John, I have tried everything to get him to keep his room neat and orderly, and nothing has worked." Oh, but you obviously haven't read him the riot act and then lowered the boom. If you had, you wouldn't have written me about the problem because it would have quickly become family history.

The riot act: "I/we will no longer tolerate the mess in the room we allow you to use. From now on, you will make your bed every morning, put your clothes in their proper places, keep the floor picked up, and otherwise maintain a clean and orderly environment. If you cooperate in this, we will reciprocate by continuing to support you in the manner to which you have become accustomed. If you refuse to cooperate, then the gravy train will come to an abrupt halt."

Lower the boom: "The very next time your room is a mess in any small sense of the term, we are disconnecting your modem and suspending your driving privileges for a minimum of a week. To re-earn these privileges, you must keep your room neat and clean, your clothes put away properly, and the bed made every morning for seven consecutive days. The next violation will result in the same consequences but will require compliance for two weeks. Every violation thereafter will require compliance for a month. Questions?"

The combination of reading the riot act and then lowering the boom constitutes a "wake-up call." Make no mistake about it, you will most definitely have to put the hammer down at least twice before His Majesty wakes up and smells the coffee.

Q: Our six-year-old constantly forgets things. He can't seem to remember things we tell him to do. In addition, he forgets to do his chores, give messages to people, and so on and on and on. We have started calling him "Foggy" because he seems to be in a fog nearly all the time. Mind you now, his teacher says it's not a problem at school, but it's constant at home. My husband says he had the same difficulty as a child, so we're wondering if it's inherited. In any case, can forgetfulness be cured, or are we just going to have to learn to live with it?

A: No, forgetfulness is not inherited. More often than not, it's enabled, meaning the parents of forgetful children complain and wring their hands and implore the gods for relief but rarely put any real consistent pressure on their kids to change their disobedient ways.

"Disobedient?" someone is exclaiming. "Oh, John, how can you be so insensitive? Forgetful and disobedient are two different things."

Quite the contrary. Note that the child in question usually forgets a responsibility, a task. I'll just bet he doesn't forget ice cream in the freezer or a promise his parents have made to him. No, this child remembers what he wants to remember and forgets what he'd rather not do, like chores. This is not a symptom of budding genius; this is a passive (and therefore less obvious) form of disobedience. Granted, the rare (emphasized!) child who *is* forgetful may have a rare learning disability. Also, I would not say that forgetfulness in a three-year-old is synonymous with disobedience, but in an otherwise able-minded six-year-old, constant forgetting is a form of disobedience and calls for discipline.

The cure you requested: Make a list of your son's favorite privileges such as riding his bike, having friends over to play, watching television, playing video games, and his normal bedtime. Post the list on the refrigerator and every time he forgets to do something he's been told to do, cross off a privilege, beginning with his favorite one. If he loses his normal bedtime, he goes to bed an hour early. Every privilege crossed off is lost until the following Monday. After you've tucked your son into bed on Sunday evening, wipe the slate clean by taking the previous week's list down, and post a new one in its place.

In the parlance of behavior modification, this is known as a "response-cost" system. In other words, your son's forgetful responses to instructions cost him things he values. (By the way, if a disciplinary method is termed behavior modification and it works, psychologists didn't invent it. Grandma did.)

The yeast in this recipe is what I call the Referee's Rule. No threats, second chances, or deals. If he forgets, he loses a privilege.

Bada-bing, bada-boom. I call this the Referee's Rule because you will never see a referee give second chances. If he or she did, the game would deteriorate into chaos in a matter of minutes.

If you are consistent, dispassionate, and ruthless in applying this age-old method, I can virtually guarantee that over the next few months you'll witness an amazing improvement in his memory!

Q: Our sixteen-year-old daughter needs to wear glasses in order to drive legally. It clearly says so on her driver's license. We have discovered recently that she keeps her glasses in her car but does not always wear them because she feels they make her look "nerdy." The chance of her not wearing them goes up, as you might imagine, if other teens are in the car with her. Should we take her driving privilege away? If so, for how long?

A: I'm going to assume you found out she was not always wearing her glasses when she drove because you happened to see her driving without them. I'm further going to assume that the odds of you catching her driving without them again are slim. If I'm correct, she will play these odds, taking the chance she won't be caught again and also taking chances with her own life and other people's lives. Such is the mind of the teen.

My point: You can't enforce this rule. Not reliably. For every time you catch her driving without her glasses, she'll get away with it at least fifty times. So there's no point in taking away her driving privilege for a little while. She'll still play the odds. The only perfect solution is to take her driving privilege away for good. Cancel her insurance and impound, then sell her car.

"Sorry, kid," you simply say, "but we are not going to aid and abet someone who insists upon breaking the law. Furthermore, when you drive without glasses, you are a risk, and I cannot in good conscience extend your driving privilege to someone who puts herself, her passengers, and other members of this community at risk when she is behind the wheel of a car."

Keep in mind that I don't believe in letting young people drive until they are eighteen, which is the law in Europe, and then only if they have graduated from high school. The current minimum-age laws were passed when sixteen-year-olds were a lot more mature than their contemporary counterparts are now. Furthermore, the roads were not as congested, and vehicles were not as powerful. The damage done to themselves and others by sixteen- to eighteen-year-old drivers is horrific. It's "American roulette," for sure.

So, if I were you, I would use this opportunity to snatch away that which was foolishly granted. If that seems too draconian, then Plan B would be to suspend your daughter's driving privileges for a month, during which time you need to see her wearing her glasses as prescribed. Then restore her privileges with two understandings: First, she will now pay her portion of the car insurance if she is not doing so already; second, the next time you discover that she has been behind the wheel of a moving vehicle without wearing her glasses will be the last time. At that point, you invoke Plan A (the "draconian" one). Make sure she understands, in advance, just what Plan A involves, adding, "That will be the last automobile you will own or drive as long as you are living under this roof."

If your daughter is not a rebellious person, then Plan B should work, although I don't know how you're going to monitor her compliance. With a sixteen-year-old, you are still throwing the dice by letting her drive at all, something I would not do in these days and times.

Q: Our son is nineteen and home for the summer from college. He goes out with his buddies and drinks and afterward decides to drive home. We have talked with him about preselecting a designated driver, staying where he is until he's sober, or calling us to come get him. He maintains that he doesn't drink enough to impair his driving ability. We think otherwise. What can we do?

A: This is one of the easiest questions a parent has ever asked me. First, thank you for giving my brain a vacation. Second, please don't be offended if I suggest that yours seems to have taken one as well.

I'm going to assume that your son is driving on your insurance policy. Therefore, it may have occurred to you that if he is busted for driving while impaired or causes an accident, you are liable. He won't be sued. Your insurance company will be, and if your coverage is insufficient, so will you. In either case, your insurance company will probably drop you like a hot potato. To say that new insurance will be costly is an understatement.

Your son is obviously intelligent, but he is still in the grips of adolescent invincibility disorder (AID). Like the typical adolescent, he thinks he is immune to disaster, impervious to harm, indestructible, immortal, and invisible. Therefore, talk will accomplish nothing other than to give you cases of blue-in-the-face. You cannot convince him that his attitude is irrational. He thinks your concerns reflect lingering parental overprotection. You cannot persuade him that his behavior involves significant risk. He just thinks you're being your typical neurotic selves. Furthermore, it should have occurred to you that at this point you cannot trust him. If his back's against the wall, he is likely to say anything to get you to lay off. Stop talking, therefore, and *do* something. Here are your options:

1. Take him off your insurance policy and inform him that he's going to have to pay for his own policy. The simple fact is, a child (and your son is obviously still a child) is more likely to take care of that for which he has toiled. He has no job? Too bad, then. Perhaps he needs to reassess his priorities.

2. If you are the owners of record, sell the car he drives. Don't discuss it with him first or warn him, just sell it.

3. Emancipate him, completely, which means you also effect option 1.

4. The next time he goes out with his buddies, have a police officer waiting at the house when he comes home. The officer could administer a Breathalyzer and if it's positive, arrest him for driving while impaired. When your son asks why, tell him that you will not aid and abet dangerous criminal behavior. Period.

If none of the above suggestions is to your liking—in other words, if you simply cannot bring yourself to dispense tough love—then look the other way, and pray a lot.

Q: Every morning, our seven-year-old drags his feet about getting out of bed and getting dressed. Both my husband and I work, and this requires that Stevie leave the house no later than 7:45 A.M. We wake him up at six-thirty, which gives him more than enough time to get ready for school. Every morning, it's the same story. We have to call him five

or six times to get him up and moving; then we have to stay behind him until he's out the door. Help!

A: First, the only person who can solve this problem is Stevie. Second, he's not going to solve it until you make him responsible for it. Third, he has no reason to accept responsibility for the problem as long as you are willing to continue accepting it for him. Stevie will solve the problem when and only when his failure to get up and get moving in the morning upsets and inconveniences him more than it upsets and inconveniences you.

The actual mechanics of the solution are as easy as ABC.

A, plan your strategy. In chapter 2, I called this "striking while the iron is cold." Make a detailed list of the things you want Stevie to do in the morning.

B, communicate the plan. Say, "Stevie, we've decided we're no longer going to yell and scream and get red in the face in the mornings. From now on, after waking you up at six-thirty, we are going down to the kitchen and setting the stove timer for seven-fifteen. That gives you forty-five minutes to do the things you see on this list, which we're going to post on the back of your bedroom door. When the timer rings, we will have inspection. If everything on the list has been done, you may do whatever you like until it's time to leave the house. If you either fail to beat the bell or haven't properly done one or more things on the list, you won't be allowed to go outside after school that day. In addition, your bedtime that night will be one hour earlier than usual. Any questions?"

C, enforce the plan. When Stevie dawdles, say and do nothing. Between 6:30 and 7:15 every morning, your job is to tend to your business and ignore whether or not your son is attending to his. I guarantee he will fail to beat the bell at least two or three mornings the first week. He may even still be in bed when the bell rings. If that happens, get him ready without fuss or frenzy (note the thirty-minute cushion built into the plan). That afternoon, if he starts outside, gently remind him of his self-imposed restriction and express your regrets. When he pleads for one more chance, say, "Sorry, Stevie, but you knew the rule." When Stevie realizes that the problem is his to do with as he pleases, he will solve it. He may be stubborn, but he's not stupid.

Q: My daughter will be seven soon. She is not an extremely social child and chooses to have only three or four friends. For her birthday she wants to invite four children she likes, but not three other children with whom she has played and whose mothers are my friends. I feel strongly that she should invite these three children to her party. If they hear about the party (which is likely), their feelings—and their moms'—will be hurt, I'm sure. My explanations have fallen on deaf ears. My daughter absolutely refuses to invite them. So, I gave her a choice: party with these three included or no party. She quickly said, "No party, thank you." Did I do the right thing, or should I have let her decide who to invite to her party without my interference?

A: Yes, you did the right thing, and for that I hereby bestow upon you Rosemond's Seldom Given Meanie Meanie Meanie Award. A child should not be allowed to use a birthday party as a platform for selfish, mean-spirited, narcissistic behavior. Unfortunately, many parents allow their children's birthday parties to be a stage for exactly that sort of obnoxious performance. A celebration of one's birthday is a time to be grateful, selfless, generous. You wanted your daughter to include, not exclude; to open her heart, not close it. You were absolutely, indisputably right, and your daughter was wrong. You explained your position. Your daughter stuck to her guns. You tried more persuasion. She stuck to her guns. At that point, you could have either laid down the law or caved in. To your everlasting credit, you laid down the law. Your daughter still stuck to her guns. Now, you stick to yours!

Q: I have a problem that is slowly driving me crazy. My two boys, ages ten and eight, bicker constantly. To make matters worse, after nearly every fracas, it's a game of who can get to Mom first with the most dramatic rendition of "Poor, pitiful me!" I know I shouldn't referee, but if I ignore them, the fighting only gets louder. If you don't have any good ideas, then at least do me the favor of referring me to a contractor who specializes in custom-designed rubber rooms. I'm going to need one.

A: Actually, you're not refereeing as much as you are emceeing a game of "Victim, victim, who's the victim?" Unfortunately, even though your intentions are good and your motives certainly understandable, by making the distinction between "villain" and "victim," you seal the inevitability of further conflict. The children aren't coming to you because they fight. They fight because you let them come to you.

When you get involved in their squabbles, you assign to one boy the role of victim and to the other the role of villain. In this upside-down set of circumstances, the victim "wins" because Mom is on his side. So, the children begin competing to be the victim. In effect, by getting involved in their bickering, you are teaching them that there is something desirable about being downtrodden. To get them to stop playing this dangerous game, you must transfer responsibility for the problem from your shoulders to theirs.

You can use the "Countdown to Confinement" method. Call a conference with the children and say something along these lines: "Guess what, kids? Mom's figured out a way for the two of you to fight all you want without driving me crazy! I call it 'Problem, problem, you have the problem!' From now on, every time you guys bicker, fight, tattle, or are rude to each other, I'm going to confine you to your respective rooms for thirty minutes. It won't matter who started the problem or who was being unfair. Regardless of who supposedly started it, you will each spend thirty minutes in your room. I'm no longer going to play 'Who done it?' with the two of you. Now listen carefully, because the third time I have to send you to your rooms on any given day, it won't be for thirty minutes. It will be for the rest of the day. You will be allowed out only to use the bathroom and to eat meals with the family.

"Oh, yes, there's one more thing. You're used to hearing me threaten, but you're not used to having me follow through on a threat. This time, I'm not threatening. I'm promising. You'll soon find that out for yourselves." Now, instead of fighting with each other for the purpose of getting you involved, the children must learn how to cooperate in order to keep you from getting involved. Aren't you clever?

Q: Our twelve-year-old son has always been well behaved, responsible, and honest. This year he started junior high school and began hanging around with several kids who are troublemakers. As soon as we found out, we forbade the association. He says we're trying to choose his friends

and seems determined to disobey. It's the first really major conflict we've ever had, and quite frankly it's a bit scary. What should we do?

A: Nothing. This is actually a great opportunity for both you and your son to learn some very important lessons. You can learn to let go, to stop being so protective. In turn, he can learn to be more responsible for the choices he makes. No one will learn anything, however, unless you allow him the freedom to make certain mistakes.

Learning generally takes place by trial and error. This means that many attempts and many mistakes must be made before a particular skill is truly mastered. If the learner is prevented from making mistakes, the learning won't ever take place. This applies to learning to hit a baseball or drive a car as well as to learning to make good decisions.

We can all recall making a decision that brought us face-to-face with the pavement. Instead of wallowing in self-pity, we picked ourselves up, dusted ourselves off, and carried on, slightly scarred perhaps, but a whole lot wiser. Looking back, we realize that even if someone had warned us we were headed for a fall, we'd probably have fallen anyway. These painfully learned lessons are necessary to growing up and learning to accept the consequences—good or bad—of the choices we make.

You should not only let your son associate with these boys, you might actually hope he does get into trouble with them. Let's face it, the worst that could happen at this age isn't likely to ruin anyone's life. Let your son make his mistakes with these boys and, as a result, learn to pick his friends more carefully.

Tell him this: "You were right. We have been trying to choose your friends. We'd really rather you didn't hang around with those boys, but we're no longer going to try to prevent it. Whether you influence them in right directions or they influence you in wrong directions is up to you. But hear this! If you get into any trouble with them, not only will you never again be allowed to associate with them, but there will also be a significant period of time in your life when you won't be allowed to associate with anyone. You have the freedom you want, but you'd better take care of it, because along with that freedom comes a lot of responsibility."

Make it clear that if he should happen to get into trouble, you're going to hold him completely responsible for his own behavior. You will not give any consideration to such excuses as "It wasn't my idea" or "I didn't do anything but stand and watch" or "They told me if I didn't help, they'd beat me up."

If he wants to bring these boys home with him, welcome them. Who knows? Maybe your example will open their eyes to a better set of values.

Q: **Our son started sixth grade this year. He's always had a problem taking responsibility for his homework. As a result, his father and I have had to make sure he's kept up with his assignments. When I went to talk with his teacher about the problem, she politely told me to stay out of it. She would take care of it, she said. With more than a little trepidation, I agreed. Unfortunately, Andrew is abusing his freedom. Most of the work I've seen has been hurriedly done. When I pointed this out to the teacher, she calmly told me she and Andrew were "working things out" and for me not to worry. Hah! I'm not supposed to worry while I see my son's grades go down the tube?**

A: You've discovered the truth in the adage "Things get worse before they get better." In fact, I'm convinced that not only do things get worse, they virtually must.

When parents assume responsibility for a problem that rightfully belongs to a child, they end up compensating for the problem without truly correcting it. These compensations have the unintended effect of allowing the child to stay irresponsible. In your case, you've taken it upon yourselves to do for Andrew what he should have been doing for himself. You've made sure he brought his books home; you've stood over him, figuratively or otherwise, while he did his homework; you've checked to make sure the work was up to par.

You've been doing what many golfers do when they develop a slice. Instead of correcting the defect in their swing that causes the ball to curve maddeningly to the right, they compensate by aiming to the left of their target. In so doing, the problem doesn't get solved, but the consequences become less noticeable. In fact, the compensation makes the problem worse, because it gives the slice time to become a habit. The longer the golfer compensates for it, the harder it is to solve.

Like the golfer, you've been "aiming farther left." As a result, Andrew has learned to rely on you to take up the slack in his academic life. Like our golfer friend, your compensations have succeeded in making Andrew's problem less noticeable. He's still irresponsible, but his grades don't show it.

If the golfer stops aiming left, his next ten shots will go in the woods. In other words, as soon as he stops compensating for it, the problem will seem to get worse. By making the problem more noticeable, however, it finally becomes possible to correct it.

Andrew's teacher realizes that in order for him to begin taking responsibility for himself, you're going to have to stop taking responsibility for him. Having done what she told you to do, you're in a panic because the problem is now more noticeable and all your past accomplishments seem to be going down the tube. That's just the point. The accomplishments were yours, not his. It's time Andrew learned to walk on his own two feet. As he does, he's bound to stumble and perhaps even fall flat on his face. That's all right. He seems blessed with a teacher who sees the problem and knows how to solve it. Trust her. She sounds like an answer to a prayer.

Q: **Our daughter is in the eighth grade at a magnet school for gifted and talented students. Over the three years she's been there, her grades have gone from A's to C's and D's, with more than a few F's. She is always on restriction but seems motivated by nothing. When we talk to her about the problem, she has no answers. Should we continue restricting her? Move her back to our neighborhood school? Have her tested? We are desperate for help!**

A: In *Teen-Proofing*, I point out something all parents need to understand: You can respond properly to a problem you're having with a child—a problem the child can obviously control—and the child's behavior still may not change. That's just another way of saying, "Your daughter has a mind of her own." She has a problem she can control. You've done all the right things; she still has the problem. In fact, it's getting worse. Therefore, you probably need to accept that in this case you are powerless.

If your daughter had a learning problem, it's unlikely she would have ever been identified as gifted and talented. Therefore, I think having her tested will probably be a waste of money, but if it makes you feel more comfortable, by all means have it done.

Yes, I'd move her back to the neighborhood school. She's taking up space in the magnet school that another child could benefit from. And, yes, I'd continue her restriction. In a situation of this sort, I don't look upon restriction as punishment. Rather, I see it as a lesson in how the real world works: If you don't accept your responsibilities, you are going to be restricted. I'd tell your daughter that you don't like restricting her, but it would be unfair to do otherwise. Stop trying to "counsel" her out of the problem. If she wants to talk to you about it, fine. Otherwise, don't waste your breath. Something I've noticed over the years is that, quite often, when parents stop agonizing over a problem, when they accept their powerlessness, the problem begins to improve. It doesn't happen that way every time, but often enough for you to give it a good college try.

Q: Our seven-year-old daughter is absolutely terrified of thunder and lightning. When a storm comes up, she becomes hysterical. We've talked, explained, and comforted, but nothing seems to work. Suggestions?

A: First, I'd suggest you read my answer to the previous question. Like those parents, you've done all the right things, and nothing has changed. Now it's time to hand the problem over to your daughter.

When my daughter, Amy, was your daughter's age, she also was terrified of thunder and lightning. She also became hysterical when storms came up. What ultimately solved the problem was telling her we understood her fright but could no longer allow her to be the center of attention during a storm. We told her that when she felt terrified by a storm, she had to go into a closet or under her bed and stay there until the storm passed. A child younger than, say, five needs to be held and comforted, but by age six, it's time to give the child some authoritative guidance and let her solve the problem on her own.

The Fruits of Frustration

Frustration, according to nearly an entire generation of child-rearing experts from 1970 to the present, is bad for children. It causes stress, insecurity, and poor self-you-know-what, not to mention warts on the vocal chords from too much screaming. Believing this fairy tale, parents have worked hard to protect their children from this supposedly terrible scourge. In the process, many parents have given their children too much too soon and have required too little too late. As a result, children have become increasingly spoiled, demanding, and ungrateful, and parents have become increasingly frustrated. What goes around comes around.

I have good news! Those child-rearing experts were wrong. Frustration isn't necessarily bad for children. In fact, a certain amount is absolutely essential to healthy character formation and emotional growth. You want proof? Here it is.

1. As I pointed out in chapter 1, the purpose of raising children is to help them out of our lives and into successful lives of their own. Parents are, therefore, obligated to raise children in a manner consistent with the reality they will eventually face as adults.

2. As we all know, adult reality involves significant amounts of frustration. We experience frustration in response not only to our own limitations, but also to the limitations other people and circumstances impose upon us.

3. Through experience with frustration, we eventually develop a tolerance for it. We accept its inevitability and determine not to let it get us down. This tolerance enables the growth of resourcefulness and other creative coping mechanisms.

4. People who learn to tolerate frustration are able to turn adversity into challenge and persevere.

5. Perseverance, that all-important "If at first you don't succeed, try, try again" attitude toward life, is the primary quality in every success story. Whether the field of endeavor is occupational, recreational, social, personal, marital, or parental, the person who perseveres is the person most likely to succeed.

6. All the aforementioned growth takes place because of—not in spite of—that supposedly dreadful f-word, *frustration*.

CONCLUSION

If you want your children to become successful adults—successful in their work, their play, their interpersonal relationships, and their feelings toward themselves—you are obligated to frustrate them.

You can begin filling this obligation by giving your children regular, daily doses of vitamin N. This vital nutrient consists simply of the most character-building two-letter word in the English language: *no*.

Vitamin N is as important to a child's healthy growth and development as vitamins A, B, and C. Unfortunately, many if not most of today's children suffer from vitamin N deficiency. They've been overindulged by well-meaning parents who've given them far too much of what they want and far too little of what they truly need.

A Self-Test

Have you given your children enough vitamin N? Let's find out. List on a sheet of paper everything you've ever dreamed of having. Let your imagination and your greed run unabashedly wild. Don't concern yourself with whether these things are practical or presently affordable, whether your spouse shares your dreams, or whether your minister would approve of them. If you've ever coveted a particular something, write it down! What about that Italian sports car you've always wanted? How about a new house? Don't hold back. You want new furniture? Write it down. A new wardrobe? A boat? Jewelry? A trip to Europe? Membership at the country club? A hot tub? Write 'em all down!

When your fantasy frenzy is over, let reality intrude. Go back over your wish list and circle the things you feel reasonably certain you'll actually be able to acquire within the next five years. When I put a workshop audience through the same exercise, the answers generally fall between 10 and 20 percent. If you circle more than 25 percent of the items on your list, you're either incredibly wealthy or you don't want much. In other words, most of us must learn to contend with the fact that from 10 to 20 percent of what we want today is about as much as we can hope to acquire within five years. Remember, too, that we get what we want by putting forth sustained effort, by making sacrifices, by doing our best. Through it all, we endure all manner of—what? That's right—frustration. Now you're catching on.

Next, on a second sheet of paper, list everything your children are going to ask for over the next twelve months. Not things they truly need, but things they simply want: the extras. Depending on their ages, they're going to want toys of every description, various items of electronic equipment, various means of fancy transportation, the latest clothing fads, and the cost of admission to movies, sports events, amusement parks, and rock 'n' roll concerts.

When you're through, go back over the second list, circling the things your children are certain to get within the next twelve months. Don't forget to circle things that will probably be forthcoming from grandparents, other well-meaning relatives, and friends of the family. Eye-opening, isn't it? If you're a typical American parent, you circled 75 percent or more of the items on your children's wish list.

What this means is that most of us accustom our children to a material standard that is completely out of kilter with what they can ever hope to achieve as adults. Consider also that many if not most children attain this level of affluence not by working, sacrificing, or doing their best, but by whining, demanding, and manipulating. So in the process of overinflating their material expectations, we also teach our children that something can be had for next to nothing. Not only is that a falsehood, it's one of the most dangerous, destructive attitudes a person can ever acquire.

Children who grow up believing in the something-for-nothing fairy tale may never realize that the really important things in life come from within, rather than without. As adults, they are likely to be emotionally stunted, immature people, fixated at a grasping, self-centered stage of development. At the very least, they will tend to confuse the giving and getting of things with a deeper and more meaningful level of sharing and trust in relationships. When they themselves become parents, they're likely to confuse their children's value systems in a like manner, by overdosing them with things. In this sense, materialism is an inherited disease, an addiction passed from one generation to the next. Materialism is not so much an addiction to things as it is an addiction to *acquiring* things. This explains why materialists are never content. No sooner than they've acquired one thing, they want another. This also explains why children who get too much of what they want rarely take proper care of anything they have. Why should they? After all, history tells them that more is on the way.

Children deserve better than this. They deserve to have parents attend conscientiously to their needs for protection, affection, and direction. Beyond that, they deserve to hear their parents say no far more often than yes when it comes to their whimsical yearnings. They deserve to learn that getting requires giving in at least equal measure. They need to learn not just the words "It is better to give than to receive," but the deeper meaning behind those words as well. They deserve to learn the value of constructive, creative effort as opposed to the value of effort expended whining, lying on the floor kicking and screaming, or playing one parent against the other. They deserve to learn that work is the only truly fulfilling way of getting anything in life, and that the harder the work—the harder the effort—the more ultimately fulfilling the outcome.

In the process of trying to protect children from frustration, parents have turned reality upside down and inside out. A child raised in this topsy-turvy manner may not have the skills needed to stand on his own two feet when the time comes.

In Pursuit of Happiness

Four years after graduating from high school, just 25 percent of the class of 1972 was still "nesting" under their parents' roofs. In

1980, the figure was 42 percent, and today the figure has climbed beyond 75 percent.

You'd think one reason all these young people stay unmarried and continue to live at home is so they can accumulate a nest egg, but that's not the case. The same study found that they save less and spend more than any previous generation. Most of these young people were raised by parents who gave lots of material things but required little in return. Having grown up in a blissful state of premature affluence, these kids can't handle the relative hardship of being out on their own. So they stay at home, which frees up lots of income for discretionary things like new cars, expensive stereo equipment, and ski trips. In other words, their childhood experience of how the world works has failed to prepare them for self-sufficiency. They aren't willing to start small, to struggle, to sacrifice, to hang in there.

By and large, today's children have been overdosed not only materially but emotionally as well. They've been given too much attention, too much praise, and too many rewards. In short, today's parents, succumbing to prevailing parenting trends, have made their children's lives too easy and have created a fantasy for them of how the world works. A family therapist once summed up the situation for me quite well. He said, "Today's parents do a wonderful job of sharing their standard of living with their children, but a miserable job of endowing those children with the skills they'll need to achieve that standard on their own."

Looked at from a slightly different perspective, the problem is that today's parents have worked too hard to keep their children happy. As a result, children grow up believing that it's someone else's responsibility to take care of their needs and wants. Never having learned to accept responsibility for their own well-being, they go through life expecting other people to make them happy and blaming everything that goes wrong on someone else. Unfortunately, as we all know, a person who fails to take full responsibility for his or her own happiness will never be fully happy. The paradox is this: The more parents take on responsibility for their children's happiness, the more they guarantee their children's eventual unhappiness.

In the second paragraph of the Declaration of Independence, it says "that all men are created equal, that they are endowed by their Creator with certain unalienable Rights; that among these are Life, Liberty, and the pursuit of Happiness."

Read it carefully. Thomas Jefferson didn't propose a right to happiness. He simply affirmed the right to *pursue* happiness, and there lies the root of the problem. When parents busy themselves in pursuit of happiness for their children, their children never learn to pursue it on their own. Yes, the pursuit is full of pitfalls and setbacks, but as bodybuilders say, "No pain, no gain." We should support children as they come to grips with the reality of frustration, but we must not protect them from it. For a child, the gain of learning to pursue happiness is measured in terms of feelings of competence, so the more we pursue happiness for our children, the less chance they have of developing a belief in their ability to overcome adversity. There is no better reason than that for making sure your parenting cabinet is stocked with ample supplies of vitamin N.

Tantrums

If common sense tells us that vitamin N is essential to our children's well-being, why do we work so hard to provide them not only with more in the way of material things than they need, but with more than they're ever going to be able to attain for themselves as adults? Part of the problem, undoubtedly, has its roots in the "My children are going to have it better than I did" thinking that became increasingly prevalent following the hardships of the Great Depression and World War II. It also has to do with the fact that many parents want to avoid the consequences of not giving in to their children's oft-agitated demands. I'm referring to tantrums of various sorts, from a two-year-old rolling on the floor, screaming and frothing at the mouth, to a sixteen-year-old stomping and slamming doors while spewing forth a steady stream of invective. Quite a few parents are intimidated, even frightened, by tantrums, so they give in. Some give in before the tantrum even starts. When asked why they give in, they often answer, "Because it's easier to give in than to deal with the hassle."

That's true, but only in the short run. Giving in solves the immediate problem. It turns off the screaming and the stomping. In that sense, giving in is certainly easier. Unfortunately, the more often parents give in to tantrums, the worse they become. Every time parents give in to a tantrum, they virtually guarantee the occurrence of at least fifty more.

If you give a child a choice between getting something the hard way and getting that same thing in what looks like the easy way, the child will always choose the easy way. To a child, working and waiting for something, not to mention doing without, always looks like the hard way. Wearing down a parent's resistance and resolve by screaming and stomping and arguing and cursing seems much easier. What the child doesn't know, and what many parents don't seem to realize, is that giving in to tantrums blocks the development of initiative, motivation, and resourcefulness. Without those survival tools, the child is destined to be a less successful and less happy adult.

Guilt is another reason parents give in to tantrums. To parents who mistakenly believe that the measure of good parenting is a happy child, a tantrum says, "You aren't doing a good job." These parents seem to reason that good parents raise happy children, and tantrums are a sign of unhappiness. Therefore, if the child throws a tantrum, the parents must have done something wrong. Thinking of this sort makes no sense, but it's very real and very common nonetheless. Take the five-year-old boy who asks for a brownie thirty minutes before dinner. When his mother says no, he begins whining and stomping around and saying absurd things like, "You never let me eat when I'm hungry!" Mom thinks the tantrum is evidence of a bad decision, one that may result in her son feeling insecure or unloved or—heaven forbid—resentful. So she hands over the brownie, knowing full well that, as a result, the boy won't eat his supper. When he doesn't, she points out the connection between the brownie and his lack of appetite, as if this information is going to render him more reasonable in the future. Mom's got a lot to learn.

All children can be counted on to throw tantrums of one sort or another. For one thing, children come into the world devoid of any tolerance for frustration. For another, their original point of view is a self-centered (egocentric) one. Whatever they want, they believe they deserve. Parents need to slowly but surely help their children dismantle that self-centeredness and replace it with a sense of social responsibility—a willingness to put personal concerns aside for the sake of family, friendship, and society. It could be said that this is a parent's most important function. It is the essence of the socialization process, and that process involves a certain amount of discomfort. A young, undersocialized child's natural reaction to discomfort and disillusionment is a tantrum. Looked at from this perspective, a tantrum expresses the pain of relinquishing self-centeredness and developing a mature understanding of how the world works. It's essential, therefore, that parents learn how to say no to their children and say it with conviction.

I chuckle inside whenever I hear a parent complain that a certain child "can't take no for an answer." I'm amused because the comment always says more about the parent than it does the child. A child who can't take no for an answer always has parents who can't really say it themselves. It's not that the child can't take no; it's that the child has been given no reason to believe it.

The fact that today's parents are not giving their children enough vitamin N is not just weakening their children's character, it also has the potential of eroding the very foundation of our democratic society. After all, it was individual resourcefulness, perseverance, and a tolerance for frustration that made this country the greatest nation on earth.

For all these reasons, the next time you give your child a dose of vitamin N and he falls on the floor screaming, consider it a job well done!

The Prescription

If you haven't already started, you can begin administering vitamin N to your children in the following ways:

- Turn their world right side up by giving them all of what they truly need, but no more than 25 percent of what they simply want. I call this the "Principle of Benign Deprivation."
- Don't do for your children what they are capable of doing for themselves. "You can do that on your own" pushes the growth of perseverance and self-sufficiency. When the child says, "I can't," don't argue. Just say, "Well, I won't." You'll be amazed at how creative and resourceful children can be under the right circumstances.
- Don't always rescue them from failure or disappointment. Remember that falling on one's face can be an invaluable learning experience (see chapter 3).

- Remember that just because a child doesn't like something doesn't mean it shouldn't happen or exist. For example, the mere fact that a child doesn't want to be left with a babysitter doesn't mean you shouldn't do so. For children to grow up it requires that parents resist the temptation to constantly protect them from the discomfort of having to divest dependency.
- Don't worry about treating children fairly. Remember that to a child, "fair" means "me first," with the biggest and best of everything.
- Remember that simply because you enjoy a good standard of living doesn't mean you're obligated to share it in full with your children. Vitamin N gives children something to strive for, along with the skills with which to strive.
- Don't overdose your children emotionally by giving them too much attention or too much praise (see chapters 1 and 2). If you pay too much attention to your children, they have no reason to pay attention to you.

Failing Is Not Final

A mother asked my advice concerning her sixteen-year-old son's academic problems. He needed nightly help with his homework, she said, and she was the self-appointed nightly helper. This had been going on since the very first day he ever came home with a homework assignment. Ten years later she feels exhausted but also afraid that if she stops helping him, he will fail.

"I simply cannot allow him to fail," she said, emphatically.

"Ever?" I asked.

"Not if I can help it."

I pointed out that failure was a necessary experience. One achieves success by trial and error. In any context, learning what *not* to do is as essential as learning what to do. In either case, experience is the teacher. Protecting a child from the experience of failure is not only counterproductive, it is ultimately impossible. Sooner or later, it will not be possible to protect the child, and he will experience failure. Unfortunately, when failure occurs, the protected child will not know what to do. The experience may be devastating.

"You're only delaying the inevitable," I said, "and making it more likely that when it occurs, he will not know how to cope."

"I know," she replied, with a heavy sigh, "but I can't just stand by and see him get hurt."

This mother's heart is certainly in the right place. She doesn't want her child to experience pain, but her head and her heart aren't working together—they're not in balance. She understands the ultimate futility of what she's doing, but she cannot reconcile what she knows in her head to be true with what she feels in her heart she must do.

One of the keys to the successful discipline of a child (and there is no aspect of child rearing that does not fall under the heading of discipline) is keeping the head and the heart in balance. Sadly, this imbalance is ubiquitous among today's parents. I risk accusations of sexism, but I will venture what I have noticed: Fathers are more likely to be ruled by their heads, and mothers are more likely to be ruled by their hearts. Perhaps this is one reason why God intended for children to be raised by both, together.

The mom in our example is ruled by her heart. She loves a lot, but her love is not tempered by her head. A parent who justified refusing the child any help, saying, "He's got to learn that in the real world, you succeed and fail on your own, not because of someone else," would be right-headed but wrong-hearted. No one could argue with the statement. It's fact, but facts alone do not mean a parent's decision is functional.

So, how could the above mom manage the homework issue in a way that would reflect balance between head and heart? Well, she could tell him, for example, that she will help him with three homework problems (not assignments, but individual problems) per night, and that in each instance her help would not exceed ten minutes.

"So choose your requests carefully," she could say, "so that they count."

This would expose her son to failure, which he needs to experience, but in doses that mitigate demoralization. Furthermore, her policy would cause him to stop asking for her help at a knee-jerk level, but to exhaust his resources before doing so, in the course of which he would no doubt discover that he was more capable than he currently thinks he is.

And the story would end well, which it is supposed to do.

Questions?

Q: Our three-year-old daughter throws a tantrum whenever she doesn't get her way. How should we handle this?

A: I'll answer your question by telling you a story about my daughter, Amy: When she was two, and throughout the third year of her life, Amy was remarkably easy to get along with. Looking back, compared to most two-year-olds, she was relatively maintenance-free. If we told her to straighten her room, she straightened her room. Sometimes she did it without even being asked. If she wanted something, and we said no, she shrugged it off without a whimper. She demanded very little attention from us and was quite adept at occupying herself for long periods of time.

Then, just about the time Willie and I were preparing to heave a sigh of relief and give thanks for this unexpected reprieve, the tantrums began—and did they ever! As though determined to make up for lost time, three-year-old Amy searched high and low for excuses to do the terrible-tantrum thing. She screamed whenever we stopped her from doing what she wanted to do. She screamed whenever we refused to meet her demands, which became legion. She screamed whenever we assigned her a task, no matter how small. Sometimes she screamed for no apparent reason. Screaming wasn't all she did. Amy began a tantrum by becoming rigid and then bouncing up and down on the balls of her feet while making a rapid "uh-uh-uh" sound that got progressively louder and longer until it became a full-blown wail. By then, she was usually flapping her arms and running around in circles like a whirling dervish. At some point, she would collapse on the floor in a heap and begin thrashing about.

Having been desensitized to tantrums by Eric—his scenes were worse than Amy's—Willie and I usually sat reading the paper or some such thing until the storm blew over. After several months we noticed that despite our careless attitude toward Amy's tantrums, they were getting worse. We decided to take another approach.

One fairly peaceful afternoon, I took Amy aside for a talk. "Amy," I said, "you've been screaming a lot lately. So much that Mommy and Daddy are going to give you a special place of your very own to scream in. We have lots of special places in the house. We have special places to sleep, special places to eat, and special places to go to the toilet and take baths. Now you're going to have a special place to scream. Come with me, and I'll show you where it is."

I led her to the downstairs bathroom, opened the door, and ushered her inside. "This is it, Amy, your very own screaming place, and it's a fine screaming place. Just look! The walls are nice and close to make the screams louder, and there's soft carpet on the floor for you to roll around on. If you scream so loud that you have to go to the bathroom, the toilet is right over here. If you scream your throat dry, here's a sink and a cup for you to drink from.

"From now on, whenever you want to scream, just come in here and scream all you want. If you start to scream but forget to come here, Mommy and Daddy will help you remember and help you get here."

During my monologue, Amy just stood there with a "You must be crazy!" look on her face. Never one to pass up a challenge, it wasn't fifteen minutes before she was screaming and thrashing around over something. I said quickly, "That's some very fine screaming, Amy, but you must scream in your special place," and I dragged her kicking and screaming into the bathroom.

The first few times this happened, as soon as she was in the bathroom she would stop screaming, come out, and begin screaming again. One of us just as promptly put her back. Once Amy realized this was going to be standard operating procedure, the screams stopped almost as soon as the door closed. Nevertheless, she would remain in the bathroom pouting and scheming (or so Willie and I surmised) for several minutes. Then she'd emerge and, without as much as a glance in our direction, go to her room.

Within a couple of months, she had her tantrums under control. One morning, I passed her room and heard what sounded like crying coming from inside. I opened the door.

"Are you all right?" I asked.

"Yes," she said, dry-eyed.

"Were you crying?"

"No. Bumpo was." Bumpo was her teddy bear.

"Oh. Where is Bumpo? I don't see him."

Amy walked over to her corner cabinet and opened the door. There sat Bumpo, looking rather forlorn.

"In his screaming place," she announced.

Q: The tantrum place idea sounds great for scenes that occur at home. What if our daughter has a tantrum in a store or some other public place?

A: First, don't try to talk her out of it. Second, don't try to ignore it, because you can't. Third, get her out of the public eye. As quickly as possible, take her either to a remote part of the store or outside and wait there until the tantrum runs its course. If she seems determined to keep it up, go home and use the tantrum place. In the long run, it's worth the inconvenience. My experience, both personal and professional, suggests that two or three such episodes—leaving the public place, going home, and doing time in the tantrum place—will be all it takes.

Q: What should we say to our children when they point out that all their friends have a certain thing but they do not?

A: When they were younger, one of our children's favorite litanies was, "But all my friends have one!" Willie and I never argued. Instead, we said, "We know. We know how it feels to not have something your friends have. Your friends will share their good fortune with you, just as you will share what you have with them. That's what friends are for. In any case, you'll live."

Sometimes, however, when we were not in the mood to provide the kids with a lesson in life, we simply said, "Then you are going to be the most special child in your peer group." The fact is, they didn't like either answer, but they seem not to have suffered in the long run.

Q: My daughter is almost six. She is smart, outgoing, verbal, and very sensitive. The other day she told me that her very good friend, was not playing with her but instead had a new friend, and she told me it made her sad. Can you help me with a response to this? I know it will only get worse and would like to offer something thoughtful.

A: My approach to a situation of this sort would be to ask questions rather than offer advice. A sample:

"Do you only have one friend?"

"Can you think of other children you can play with?"

"Do you think you have done anything to make your friend upset with you?"

"Is there something you need to apologize to your friend about?"

"Can the three of you play together and get along?"

"Can you make friends with the other girl?"

Act as a "facilitator," asking questions that will cause your daughter to think. Under the circumstances, I'll bet that she will come up with her own solution to this problem. For sure, you can't solve it for her.

Q: Our nine-year-old son has been taking martial arts instruction for several years now and has become good enough to begin participating in large competitions, one of which is

coming up soon. He is convinced he is going to win, although many of the boys in his class have a lot more competitive experience than he does. I don't want to dampen his spirit, but on the other hand I want to prepare him for the possibility that he will not win so that he won't be greatly disappointed when it happens. What can/should I say or do?

A: I strongly recommend that you say and do nothing whatsoever about these concerns of yours. Whatever you say about the competition should be positive and encouraging. On the other hand, you needn't act as if you completely share his optimism. If you play Pollyanna, and he doesn't do as well in the tournament as he thinks he will, he may end up feeling he's disappointed you. Disappointing himself will be quite enough for him to deal with.

When your son says something to the effect that he's going to win his class, you could respond along these lines: "I have all the confidence in the world that you're going to make your coach proud." Leave it at that.

You may be inclined to tack on something like, "Just remember that in any sport, even the best players and teams sometimes lose." Don't. Save that for after the competition if in fact he loses. He might just surprise you—he might win. Remember, if the best players sometimes lose, then players that aren't top-ranked sometimes win.

Why in the world would anyone play a competitive sport if they weren't convinced they were capable of winning? Having played competitive golf in high school, I can say for sure that confidence in one's ability is essential to carrying the day. Indeed, self-confidence does not guarantee one is going to win, but lack of self-confidence definitely guarantees one is going to lose. I applaud your son's self-assurance and encourage you to do the same. What spirit!

Like many a modern mom, you obviously feel it's your responsibility to protect your child from the emotional consequences—in this case, disappointment—of any negative outcome. Today's parents seem to feel they're not doing their job if they don't anticipate and proactively help their children deal with any curveball life may throw at them. Efforts along these lines are certainly well-intentioned, but let's face it, life always throws curveballs, and the earlier a child discovers the reality of this, the better. Protecting a child from disappointment serves only to prevent him from learning to deal with disappointment. In the final analysis, it is a kindness to a child to let him learn what life is all about while providing the support he needs to learn to come to grips with its inevitable slings and arrows.

Losing is not the end of the world, as I'm sure your son has already discovered. In fact, one can't learn a sport without losing at it. It may be time for your son to learn that losing doesn't mean one is a loser. That's where you can help.

Q: If I say no to my daughter and later realize I should have said yes, should I change my mind and let her do or have what she wanted, or should I stick to my original decision?

A: It depends. If your daughter handled the no fairly well, and you said it only because of stresses that had nothing to do with her, feel free to change your mind. On the other hand, if she threw a tantrum or needs more vitamin N in her life anyway, stick to your guns. Rest assured, it won't kill her or do her any psychological damage to live with parents who occasionally make irrational decisions. Isn't life a bit irrational at times?

Q: For purposes of convenience, I recently changed my four-year-old son's preschool program. The new program is as highly rated and well staffed as the previous one. Once fearless, my son has become reticent about getting out of the car in the morning when I drive him to school. There's always a teacher (usually two or three) at curbside, welcoming the kids. At the old school, he'd just get out of the car and go in. Now, I have to get out and walk him in, at which point he doesn't want me to leave. Once I go, however, he's fine. Did I make a mistake changing his school?

A: First, I want to comment on your feeling that you may have made a mistake. Today's mothers tend to feel that if a child has a negative reaction to a decision she has made, the decision not only was wrong, but also may well cause psychological problems. This is tantamount to believing that a child's emotional reactions are accurate barometers of the correctness or incorrectness of parental decisions, when in fact a child's emotions are as undisciplined as his behavior.

Please hear me loudly and clearly: *A child is not in any position to know what is in his best interest.* He may know when he is thirsty, but he does not know whether he should have water or a soda. If you give him water and he cries for soda, this does not mean you have done the wrong thing, much less that he will develop psychological issues concerning water. In this case, your son may know that he is anxious, but he does not know that the solution to his anxiety is for him to simply get out of the car and walk inside. In fact, he will be able to get rid of his anxiety only if you stop walking him in.

Now, as you have already discovered (but may be reluctant to admit), you cannot talk your son into opening the car door and walking in on his own. No anxious child has ever been *talked* out of his anxieties. Older children can sometimes be talked into doing what is necessary to test their anxieties against reality and therefore overcoming them (e.g., riding a horse), but when it comes to the anxieties of a young child, there are but two paths for parents to take: Forget it or force it.

Forgetting it means deciding that the issue isn't really that important (e.g., riding a horse), and that it is in the best interest of all concerned to wait until the child is older before reintroducing him to the anxiety-arousing event or thing. When the issue is important (e.g., getting out of the car and walking into school), then forcing it becomes necessary. In this case, forcing it means insisting that when you pull up in front of school, your son must open the door, get out of the car, and walk into the building. If you continue to walk him into the building, he may soon begin screaming and clinging to you when you try to leave. Taking this to its logical conclusion, you become your son's bodyguard 24-7.

Redefine the problem. This amounts to verbal sleight of hand that allows a parent to force a change in behavior without putting on the role of serious disciplinarian. Tell your son you've spoken to his doctor about the problem, and the doctor says reluctance to get out of the car in the morning means your son is not getting enough sleep. So, if he doesn't simply get out of the car at your first prompt (i.e., if he hesitates, requiring you to tell him twice), the doctor says you need to make sure he gets more sleep that night by putting him to bed immediately after supper. Be sure to remind your son that you have to do what the doctor says.

When you pull up to the school the next day, if he does not seem to want to get out of the car, you simply say, "Oh, you're tired. C'mon. I'll walk you in." Make no big deal of it at all, but put him to bed after supper that evening. Not one of the many parents to whom I've recommended this approach has told me it failed. Furthermore, I have never spoken to a pediatrician who disapproved of his authority being invoked in this creative manner. In fact, most of them think it's funny.

Q: Our seven-year-old son often becomes very frustrated doing his homework. If he encounters a problem that gives him difficulty, he yells, pounds his fist on the kitchen table, and even cries. One of us will sit down with him and try to calm him down and help him work through the problem. This usually works, but he might have as many as four or five of these meltdowns a night. His teacher says he is smart and capable of doing the work; furthermore, she has never seen anything of this sort in class, where he finishes most of his assignments on time without regular assistance from her. She sends home practice work, meaning he's already had experience in class with assignments of the same sort. Also, he is generally not easily frustrated; rather, in other situations he's a fairly happy-go-lucky kid. What might be causing his frustration, and what can we do about it?

A: In this case, the context might be the cause. Before I elaborate on that remark, it would help to pin down the problem. What is it? Not his ability, according to his teacher. Nor is it a lack of tolerance for frustration, since he does equally demanding work in class without meltdowns and generally finishes on time. In fact, his emotional eruptions over schoolwork occur only at the kitchen table. There we have it—the kitchen table causes his meltdowns!

You might think I'm kidding, but I'm not. The fact that he is allowed to do homework at the kitchen table places him in a situation where he can instantly receive your well-intentioned—nevertheless enabling—attention whenever he has a knee jerk of frustration concerning homework. He encounters a bit of difficulty with an assignment, begins playing the victim, and you immediately rescue him. Get him out of there! He needs to be doing his homework in a relatively private, personal area specially designated for homework, such as at a desk in his room. Yes, I know most of his classmates' parents are hovering over them while they do their homework, which simply means most of his classmates have parents who are making the same mistake you are.

Ask yourself: Does he do his work independently in class? The answer is obviously yes; therefore, he can do his homework independently. The kitchen has become a stage from which he can get attention by playing the victim. Thus, the context is the cause of the problem. It follows that if you change the context, you will eliminate the cause.

I'm not suggesting that your son's homework meltdowns are a means of manipulating or controlling you. He's not, I'm sure, sitting at the kitchen table planning his next meltdown. It's simply a matter of Rosemond's Third Law of Parenting Physics: The more available the parent is to a young child, the more likely it is the child will act helpless when frustrated. Conversely, the more space there is between parent and child, the more likely it is that the child will act competent when frustrated.

If your son doesn't already have one, put a desk in his room and stock it with everything he needs to do his homework. Tell him that he can do his homework only at his desk and not to yell for you if he has a problem, because you won't come. If he needs help, he has to bring the problem to you. Make a rule that he can receive your help only three times on any given evening. That will cause him to be very selective when it comes to seeking your assistance. For more on all of this, I recommend my book *Ending the Homework Hassle.*

Q: I recently read an article on "the family bed." The author maintained that children who sleep with their parents are more self-reliant, happy, and secure than children who do not. Should we bring our children, ages seven and four, into our bed?

A: Not unless you want two children who are less self-reliant and secure, and happy only if they are able to sleep with you. The claims of "family bed" advocates are without basis. There is not a shred of evidence to support them, but there is plenty with which to refute them.

The point of assigning a specific bedtime for children and having them sleep in their own beds is twofold. First, it gives parents much-needed time for themselves and each other. Second, bedtime is an exercise in separation and independence. It is the first of many such exercises to come, and how parents handle it sets an important and enduring precedent.

Separation involves a certain amount of anxiety for parents and children, especially young ones. Because it demands that children become less dependent and more self-sufficient, the issue of separation is inseparable from the task of growing up.

In his best-selling book *The Road Less Traveled,* psychiatrist M. Scott Peck says that many people never learn to accept the inherent pain of living. When confronted with a problem, they either attempt an impatient knee-jerk solution or try to ignore it altogether. Those who spank children for crying at bedtime fall into the first category. Parents who let their children sleep with them fall into the second. Both are failing to deal with the issue.

In thirty-odd years of working with families, I've talked with many parents who have slept with their children, but rarely have I talked with one who has been comfortable with the arrangement. Why aren't these children sleeping alone? The usual answer is that the child in question screams when the parents try to put him in his own bed. What these parents don't realize is that the longer they avoid dealing with the issue of separation, the more anxiety their children will attach to it, and the more screams it will provoke.

In Peck's terms, family sleeping is a way of avoiding a problem in the hope that somehow, someday, the problem will miraculously resolve itself. Unfortunately, life will probably deal a different hand to family sleepers.

The child whose parents avoid confronting the pain of separation never receives complete implicit permission to separate from them. As the years go by, the parents' continued failure to resolve this fundamental issue becomes an obstacle to healthy growth and development. In my experience and that of most other clinicians, these children are generally excessively dependent, fearful, socially immature, and undisciplined.

At some point, nearly all young children cry at bedtime, and their cries make us want to draw them protectively closer. Protection of this nature is not always in the children's best interests. They must learn to deal with separation, parents must show the way, and bedtime is a logical first place to begin the lessons. It's not as hard as it may sound. Establish a predictable bedtime and a routine to precede it. If the child cries, do not—as some pediatricians and child psychologists advise—let him cry it out. Return to the bedroom at regular intervals to provide reassurance that you are still here, watching over him. If, along with your reassurances, the child hears a steadfast insistence to stay in bed, it won't be long before bedtime is accepted as routine.

Q: My eight-year-old daughter is afraid to try new things. She also becomes easily discouraged when her first attempt at something doesn't succeed. For example, if I try to encourage her to swim three laps of the pool instead of two, she'll say, "I can't." No matter how much I encourage, or try to pump up her self-confidence, she won't make the attempt. If her piano teacher assigns her a difficult piece, she'll hardly try it before giving up. I can't understand why this otherwise capable child has such low self-esteem. How can I help her?

A: Your daughter's problem has less to do with self-esteem and more to do with the way you're responding to her frustrations. You're letting yourself get too emotionally involved in your daughter's performance, whether swimming or piano or whatever.

Learning any new skill involves a certain amount of frustration. When your daughter encounters it, you go to her rescue. Although your intentions are good, you're actually preventing her from working through the frustration on her own, in her own way, and in her own time. Her stubborn refusal to heed your words of encouragement is a way of saying, "Back off, Mom." You see, when you get involved in these situations, your daughter has to deal not only with her frustrations but with yours as well. To her, your encouragement feels like pressure. So the more you encourage, the more she resists.

Let your daughter work these things out. If she wants to talk to you about problems she's having learning a piano piece or swimming the length of the pool, listen to her but let her do most of the talking. When it's time for you to talk, say, "Learning new things takes a lot of effort and patience. Losing patience means it's time to set the thing aside for a while and come back to it later." In other words, give her permission to be frustrated and even to give up, at least temporarily.

If she still insists that she "can't," shrug your shoulders and say, "Well, then don't. If you think you've done your best, and you're convinced you can't do it, maybe you should give up. After all, if you've tried your best, giving up makes sense." Whatever you say, make it short and sweet, and then walk away.

By not getting emotionally involved in her frustrations, you let her be completely responsible for her own feelings. My parents called it "stewing in your own juices." When you stay out of it, you also give her freedom to try again, because now she can make the attempt on her terms rather than yours. Chances are, she will.

Q: Our daughter started kindergarten this year. Every evening, after supper, I sit with her at the kitchen table while she does her homework, which never amounts to much. Missy's problem is, she doesn't make numbers and letters well enough to suit herself and thinks her coloring is ugly. Consequently, she ends up doing everything over three or four times, when her first attempt was perfectly

fine. **The more I reassure her, the madder she gets. At times, she's made statements such as "I'm dumb!" and "I can't do anything!" Her teacher sees none of this at school. How can I help her?**

A: Let's keep things in their proper perspective: Missy is going through some major changes. She's in school for the first time; she's learning new skills; she's trying to please you; she's trying to please the teacher; she's trying to please herself; and, on top of all this, she has homework to do. Little wonder that she's feeling some pressure.

The way you manage this homework problem will be precedent-setting. In the final analysis, you want her to accept responsibility for her homework, set realistic goals for herself, and take pride in what she accomplishes. You don't want her to become a neurotic perfectionist at age five.

Two things are clear: First, you know she can do the work and do it well. Second, she doesn't get bent out of shape about her work in front of the teacher. Why? Because the teacher can't (and probably won't) give her as much attention as you can. Ah-ha! Now we know that the less attention Missy gets, the better her attitude toward herself and her work becomes. So stop overseeing her homework. Make three rules:

1. Missy does her homework in her room. No more kitchen table.
2. If she wants help, she must ask for it. If you know she's capable of doing it on her own, tell her so in a supportive, encouraging way: "Oh, you can do that by yourself. You don't really need my help."
3. She can work on homework for only thirty minutes. Set a timer. When it goes off, make her stop, whether she's finished

or not. This will limit her obsessing and prevent homework from becoming a marathon.

If she complains of not being able to do this or that, just say, "I won't listen to things I know aren't true. I love you and trust you to do your best." Don't labor over this issue. The more you try to persuade her that she's capable, the more she'll complain.

Without intending to do so, Missy has manufactured this problem. There is no evidence whatsoever that it exists outside her imagination, or even outside of the kitchen. It's a soap opera, and she's the producer. When you stop being the audience, it will quickly go off the air.

Q: We have two boys, ages ten and seven. We've always done the same for both, thinking this was the way to prevent jealousy. It hasn't worked. They're constantly on the lookout for things one has or gets that the other doesn't. The situation is getting completely out of hand. What should we do?

A: If it's any consolation, the same plan has backfired for thousands of parents before you and will continue to backfire for thousands yet to come.

The solution is to stop treating them fairly. In the first place, your well-intentioned fairness is actually unfair, because no one will ever make any effort to treat them so fairly again. The more accustomed they get to the idea that fair is the normal way of the world, the ruder their awakening will eventually be. In the process of being fair, you've become a slave to their demands. They find your omissions, and you dutifully correct them. So, I ask you, who's running the show?

Q: So how do I go about undoing five years of fairness?

A: Sit your children down and read them your proclamation of independence: "Hear ye! Hear ye! Let it be henceforth known and proclaimed throughout the household that your parents are no longer going to be fair. Since it has become increasingly obvious to us that you are two different people, we are going to treat you differently! For instance, if we buy you"—point dramatically at one of them—"something, we may not buy you"—point, with a flourish, at the other—"anything at all. If we do something with or for you"—point accusingly—"we may not do anything with or for you"—point menacingly—"and if that's not fair, so be it. If you don't like it, that's life! Get the point?"

You're in the habit of being fair and your boys are in the habit of expecting it. There's only one way to break a habit, and that's cold turkey. From now on, you and your husband should conspire to plan instances of unfairness. For example, take one son to the store and buy him a new pair of shoes. Several days later, take the other to the store and buy him a new sweatshirt. In other words, plan things for them individually, rather than collectively. It's the only way they're ever going to find out that unfair isn't terminal.

They won't like it. They will scream, rant, rave, act pitiful, and blaspheme you, and that's just for starters. When they do, you will have the urge to sit them down and explain why you're doing what you're doing and how it's in their best interest blah-blah-blah. Don't! They won't agree with you, much less even listen. The harder you try to get them to understand, the more they'll rant. Pretty soon you'll begin to feel that maybe you're doing the wrong thing, and you'll try to be fair to make up for your awfulness. Zap—you'll be right back where you started. Instead of entertaining their misery, just request that they take it to their rooms and vent it against their pillows and mattresses.

Q: Are there ever times when we should be fair?

A: If by that you mean, "Are there ever times when we should do the same thing for both of them?" the answer is yes. I'm not suggesting that you never do the same thing for both of them or include them in the same activity. You wouldn't be a family anymore if you did that.

Q: How long will it take before our children adjust to our unfairness?

A: I'd say it will take three to six months for the screaming to stop, another three to six years for them to get completely used to the idea, and adulthood before they understand why you did it and forgive you.

Q: At least ten times a day, every day, my four-year-old daughter asks me if I love her. I always tell her I love her very much and always will. Several months ago, when this first started, I thought it was a phase that would pass quickly. Instead of tapering off, it's gotten steadily worse. I can't figure out what might have caused her to become so insecure. What would you advise?

A: I'd advise that you help your daughter stop asking the question so much. Asking "Do you love me?" ten times a day doesn't mean your daughter is insecure. She's probably just trying to figure out what love means and how long it lasts. Repetition is one way children answer questions of this sort for themselves.

For example, if you move a brightly colored object through a six-month-old's field of vision and then hide it behind your back, the infant won't look any further for it—out of sight, out of mind. Several months later, the same child will respond to this tease by crawling behind you to find it. Around age eight months, an infant realizes that objects don't cease to exist when they're out of sight.

I once watched a ten-month-old amuse himself by placing a block inside a kitchen pot, putting the lid on the pot, and then immediately taking it off to rediscover the "lost" toy. Like a scientist, he repeated this simple experiment over and over again until he had proved to himself that the block was forever.

Your daughter is trying to establish the identity and permanence of an intangible concept—an invisible idea—by taking the lid off the question "Do you love me?" time and time again.

The problem isn't the question. It's that adults are generally insecure about their ability to raise children and tend, therefore, to look for any possible indication that something is terribly wrong. We overanalyze and misinterpret events; we blow the significance of things completely out of proportion; we misplace common sense and replace it with nonsense.

At some point, your daughter probably began to sense that the question made you feel somewhat uncomfortable. Needing to understand why Mommy got flustered, she began asking the question more and more often. The more she asked, the more flustered you became, the more she asked—and so on.

The two of you are riding the same merry-go-round. You don't know how to stop getting flustered, and she doesn't know how to stop asking the question. She can't help you. So, you've got to help her.

Find a peaceful, relaxed time for the two of you to sit down and talk. Tell her that "I love you" is like a piece of candy people surprise one another with, and that you would like to begin surprising her with it, too. Help her understand that you can't surprise her as long as she asks the question.

The next time she asks, say something like, "Oh-oh, now it's not a surprise."

Meanwhile, make it a point to call her over to you several times a day to play "Guess what?"

"Guess what?"

"What?"

"I love you."

Personally, I can't think of a nicer surprise.

Q: Is it ever okay to let an adult child live at home? If so, what understandings should exist between the parents and the child?

A: Valid reasons for letting a grown child come home to nest include such things as divorce, job loss, and prolonged illness. Stressful circumstances such as these might temporarily interfere with the young person's ability to be self-supporting, in which case equally temporary parental help might be necessary.

"Nesting" is also perfectly acceptable during major, but not necessarily stressful, transitions in the child's life. This would include the time between college graduation or the end of military service and a job. If living at home for a few months before getting married would help the young person build a nest egg, that's fine, too.

Whatever the circumstances, the arrangement should not be open-ended. Parents and child should establish goals, a specific plan of action, and time frames for reaching those goals. For example, the agreement might stipulate that the young person will be out of the house in six months. The first month will be spent finding a job, the second and third paying off debts, the fourth and fifth building a financial cushion, and the sixth finding an affordable place to live.

During this period of dependency, the young person should be required to make some form of contribution to the household. If unable to contribute financially, he should perform services around the home that function as payment. Once the young person has income, a sliding scale of financial reimbursement can be worked out. Grown children should, in other words, "earn their keep."

Q: How much control should parents exercise over an adult child who lives at home?

A: No more than they would exercise over any other temporary boarder. This arrangement involves three adults, not two adults and one child. The young person should be treated as an adult and be expected to act as such. Likewise, the parents should act as adults, not parents. This means, for example, that the parents should set no specific restrictions on the young person's comings and goings. It also means that the young person should come and go with due respect for the parents' lifestyle and values.

Q: What if the adult child violates the agreement or behaves in a manner that's annoying or offensive to the parents?

A: The parents shouldn't lecture or punish the young person for behavior they don't like, but should express their concerns in a straightforward manner. Violations of the agreement should be openly discussed, the goal being to reach an understanding as to why the violation occurred and thus prevent a repeat performance. Perhaps the violation was the result of a misunderstanding, or perhaps the agreement was unrealistic to begin with and needs to be modified. If conflict continues between parents and grown child, family counseling is the next step.

Q: What if the agreed-upon time for leaving comes and the adult child isn't financially able to move away?

A: Inventory what went wrong and why. Set new goals based on the mistakes and miscalculations that were made and try again. If the young person fails a second time to emancipate on schedule, there may be more going on than meets the eye. At that point, it may be appropriate to explore the issues and problems with a family counselor.

Q: We have a twenty-year-old daughter—an only child—who feels we have no right to restrict her behavior. For one, she refuses to go to church with us. After several nasty fights, I gave up on this. Her curfew is 1:00 A.M., but she often stays out later and has recently told me she will stay out as long as she pleases. I've discovered that she occasionally drinks. Her father thinks we should let go of this because "she'll soon be twenty-one and is going to drink anyway." My husband thinks we should overlook everything. He just wants peace. I think we should start enforcing the rules or tell her to leave. Believe it or not, my daughter is very responsible

(she attends college, has a part-time job, and owns and takes care of her own car), and communication between us is usually good. It's just the rules thing. She contends that when she turned nineteen, she graduated from having to follow our rules. Am I being unreasonable? If not, how can I get my husband to support me?

A: I take no pleasure in informing people of such things, but you are your own worst enemy. Your surveillance and obviously vain attempts to control decisions made by a twenty-year-old put you in the running for my Magnificent Maternal Micromanager Award, the Triple-M of parenting.

There is a difference between not liking decisions an adult child is making and trying to control them. If the issue is simply a matter of who's right, you are. Church is good (research finds that young people who attend church are much less likely to engage in all manner of self-destructive behavior), underage drinking is bad, and then there's the matter of living at home and having defiant disrespect for the fact that coming in at all hours of the night is disturbing to one's parents. Unfortunately, being right does not justify your hypervigilant attempts to micromanage your daughter. All you've managed to do is create a power struggle that you cannot possibly win. I agree with your husband: You need to let it go.

That said, your daughter definitely does not need to be living at home any longer. She is responsible enough to support herself and obviously does not want to abide by anyone else's rules. Therefore, she needs to be emancipated. Not ejected, but emancipated—joyously.

Toys and Play—
The Right Stuff

I remember being five years old. My life was chock-full of stone
walls and trees to climb, lizards to catch, nooks and crannies to
explore, and parks and empty lots in which to play. I had no television during those early years and very few store-bought toys. My
imagination had wings and I flew to whatever place and became
whatever pretend person I pleased.

I lived the first seven years of my life in Charleston, South
Carolina. There was a waterfront park not far from our house, and
I spent many an afternoon there, watching the big ships and
dreaming of faraway places like London, where the queen lived,
and Africa, where Tarzan swung through the trees with the apes.
Every night, either my mother or my grandmother would read to
me from children's classics like Kipling's *Just So Stories* and
Grahame's *The Wind in the Willows*. Because my mother worked
part-time in addition to attending college, I went to a preschool
where we played games, and painted pictures with our fingers, and
made castles out of empty oatmeal boxes and soldiers out of
clothespins. Mom used to tell me we were "dirt poor," but looking
back, the standard of my living was high. It was a special time but

not out of the ordinary, because that's what childhood was all about.

Time has taken its toll on childhood—so much so that I fear we may be poised on the brink of childhood's end. Not the final apocalyptic end of children, but the loss of what being a child once was and still should be all about.

Today, instead of sending children outdoors to play, parents let them sit in front of TV sets for thousands of hours during their formative years, staring at a constantly blinking, tasteless, odor-free, hands-off counterfeit of the real world. Meanwhile, their imaginations atrophy from disuse along with their initiative, their curiosity, their resourcefulness, and their creativity.

Today, instead of providing children with ample opportunity and the raw materials with which to create handmade playthings, adults overdose them with mass-produced toys that stimulate relatively little imaginative thought—toys that are nothing more than what the labels on their boxes say they are.

Today, instead of reading to children and letting time and teachers do the rest, adults push letters and numbers at preschoolers, completely disregarding the fact that early childhood has nothing to do with letters and numbers and everything to do with play. We have lost nearly all respect for the enormous contribution play makes to healthy growth and development. "He's just playing," a parent is apt to say, when "just playing" is the very essence of childhood.

Charlie's Magical Make-Do Marker

Somewhere, in a present place and a present time, there lives a five-year-old boy named Charlie. One day, Charlie's parents hear strange noises coming from his room: "Sssssssszzzzzoooommmmm! Pow! Pow! Pow! Pow! Nnnnneeeeeyyyooow!"

Charlie's parents tiptoe quietly down the hall to check things out. As they get closer, the sounds get louder. Quietly, they open Charlie's door just enough to see without being seen. Charlie is running excitedly around his room, tracing sweeping arcs in the air with an empty felt-tip marker–turned–rocketship he managed to rescue from the trash. Suddenly, Charlie stops. The sound becomes a high-pitched whine as the "spaceship" begins its vertical descent to the surface of Planet Chest-of-Drawers. It lands, and for a moment nothing moves. Then "Click, click, click," says Charlie, and his parents can almost see the hatch of the spaceship open and its alien commander emerge.

Instantly, the marker becomes the alien and begins to lumber ominously across the surface of the planet, looking for something to eat. The alien doesn't get very far, when suddenly, from behind a wad of rolled-up underwear, there jumps a plastic Indian, with bow drawn. "Whooooooosssshh!" the Indian lets fly an arrow at the alien. As the alien intruder moves to defend itself, the marker becomes a ray gun, which the alien begins firing at the Indian, making a rapid shoom-shoom! sound. For the next three or four minutes, the battle rages. Finally, sensing the advantage, the Indian emerges from behind the shelter of his underwear rocks, shouts a ferocious war cry, and charges at the startled alien. Realizing that death rays are no match for a crazed Indian with bow and arrow, the alien beats a hasty retreat and blasts off in search of a more hospitable planet.

Closing Charlie's door, his parents tiptoe back to the living room. "Well," says Charlie's father. "Now we know what to get Charlie for Christmas."

"We certainly do," says Charlie's mother, and together they chorus, "A rocket ship!"

On Christmas morning, Charlie wakes up to find a huge box under the tree labeled *To Charlie from Santa*. Inside, he finds a replica of the space shuttle, complete with cargo hatch, command module with seating for seven astronauts, and retractable landing gear. Inside the box, Charlie finds a plastic drop-cloth printed to look like the surface of the moon. The box itself, when folded in a certain manner, makes a ridge of moon mountains. Charlie is absolutely consumed with joy. The spaceship isn't all Charlie gets on Christmas morning. There's also a battery-operated car he can steer by remote control. There's a slot-car racing set. There's a man on a motorcycle that winds up and leaps from ramp to ramp. Finally, there's a suitcase that opens to reveal a miniature city and comes complete with tiny cars to drive around the city's streets. Oh, joy! Charlie really rakes it in on Christmas morning.

Three weeks later, Charlie's mother is in the kitchen fixing dinner, when Charlie drags in, looking dejected. His mother asks, "Charlie? What's the matter with you?"

Charlie scuffs the floor with his toe and whines, "I've got nothin' to do."

Charlie's mother has a spontaneous cerebral event. She turns on him and shrieks, "What do you mean, you've got nothing to do? You've got a new space shuttle, a remote-controlled car, a slot-car racing set, a man on a motorcycle, and a city in a suitcase, not to mention all the other toys you have back in your room from birthdays and Christmases past! How dare you tell me you've got nothing to do!"

What Charlie's mother fails to realize is that Charlie is telling the truth. He really doesn't have anything to do. He's done everything that can be done with a space shuttle, a remote-controlled car, a slot-car racing set, a man on a motorcycle, and a city in a suitcase. What Charlie really needed on Christmas morning were toys he could *do* things with, rather than toys that are nice to look at, cost a lot of money, and perform at the flip of a switch. You see, the difference between Charlie's marvelous magical marker and a $75 plastic replica of the space shuttle is that the magical marker was anything Charlie wanted it to be. In the span of a mere few minutes, it was a spaceship, an alien, and a ray gun. And all Charlie did to effect these transformations was zap it with the alchemy of his imagination. No matter how much Charlie imagines his space shuttle to be something else, it remains a space shuttle, forever and ever. Within three weeks, Charlie has exhausted all the creative potential not only of the space shuttle, but also of the remote-controlled car, the slot-car racing set, the man on the motorcycle, and the city in the suitcase. Three weeks after Christmas, Charlie truly has nothing to do.

With the best of intentions, adults are successfully preventing today's children from getting in touch with the magical make-do of childhood. When I was a child, play was largely a matter of making do. For instance, if "pirates" was the game of the day, I'd borrow one of my mother's brightly colored scarves for a sash and her black galoshes for ten-league boots. A stick became my broadsword. Mom helped me make a hat by folding a sheet of newspaper. A few pieces of her costume jewelry completed the disguise. Looking at myself in the mirror, I was Captain Blood! Together, my mates and I sailed the seven backyards in search of milk and cookies. Oh, joy!

Through the magic of making do, children exercise imagination, initiative, creativity, intelligence, resourcefulness, and self-reliance. In the process, they practice discovery and invention, which are the basics of science. Making do is not only the essence of truly creative play—which is the essence of childhood—it's also the story of the advancement of the human race. Throughout the parade of history, the art of making do has been significant to nearly every important invention and nearly every famous discovery. The child who discovers the magic of making do is on the road to success! Who knows, that same child might be our next Marie Curie, Louis Pasteur, Jonas Salk, Ferdinand Magellan, Thomas Edison, or Alexander Graham Bell. Who knows?

Transformations

Like Charlie's empty felt-tip marker, all truly creative toys have one characteristic in common: They encourage and enable children to perform what developmental psychologists call "transformations." A child performs a transformation by using one thing to represent something else. For instance, when a child takes a pinecone and sets it upright on the ground and calls it a tree, that's a transformation. Transformations are the essence of fantasy, which is the essence of play. An empty box becomes a boat, a car, a table, or anything else the child wills it to be. A child can also become someone else at will: Tarzan, Jane, or the neighborhood grocer. If a toy aids a child in making transformations, it is well worth the money spent on it, not to mention the time the child spends playing with it.

Toys that encourage transformation include creative materials such as clay, finger paint, and crayons. Inside, there's the everyday household stuff of empty oatmeal cartons, Popsicle sticks, spoons, shoe boxes, empty spools of thread, straws, paper bags, buttons, pots and pans, and empty toilet paper rolls. Don't forget how much fun children have turning large appliance cartons into houses. Outside, there are leaves, sticks, pinecones, rocks, and mud, glorious mud! The list goes on and on, limited only by the child's virtually limitless imagination.

As a child, one of my favorite toys was a Quaker oats carton. I could make it into just about anything I wanted. I'd turn it upside down, thread a neck band of string through two holes punched in the sides, and it became a drum that I played with wooden spoons. Or I'd cut rectangular notches in the top and a drawbridge in the side and it became a castle. Or I'd tape a brim to it and it became a top hat. How much did these toys cost? The price of a carton of oatmeal. How much did I gain from them? An incredible amount. After all, I'd made them with my own hands.

While your children are young, show them how to use things like pots and pans, empty boxes, pipe cleaners, and other odds and ends to make their own toys. Once you show what can be done with a box, some tape, a few sheets of construction paper, and a pair of scissors, there'll be no stopping them! Children who make their own playthings are not only learning how to entertain themselves, but also exercising and strengthening independence, self-sufficiency, initiative, resourcefulness, eye-hand coordination, intelligence, imagination, a sense of achievement, motivation, and creativity. What more could a parent want? There are few investments of a parent's time and energy that will pay off better than this one.

Buying Worthwhile Toys

Realizing that the average American child is a toy addict, many companies make toys with purposefully (and profitably) short life spans. After all, why make toys that last when the average child is more concerned with getting than with the quality of what's gotten?

When buying toys for children, consider first the fact that children are inquisitive. The first question that pops into their minds when they're given something is "How does it work?" In most cases, you find out how something works by taking it apart. Unfortunately, most toys are not made to be taken apart. If you try, they will break.

Consider also that most toys are designed to attract a child's attention and curiosity, but not to hold his interest. This obviously profitable marketing philosophy is to blame for the fact that children lose interest in most toys within a few weeks, if not days.

Not all toy companies are into making schlock, but many are. How are parents to know whether the toys they are buying their children are good investments? In addition to being safe, a toy embodies four qualities by which to measure its play value:

1. The toy presents a wide range of creative possibilities. It is capable of being many things, as defined by the child's imagination, rather than one thing, as defined by the manufacturer. In other words, it enables transformations.

2. The toy encourages manipulation. It can be taken apart and put together in various ways. Toys of this kind hold a child's interest because they stimulate creative behavior.

3. The toy is age appropriate. You don't give a rubber duck to a ten-year-old any more than you give an electric train to a two-year-old. Most manufacturers publish the age range of a toy on its box. While not always entirely accurate, this gives a fairly good idea of whether the toy and the child will "match."

4. The toy is durable. It will withstand lots of abuse.

When parents ask me for examples of manufactured toys high in play value, the first that come to mind are the construction sets manufactured by LEGO. In my estimation, these are the only toy systems that score a perfect ten in all four categories. Coming in a close second are building sets like Lincoln Logs, Tinkertoy, and

Erector. Art materials—clay, finger paint, construction paper, crayons, scissors—should be staples in every child's life.

Cuddly dolls (ones that perform no quasi-human functions) enable children to explore parental feelings and act out parental behavior. They're far more imaginative and creative than dolls that walk, talk, drink from a bottle, and wet their pants.

While we're on the subject of dolls, I should mention how important it is that parents not limit children to toys traditionally considered suitable for only one gender. Dolls and stuffed animals are just as appropriate for boys as they are for girls. If a boy wants to play with dolls, buy him dolls. Believe it or not, dolls do not compromise a boy's sexual development any more than a baseball bat compromises a girl's sexual development. If a girl wants to play baseball, buy her a bat and a ball. The freer children are to explore the possibilities of life, the better the choices they will make later on.

Surprisingly, most toys that are advertised as educational rate low on the play-value scale. They are typically one-dimensional and challenge a child's imagination and intellect for a relatively short period of time. Educational toys appeal primarily to parents, who mistakenly think that toys of this type will speed their children's development or get them ready for school more rapidly. For the most part, however, their educational value is shallow, contrived, and either irrelevant to a child's development or a poor substitute for cheaper but more interesting materials and activities.

Notice that the toys mentioned above as being high in play value have been on the market for fifty years or more. In addition to those already mentioned, toys that fit this criterion include blocks, electric trains (the child can use sets such as LEGO and Lincoln Logs to make the train station and other buildings and Tinkertoy to make bridges and tunnels), Matchbox cars, small plastic figures (a bag of plastic army men or cowboys and Indians), dolls, dollhouses (the child can be taught to make furniture out of construction paper), and marbles. For the older child, buy toys that can form the nucleus of a hobby, such as chemistry sets, telescopes and microscopes, rock-collecting sets, and models. A child will get a lot more mileage from a handful of old-fashioned toys than from all the newfangled junk in the world.

Less Is More, Part One

One of the more consistent things grandparents notice is that sibling rivalry seems to have become a lot more intense since we were kids. I have a theory. Ironically, it's one most grandparents aren't going to like, because if I'm right, then today's grandparents are part of the problem. I believe that the force driving most sibling rivalry is greed. Today's parents, with more than a little assistance from many grandparents, turn their children into greedy little materialists by buying them toy after toy after gadget after game after vehicle after gizmo, beginning before they're born and lasting forever.

Because today's parents feed the self-centered spark that resides in the heart of every newborn, it grows into a flame, a fire, and then a raging inferno. By age four or five, today's all-too-typical child is infected with King Midas syndrome—he is a greedy little hoarder who can't share unless forced to do so, which means the child can't really share at all.

When I was five, I had five toys I could call my own. Most people my age report between none and ten. According to our parents, we didn't fight much over toys. That's pretty much a cause-and-effect thing. To paraphrase a line from Bob Dylan's "Like a Rolling Stone," when you haven't got much, you haven't got much to lose. So sharing is not a problem. When you have a lot, however, you have a lot to lose, which means you're probably going to have difficulty when it comes to sharing.

The more material things a child acquires, the more likely he is to resent it when someone else acquires something he doesn't have, especially if the something is unaffordable; or the more likely he is to feel the other person's good fortune isn't fair, and to be jealous, envious, and covetous. Aren't these the themes around which today's high levels of sibling conflict spin?

Take note, parents! Stop buying your children so many things! Stop throwing fuel on the fires of narcissism and materialism. At a certain relatively low level, things become a drug that anesthetizes the spirit. Make strong your children's spirits by keeping them poor.

Need I repeat myself for the benefit of the grandparents in the audience?

The Gift of Grandparents

A fellow in Traverse City, Michigan, once asked me if I thought today's grandparents give too much to their grandchildren. If grandparents give mostly time and attention, I told him, then the answer is no, because while parents can give too much time and attention to their children, grandparents cannot. That is one of parenting's more delightful paradoxes. On the other hand, if grandparents give mostly material things, then the answer is definitely yes.

At this writing, I've been a grand for nearly twelve years. During that time, our two children have gifted Willie and me with five grand boys and one grand girl. Early on, we made our best grandparent decision ever, possibly the best we will ever make. We resolved that we would not cause our grandkids to expect material things from us. We would take them to places they'd never been and might otherwise never go, expose them to new experiences, give them vacations from the rules and routines of their own homes, read to them, play games with them, and take them traveling with us. We would not give them lots of things. And we haven't.

One typical Christmas, for example, we gave each of Eric and Nancy's three children a fleece pullover. That was it! If you sense that I'm bragging, you're right on. Not only am I proud of us for not joining in the general genuflect to the gods of the mall, but I am also proud to say that our pullovers were the only Christmas gifts the kids were still using in March.

Never has one of our grandchildren asked, "What did you bring me?" When we call, they can't wait to talk to us. When they see us, they break out in big smiles, run to us, and jump into our arms. They ask to spend the night at our house, where we have a bedroom/playroom for them that offers about a dozen toys, none of which are electronic. There will never be electronic toys in our house. We have not added a toy to the bedroom/playroom in probably two years. They don't care. They want to spend the night with us because it's an adventure. One of their favorite things to do at our house is to draw chalk figures all over our driveway. Now *that's* what a truly authentic childhood is like.

Make no mistake, we have rules, and the kids are very conscious of them. I honestly think they are on their very best behavior at our house for the simple reason that we do not tolerate misbehavior. Our intolerance is always conveyed calmly, and as a consequence, the kids don't misbehave. Therefore, time spent at our house is always relaxed and enjoyable.

Our experience causes me to feel sorry for grandparents who think their role is to shower their grandchildren with material things. If they never change their worldly ways, their relationships with their grandchildren are never going to be more than superficial, if they have relationships at all. I pray these folks someday discover that the richest grandparenthood is not expensive at all.

Less Is More, Part Two

A number of years ago, a couple consulted me concerning their almost-three-year-old daughter. Most of the problems they described were typical of children of this age, but one was especially intriguing.

"Molly won't let us out of her sight," they said. "In addition to following us wherever we go in the house, she's constantly asking us to play with her and whining if we can't. Neither of us minds playing with her some, but we feel that with all the toys she has, she ought to have no trouble entertaining herself."

My ears perked up. "How many toys does she have?" I asked. "And what kind are they?"

"She's got so many toys, you can hardly walk into her room without stepping on one," said her father. "I guess they're mostly the ones you see advertised on television."

That was all I needed to hear to know what the problem was.

First, I helped Molly's parents rate the play value of Molly's toys on a scale of one to ten. Those with ratings of less than seven were boxed and given to charity. Not surprisingly, that reduced the pile by nine-tenths. Those that remained included soft gimmick-free dolls, some stuffed animals, a set of blocks, and a dollhouse.

Next, Molly's parents went toy shopping. Instead of the junk that constitutes most of the toys advertised on television, they bought a few toys that measured up to the four criteria set forth earlier in this chapter.

To create a household environment that encouraged exploration, Molly's parents childproofed their home. They put up anything that was potentially dangerous as well as anything that couldn't be easily replaced if broken. This ensured that Molly would be able to roam through most of the house without needing much supervision. Childproofing also minimized the number of times Molly had to hear the word no, making obedience more likely.

Molly's parents also put safety latches on all the kitchen cabinets but one, which became Molly's cabinet. Her parents stocked this special place with empty oatmeal boxes, large spools, old pots and pans, boxes of all sorts and sizes, and other safe household items that might otherwise have been discarded. Here was a place where Molly could come and rummage to her heart's content.

Last, but not least, Molly's parents went to an appliance store and obtained a large sturdy box into which they cut windows and a door. A small chair went inside, along with a few dolls and other housekeeping items—just the place for hours of imaginative play.

I saw Molly's parents several weeks later. Sure enough, Molly was entertaining herself much better than before and demanding far less of her parents' attention. "She seems bright and happy again," said her mother.

Molly's story isn't unique. In the last ten years, I've made the same basic set of recommendations to at least twenty individual parents. Of those, perhaps ten have had the gumption to follow through. The experiment has yet to fail. Every parent has reported the same basic results: The fewer the toys and the more space the child has in which to explore and create, the more successful the child is at occupying his time. The more success the child experiences at what comes more naturally than anything else—play—the happier the child is. These success stories simply show us that sometimes less is more.

Spoiled, Part One

Journalists frequently ask me, "Are America's kids spoiled?"

I certainly think so, but America's parents would deny it. The problem, I think, is with the word itself. *Spoiled* is synonymous with *rotten,* which means being in a state of decay—i.e., smelling bad. Perhaps if we redenominate the problem, calling it something that isn't so putrid, parents would be willing to admit they are creating a problem and change their ways. With that in mind, I propose changing the term *spoiled children* to *ungrateful, demanding, petulant brats.* The question then becomes, are you raising an ungrateful, demanding, petulant brat (UDPB)?

If you're having trouble figuring it out, here's a quick self-test to determine whether or not your child is a UDPB. Answer each question simply "True" or "False":

1. When I buy my child something he wants, but does not need—a new toy, for example—he acts like it's about time I did something for him.

2. If I don't do what my child wants me to do, he is likely to cry or scream at me that I'm a bad parent.

3. I have to virtually get down on my knees and beg my child to accept any responsibility at all, and even then it's a crapshoot.

Okay, if you answered "True" to even one of the above questions, you have a UDPB. Why does just one "True" answer qualify a child? Because one "True" means you should have answered "True" to the other two questions but didn't because, like most American parents, you're in heavy denial concerning your child.

Then what does a non-UDPB act like?

My church's newsletter once published a letter by a young man who grew up in the church and was giving a year of his life serving disadvantaged children at an orphanage in Honduras. The young man was definitely *not* a UDPB and neither were the children with whom he worked. He wrote: "The second image that struck me was watching a child and a dog fight over what looked to be a chicken carcass. The child won and tore at it greedily. I wish I could paint with words what the city is like. However, the actual orphanage is heaven for these children. Never in my life have I met more respectful and grateful children. A far cry from what I saw working up in [a small eastern city]. These children know how lucky they are to have even the opportunity to take responsibility for their lives. An outlook many children in the States lack."

Amen. I'm sure every American parent, if asked, would say they wanted their children to be respectful and grateful. This young man put his finger on the key to raising a non-UDPB. If you want your child to be grateful and respectful, don't give him a lot. Say no more often than you say yes—a lot more often, in fact. At least four noes to every yes is my suggestion. And while you're at it, be a model of frugality, patience, and service to others. Children are more impressed, in every sense of the term, by someone who serves others than by someone who serves them. Put your children to work around the house, and work alongside them. Our young missionary rose at the crack of dawn every morning and went to work with the boys who lived in the orphanage. Together they slopped hogs and shoveled manure and weeded fields by hand until it was time for supper, at which point they all bowed their heads and thanked the good Lord for each and every small blessing in their lives—rich lives, indeed.

Spoiled, Part Two

A producer for a popular talk show called me to ask if I'd be interested in appearing on a segment they were doing on spoiled children and how *not* to raise one. I said I would consider it, and she began the preinterview, which is for the purpose of making sure that the potential guest has a viewpoint that will fit the show's purpose.

"How does one spoil a child?" she asked.

"By saying yes to most of the child's requests for things," I replied, "the end result of which is that the child becomes increasingly demanding, petulant, ungrateful, and intolerant. The aforementioned qualities reflect self-centeredness, which is the antithesis of positive character development."

"Can a child be spoiled in other ways?" she asked.

"Well," I said, "you can add catering, enabling, and rescuing, but no one of those attributes ever stands alone. The parent who caters always is a parent who enables and rescues. Furthermore, the parent who enables and rescues is a parent who feeds his or her child a constant diet of yes. Oh, and by the way," I added, "children who are catered to and enabled and so on always develop bad manners, which is how you can spot them."

She then asked the question that headed the interview south: "Can you give me an example?"

I gave the example of a parent who permits a child to complain about the food he is served at the dinner table and then, taking it one step further, "customizes" the evening meal for the child.

"I don't understand that at all, John," she replied, with an edge in her voice. "Why shouldn't a child be allowed to express dislike of food at the dinner table?"

"Because it's rude," I said. "You are training your child, during the evening meal, to display good manners when he is a guest in someone else's home, and it's downright rude to tell someone who has prepared food for you that you don't like it."

"So what should a child do if he doesn't like something that's served to him?" said producer queried, but I could tell from her tone that she took issue with my example.

I said that parents should teach their children to eat all sorts of food, and that there's a way of doing just that, a tried-and-true way of making sure that your child does not develop into a picky eater.

How? Put a ridiculously small amount of each item being served on the child's plate—e.g., one teaspoon of mashed potatoes, one bite of roast beef, and one-half of a dreaded green bean—and inform the child he can have seconds of anything he wants when he has eaten everything on his plate.

"What if the child eats the mashed potatoes and the roast beef and leaves the green bean?" she asked, to which I replied that the parents should cover the bean and set it aside. If the child complained of being hungry later in the evening, he would be told that when he ate the dreaded bean, he could have pretty much anything he wanted. "So the child might go to bed hungry?" she asked, testy now, and I said yes, but that would obviously be the child's choice. Furthermore, I told her, I'd never heard of a child making that choice for long. In short order, the child discovers that green beans are not nearly as noxious as he imagined them to be, and that is how one rears a child who is not a picky eater and who also has good table manners.

"Well," she said, "I just don't agree with that at all!"

"I'm sorry," I said. "Am I talking about you and your child?"

There was a pause. Finally, she said, "Well, if my children don't like something, I respect that and I fix them something else."

Catering to a child's irrational, arbitrary whims is not respect. Respect is helping a child understand that the world does not revolve around him. Respect is helping the child develop good social manners. Respect is discipline. I said none of that, of course, because I work at being well mannered.

Anyway, the producer ultimately decided I wasn't a good fit for the show, and I respected her decision. In fact, I agreed.

Play-Fullness

Before I leave the topic, I want to count the ways in which play is important to healthy development.

First, play exercises the skills a child needs in order to become a fully competent individual. It is a multidimensional experience, involving nearly all of a child's perceptual, motor, sensory, and cognitive equipment. It is a total learning experience, unlike any other. Play is the catalyst of growth, as well as the medium, during early and middle childhood.

Second, as a number of studies have demonstrated, unstructured playtime during early childhood is vitally important to the development of a well-rounded personality and healthy social skills. Children who are deprived of imaginative playtime are more likely to become overly aggressive or depressed.

Third, play provides a nonthreatening context within which a child can explore and begin to understand the adult world. It is through fantasy play that children come to understand and work through things that might otherwise remain confusing, like divorce, parental anger, and death.

Fourth, play helps children relieve stress and develop a sense of humor. It also helps them grow up to become adults who are capable of having fun.

Play is also a vehicle for significant learning, especially learning how to learn. Through play, children ask questions, explore their environments, learn essential problem-solving skills, practice social roles, and strengthen all the faculties that will enable them to realize their potential.

Unfortunately, over the last forty or more years, we have managed to place a number of obstacles in the path of the young child's innate desire to express imagination and growth through play. We have inundated young children with toys that smother their powers of creativity. We have let them sit in front of TV sets for hours upon hours while their imaginations atrophy from disuse. Instead of reading to children and letting time and the schools do the rest, we push flash cards and letters and numbers at preschool children, having lost sight of the fact that those activities are completely irrelevant to healthy growth and development.

The trend in recent years has been toward structuring the young child's time with such activities as organized sports, music lessons, classes in etiquette, and early academic instruction. We mistakenly believe that these things are more meaningful than play, when exactly the opposite is true. Furthermore, because so much has been planned and done for them, many of today's children have forgotten how to plan and do for themselves.

Give the Kids Their Games Back

One of the most disturbing aspects of the after-school activities craze is the trend toward enrolling children, at younger and younger ages, in organized sports programs. In my hometown, for example, children as young as four are participating in T-ball, soccer, and competitive swimming. These programs are absolutely irrelevant to the developmental needs—social, physical, and otherwise—of young children. Moreover, they can actually be detrimental, especially during middle childhood, ages six to ten.

The psychology of the young school-age child can be summarized in two words: *acceptance* and *achievement.* A lot hinges on how successful these kids are at creating a secure place for themselves among their peers and at establishing and attaining specific goals of excellence.

Organized sports would seem to be an ideal complement to the needs of this age child, the perfect medium in which to nurture both the inner and outer self. Not so. The primary problem is adult involvement. Adults organize these programs, raise the money to fund them, and draw up the playing schedule. Adults pick the teams, coach them, referee them, decide who plays and who doesn't, give out awards, and make up the biggest share of the audience.

But it doesn't stop there. Not only do adults play too prominent a role in planning and organizing these events, they also take it upon themselves to mediate such things as which children acquire what status within the peer group, how conflict between children is resolved, and so on.

Adults have absolutely no business being so involved in the play of children. Their presence is a complicating factor that prevents children from learning to negotiate social issues on their own. All too often, instead of being activities for children, these events become theaters where youngsters are manipulated for the gratification of adults.

The fact that these sports are competitive is not, in and of itself, disturbing. A child this age needs appropriate competitive experiences and if left alone will seek them out. What is disturbing is that because adults are so entangled in the proceedings, the children will play no longer for fun but to obtain adult approval. They are not really playing at all. They are working, performing for an adult audience.

The difference between competitive play and competitive work can be measured in terms of emotional outcome. When children band together to play a sandlot game, one team wins and one team loses, but everyone usually manages to leave the field feeling okay. When adults direct children in an organized sports event, the children on the losing team often end up feeling angry, dejected, frustrated, ashamed, or depressed. This isn't play. This is serious business, and the stakes are high. Too high.

In this context, the child athlete's sense of achievement and self-ahem becomes defined in terms of winning and losing. Process and participation take a backseat to outcome, which isn't what childhood is all about. Everyone suffers, but the biggest losers are the children who don't get to play because they aren't good enough.

The basic problem is one that isn't limited to this issue. It is the adult tendency to act as though children will botch the job of growing up unless we engineer the process for them. The exact opposite is true. When we place ourselves between the child and the task of growing up, we are no longer in a helpful position. We are interfering, and the child is ultimately less capable of dealing with life in the raw.

When I was a kid, sports was one of the most important things in my life. Along with the other boys in my suburban Chicago neighborhood, I played football in the fall, basketball in the winter, and baseball through the glory days of spring and summer. Our games were all pickup games played on fields at the local school or park. We got there on our bicycles. There were hardly ever enough players to make up two bona fide teams, so we modified the rules to suit the situation.

There were never any adults at our games. We were the players, the coaches, and the referees. We yelled at one another to hustle; we praised and criticized one another's play; we razzed one another. Despite all this, hard feelings were rare. It was all part of the game, and since the game was exclusively ours, we could do with it as we pleased. In the process, we learned how to subordinate our own desires to the best interests of the group, how to be good winners and good losers, how to resolve conflict, and how to begin running our own lives.

Little League baseball was the only organized sport available outside of school sports, which didn't start until the seventh grade. Through our early teenage years, my buddies and I watched as the organized sports programs grew and began taking over the hallowed ground of our playing fields. The turning point for us came the day we were politely but firmly told to vacate a field we were playing on because a Little League team needed it for practice.

I'm aware that children rarely play pickup games anymore. Somewhere along the line, someone got the brilliant idea that sports would be more of a meaningful learning experience for children if the games were managed by adults. The adults could see to it that rules were followed, that play was fair, that the children's skills improved through proper coaching, and that conflicts were resolved properly. The end result of all this well-intentioned meddling is that children don't have the opportunity to discover and work these issues out on their own.

I voice my objections, but people respond by saying things like, "I know, I know, but, John, sports are so competitive these days that if you don't start the kids out young, they won't be able to make the teams when they get to high school." Hogwash! The same lame argument is used to justify teaching reading skills to preschool children. Studies show that the earlier you push reading at children, the less joy they bring to the task and the less successful they ultimately are. I suspect the same may be true of organized children's sports. Let's face it. Joy, not parental pressure, is the essence of success, whether that success is in the classroom or on the athletic field.

I say let the kids have their games back.

Parents Should Take Their Families Back

I once told one of my audiences, some 450 strong, "I can virtually guarantee that by making one simple decision, you can reduce parenting stress by more than half, create a more relaxed, harmonious family environment, and provide your children with more carefree childhoods. Raise your hands if that sounds good to you."

Nearly everyone raised a hand. I then said, "Great! All you have to do is take your children out of all after-school activities—sports, music, gymnastics, martial arts, and so on. Do I have any takers?"

No one raised a hand. There was total silence. Four-hundred and fifty pairs of eyes just stared at me, as if I'd just proposed they join me in committing mass suicide. Come to think of it, for the contemporary American parent, the idea of taking one's children out of all after-school activities is probably akin to committing parenting suicide. How would they demonstrate their commitment to their children without the aforementioned public display?

I have yet to hear a good counterargument to my proposal. One riposte states that children like some if not all of these activities. So what? The needs of the family unit are more important than what children want or like. Everyone agrees that the family benefits greatly if parents are relaxed instead of in almost constant "Hurry up, we gotta go" mode. Besides, when your children are no longer young, no one is going to make sure they get to do whatever they like.

Let's face it, children do not need these activities, a statement to which someone recently rejoined, "But what if Tiger Woods's parents hadn't started him in golf so early?" Then maybe Tiger would have grown up to become a virologist, and maybe he would have discovered a cure for AIDS. Tiger Woods is not making a great and wonderful contribution to mankind. It's a sad comment on our collectively misplaced values that the average American regards Tiger as a hero.

"What if my child has a lot of innate talent for, say, music, and I never let him develop that talent?"

Then your child will take his talents—there's no such thing as having only one talent, you know—and put them into some other area. And by the time he's forty, there's little doubt he'll be as successful in whatever path he's chosen as he would have been if he'd walked the path you chose for him.

Here's another guarantee: The more relaxed the family unit, the fewer discipline problems you'll have to manage. Furthermore, the less stress you're under, the more relaxed will be your approach to discipline. So by taking your children out of after-school activities, they will be better behaved. With more discretionary time, they'll be better able to focus on homework and need less help (aka enabling) from you. They'll even have time for chores. Your children may actually earn their keep and acquire a solid service ethic at the same time.

Here's one more guarantee: Less focus on children, combined with a more relaxed family atmosphere and more relaxed parents, translates to a stronger marriage. No reasonable person would argue that relaxation does not lend itself to better communication and intimacy.

How about it? If you don't eliminate after school activities, how about limiting them to one per year? What a wonderful world it would be if the typical American family's number one after-school pastime was just relaxing and enjoying its happy home.

Just relax. What a concept!

How to Grow a "Team Player"

A father recently told me one reason his ten-year-old son was active in a different sport every season was that he needed to learn how to be a team player. It's an odd notion that a child learns to be a team player by participating in sports events where the level of adult involvement effectively eliminates decision-making on the part of the children.

Like many American families, the one in question spends significant after-school and weekend hours carting two children to team sports' practices and games. In the course of all this driving and cheering, they consume more time than they spend in any other family activity, except that watching a child play a sport and cheering from the sidelines does not constitute a family activity. A picnic is a family activity, as is a nature hike, spending the afternoon in a museum, or taking a trip to Niagara Falls or Disney World; watching a child play a sport does not qualify.

A family is also engaged in a truly *family* activity when everyone pitches in to clean the house, weed planting areas, or plant a garden that will help put food on the table. Sadly, few of today's families can be found doing those sorts of things on any sort of regular basis. What with all the after-school sports and activities the kids are involved in, not to mention homework, there's just no time. I contend that many children are growing up without an adequate sense of what family really and truly means. They know what the word *team* means, but they do not know that one's family is the greatest team one can ever be a member of, and that membership on that team is the best of all ways to learn how to be a team player.

A child learns how to be a family-team player by having a meaningful role consisting of real responsibilities, within his family. By the time the child is four years old, for example, his parents have assigned him to a daily routine of chores that contribute to the cleanliness and orderliness of the family environment, or that even help sustain the family's standard of living. In the course of performing his chores, he learns that his role in the family is important, that he has value within his family. In response, he develops a sense of personal dignity, attaches importance to his family, and begins to bond with the values the family holds dear. That is the essence of learning to be a team player.

Unfortunately, most of today's kids are making no contribution to their families other than their presence, which means they are only consumers. Another way of saying the same thing: In today's all-too-typical family, the only persons who are acting as if they have obligations are the parents. The problem with this one-sided state of affairs is that consumption without contribution inevitably engenders a feeling of entitlement, the feeling that "I deserve." Under the circumstances, individualism and materialism rule, hobbling the development of more functional pro-social values as well as a valid sense of self-worth. The child so hobbled ends up feeling okay when he is getting what he wants and not okay when he is not getting what he wants. Thus, the ubiquitous effort to make children happy is putting them at risk for becoming perpetual malcontents. It has no doubt played a significant role in the steady rise in the rate of child and teen depression since the 1960s, when "You can go outside after you've finished your chores" began its slide into obscurity, to be replaced by "Hurry up, we've got to get you to football practice on time."

Questions?

Q: Not including thirty minutes of reading and snuggling before bed, how much time each day should I spend involved in activities with my two toddlers? Also, does it matter how they play? They chase each other around the house a lot, roughhouse, and sometimes ride their riding toys, but they hardly ever play with developmental toys like blocks and puzzles. Is there some way I can stimulate interest in these things?

A: Regarding how much time you spend involved in activities with them, keep in mind that the most important thing parents can do with young children is read to them, which you are already doing.

The notion that parents need to get down on the floor and play with toddlers for a certain amount of time each day is very recent and without substance. If you feel like getting down on the floor and making a block castle with one of your children, do it. On the other hand, if you don't feel like it, then don't. Your children should not learn that you are an on-call antidote for boredom—a playmate. Don't try to fill some Play with the Kids quota, and when you do play with them, don't conduct activities. Just play. Have fun. When you've had enough, simply excuse yourself and go do your own thing. In the long run, it is best that they learn to play by themselves. If you feel the need to be involved several times a day, read to them for thirty minutes per session. In addition to developing their imaginations, reading will also calm them down for a while—a benefit to you.

At this age, a child's play is not very organized, nor should someone take pains to organize it or turn it into a specific learning experience. The play of a toddler is spontaneous, active, and generally not goal-directed. In short, the running, chasing, and jumping that your children are doing is very toddlerlike and in their own boisterous way, they're learning a lot. Another way of bringing some peace into your life is to mandate several quiet-time periods a day during which the children are separated and must play quietly for, say, fifteen minutes. Use a timer to define the period of quiet. When they are able to handle fifteen minutes, extend it to twenty, and so on. If you persist at this, you just might get to an hour by the time the older child is three.

As for their toys, I recommend that you remove the toys they aren't playing with. As I've said, most of the manufactured toys on the shelves today should remain there. They're worthless. The packaging and bright colors attract a child's attention, but once the toy is in his hands, it might have a play life of less than fifteen minutes, and sometimes that's a stretch. The toys they aren't playing with should disappear quietly, one or two at a time, and be replaced with boxes and pots and pans and wooden spoons and so on. Give the junk to charity.

Once you find five or ten toys that your children will play with, start a toy library. Store the toys in a closet, and let each child have only one toy at a time. When he's finished with the one he has, he can turn it in for another one. This will slowly help their play become more focused and organized; it will also dramatically reduce toy clutter around the house.

Q: My best friend refuses to buy her children what she calls war toys: toy guns, army paraphernalia, superhero action figures, and the like. She says they reinforce the notion that force is an acceptable way of resolving conflict. I'm undecided. What do you think?

A: I can certainly appreciate your friend's point of view, but I don't think war toys have quite the impact on children she says they do. Unquestionably, if there were no such thing as war, there would be no war toys, but I doubt the reverse is true. Children have been playing with war toys and at war games for as long as battles have been waged. Nevertheless, there is no reason to believe that playing at war encourages actual aggressive behavior.

Children play at all manner of adult vocations and recreations. In fact, once children find out that adults do thus-and-such, they seek to understand that aspect of the grown-up world by playing at it. A child's play does not determine a child's values. Children who play married and end up getting a pretend divorce are only trying to understand, through enactment, why grown-ups get divorced. Those same children aren't more likely as adults to think that divorce is the way to solve marital problems.

The quality and quantity of toys parents buy children certainly do have a significant effect on their development. Too many toys of the wrong type can actually have a negative effect on the development of imagination, creativity, initiative, and resourcefulness. A child's concept of right and wrong, or value structure, is determined primarily through interaction with parents, not through interaction with toys.

The same is true of war toys and war games. They are tools, not of menace, but of understanding. By themselves, they are harmless. A child who plays at games like war and cops and robbers may even come to better grips with the reality of violence than a child who does not. A child who grows up in a climate of violence, however, is an altogether different situation.

For the most part, I don't like war toys for the same reason I don't like the majority of toys in today's marketplace: They're too literal and therefore require little imagination. A toy gun made out of LEGO pieces or a stick is far superior to a plastic gun bought in a store.

I should hasten to mention that real guns, including BB guns and air rifles, are not toys. They are weapons, plain and simple. As such, they don't belong in the hands of a child, and putting one of them there does nothing but court disaster. If you want to teach a child to aim and shoot, buy a camera.

Q: Our seven-year-old son has been obsessed with airplanes since he was two. I do not use the term lightly—anyone who meets him is floored by his knowledge of planes. He is especially into WWII aircraft and the attack on Pearl

Harbor. He builds models, reenacts the attack, and so on. He talks nonstop about the various Japanese pilots, planes, and aircraft carriers. We have told him to cool it when it comes to talking about his interest with adults he's just met, because once he gets going, he doesn't know how to stop. He knows that no other local kids have this interest and wonders why he is so "weird" (his term). Is this something to be concerned about? I will admit to being numb from hearing him rattle on about this.

A: I don't think this is anything to be concerned about, but there are psychologists who would disagree with me. Indeed, your son's interest in airplanes and air battles is a bit obsessive, but whether or not a given obsession is unhealthy is a matter of the extent to which it interferes with normal social, intellectual, and emotional functioning. If your son is not withdrawing socially into his own little world of WWII airplanes, if he readily participates in social activities, if he's doing fine in school, and if his emotional reactions are appropriate, then this degree of interest in one subject cannot really be said to be unhealthy.

It's unfortunate that your son thinks he's weird. That may be because he feels your anxiety rather than any message he's getting from his peers. In fact, it's hard for me to imagine that other seven-year-olds think something like this is strange. Like most parents today, you are thinking psychologically about something that may be no more significant than the level of interest some of my childhood peers had in collecting baseball cards. Many of today's parents tend to see a psychological issue behind any behavior or interest that is even slightly out of the ordinary.

You should definitely let your son know that dominating conversation with adults is not appropriate, that most adults will listen to him politely because they don't want to hurt his feelings, but that he needs to realize that listening to a long description of someone else's interest can be significantly boring, even irritating.

Tell him this in kind but direct terms: "Your interest in airplanes is not a problem at all, and you are not weird because of it any more than someone who spends all day designing airplanes is weird. We encourage you to continue developing this interest. We are certain that someday you will write an excellent book on the attack at Pearl Harbor and be regarded as a leading expert on the subject. For now, however, you need to respect the fact that not everyone wants to hear you go on and on about it. Daddy is interested in [whatever], but you'll notice that he only talks about it with people who express an interest, and not with just anyone. To help you learn this, we are going to give you a secret signal when we feel that you're starting to bore someone with your knowledge. When we give you the signal, we want you to stop and find something else to do. If you have a problem doing that, we will direct you toward something else."

I'm recommending that you help him develop self-discipline where this issue is concerned. Let this be a lesson to you: When parents think a problem is psychological in nature, their ability to discipline becomes paralyzed. So, loosen up!

Q: My husband and I have a four-year-old boy and an eight-year-old girl. They both whine and cry when they do not get their way, and they do not seem to understand what no means. In addition, there is lots of sibling rivalry and hassles when it comes to doing what they are told. Because of the demands of our jobs, my husband and I end up doing a lot of tag team parenting, especially when it comes to getting the

kids to their after-school programs, getting them fed, and seeing that they do their homework. I feel like all we do is yell. I realize this is a tall order, but can you give us some useful suggestions?

A: You are describing what I call the "frantic family syndrome," the result of emotional resources that are stretched to the max by an overload of outside commitments. It's fairly clear that you and your husband spend most of your time dashing from one obligation to another, somewhat like the plate spinners on the old *Ed Sullivan Show* would dash from one spinning plate to another. As a consequence, you are a family in name only. I'll wager that you rarely sit down to a peaceful, unhurried dinner together, that the last time you went on a family picnic or took a leisurely stroll through a zoo was too long ago to clearly remember, and that by the time the kids get to bed, you're too exhausted to be husband and wife.

An adult or adults and children who are bound by biological or legal ties can claim the title of family, but to actually *be* a family in the true sense of the term requires a commitment to spending a good amount of time in the pursuit of nothing more than being together, enjoying one another's company as well as what you're doing. Sitting in the same room, staring at a television set, doesn't count.

I do indeed have some useful suggestions. First, I have to believe that if one of you quit his or her job, the overall level of stress in your family would come down considerably. Studies have shown that most second incomes do nothing but increase family expenditures and push the family into a higher tax bracket, all the while creating the illusion that the family is enjoying a higher standard of living than is actually the case. The end result is a significant increase in the family's debt load, which makes necessary a second income that was not essential at all to begin with. If you don't see how you can do that, given the debt you've already accumulated, then I recommend seeing a financial counselor. In the final analysis, you may have to make a choice between ever-diminishing financial stress and ever-increasing family chaos. I don't see this going anywhere but down if you try to maintain the status quo.

Second, I recommend taking the kids out of most of their after-school activities, or at the very least, not replacing one when it expires. In the future, limit after-school activities to one per child per season excepting summer, which should be reserved solely for family activities. The end result is that no activity can interfere with your ability to sit down together every evening to a relaxed family supper.

I have to believe that the discipline problems you're having with your children will begin to fix themselves as your family gains a sense of equilibrium. In any case, you aren't going to be able to effectively discipline the kids until you have restored balance and discipline to the family unit.

Q: If a child asks to participate in an organized sport or take piano lessons and later wants to quit, should parents make the child stick it out?

A: No and maybe. Children should be free to approach such things as soccer and piano with a spirit of playfulness. In a young child, the initial desire to become involved in a sport or an activity is nothing more than an expression of curiosity. For this reason, a child should not feel obligated to participate in a sport or an activity because of parental pressure and should be as free to quit as he is free to join. "I want to" should be considered an adequate excuse for quitting.

Parents who refuse to allow a child to withdraw from something he has found unfulfilling unknowingly inhibit the experimental nature of these activities. A child who is not free to quit becomes increasingly reluctant to join for fear of becoming locked into something that might seem attractive at first but ultimately is not.

Children who are free to leave an activity they entered on their own initiative are in no danger of developing a quitter's attitude toward life. Quite the contrary. The stuff of success—initiative, achievement, motivation, and persistence—grows only when it is allowed to take root and flower within the child. Parents who appropriate those attributes and then attempt to impose them on a child are unintentionally doing more harm than good.

That being the rule, here is the exception. There is occasional value to be had from contracting with a child for specified periods of commitment regarding certain activities, especially those that involve significant monetary investment. For example, parents might require that a child agree to two years of lessons before buying a musical instrument that the child has expressed interest in learning to play. In these cases, the child learns something about obligation and responsibility.

Q: Our first child is seven months old. When should we begin reading to her?

A: Last month. Seriously, folks, a child is never too young for reading. Parents should begin reading to a child by no later than six months of age, but six weeks is even better.

"But," you say, "she might not even be able to see the pictures." That's okay. Pictures are not necessary to reading anyway.

My mother or grandmother read to me every night before bed until I was at least six years old. The books had few pictures. Some had none. I didn't know any better, so I never complained. But I did pay attention, and I did use my imagination. In fact, I probably exercised my imagination lots more than I would have had there been more pictures. I'm not saying that pictures are in any way detrimental, only that they aren't essential.

When I read to Eric or Amy, I generally preferred books with lots of pictures because that forced us to cuddle. The pictures also became the occasion for games of "Show me . . ." and "What's this?"

Early reading stimulates language, perceptual, and cognitive development. Studies have also shown that as a child's communication skills improve, so does motor coordination. This makes sense, not only because an enriching environment stimulates a child's abilities in all areas, but also because language development and motor behavior are interwoven during early childhood.

The nurturing that takes place when a parent reads to a child helps strengthen the child's sense of security. In turn, this contributes greatly to the growth of independence. So you see, early and ongoing reading is one of the best investments you can make toward your child's healthy development.

Don't confuse the purpose of early reading with teaching a child to read. If you start reading to your daughter now and read to her often, you will teach her that reading feels good, and that is quite enough. It isn't at all unusual for a well-read-to three- or four-year-old child suddenly to begin reading. With enough exposure, some children figure out how to read on their own. If they don't and learn to read in the first grade, that's okay, too.

Begin with books that rhyme, like those by Dr. Seuss. My favorite rhyming book is Arnold Lobel's *The Man Who Took the Indoors Out*. The natural rhythm of the words will hold an infant's attention better than prose. Poetry also lends itself to improvisational song, which—assuming you are able to make up and carry a tune—never fails to fascinate and delight the child in all of us. Diversify into prose around the same time the child begins talking. Regardless of what you select, follow these guidelines:

- Read to your child at least thirty minutes each day.
- Choose books you enjoy reading. The more you like them, the more your child will, too.
- Read slightly above your child's current vocabulary level.
- Read with feeling, with gusto. Give each character a different accent. Sing certain passages.
- Hold your child close.
- Have a wonderful time!

For more information and helpful hints on reading aloud to children of all ages, I highly recommend *The Read-Aloud Handbook* by Jim Trelease.

Q: The preschool program our four-year-old attends has always emphasized social and creative skills rather than academics. However, the board of directors recently hired a new teacher for the four-year-olds who wants to teach reading and math. According to her, a child this age is ready to begin academic instruction. The parents are divided on this issue, some eager for their children to have a head start, others resisting the change. What's your opinion?

A: The fundamental question is: What, if anything, do children gain by learning how to read and perform arithmetic problems at age four? The answer: Nothing.

Take two four-year-olds of approximately equal ability, teach one to read and do basic math, but wait to begin formal instruction with the other until he enters first grade. The result? Although the first child might outshine the second through most of first grade, by the time they both reach third grade no one will be able to determine which had the initial advantage.

The concept of readiness is at the crux of the problem. If readiness is defined in terms of whether four-year-olds can learn to read and do basic math, then most four-year-olds are ready. On the other hand, if readiness is defined in terms of the most appropriate time to begin teaching reading and math, then four-year-olds are not ready.

The observations and research of Swiss developmental psychologist Jean Piaget (1896–1980) suggest that abstract symbol systems such as those involved in reading and math need not and should not be introduced to children until age six or seven. Piaget maintained that intelligence develops within every human being according to a predictable evolutionary sequence. Each stage of intellectual (cognitive) growth, as characterized by the emergence of new and more sophisticated ways of understanding the world, is built upon previously existing modes of understanding.

Piaget said that any attempt to impose understanding of a certain concept before its time was not only fruitless but potentially harmful. He maintained that if a certain concept was introduced to a child before the appropriate developmental window was open, the child might never be able to utilize that concept effectively. Later researchers have argued that teaching four-year-olds to read is accomplished at the expense of doing permanent damage to the very nature of intelligence.

Q: I am an educator who disagrees with your stand on early reading instruction. Recent studies have demonstrated that preschool children have a far greater capacity for learning than was previously suspected. By exposing preschoolers to educational opportunities such as early reading instruction, we acknowledge and nurture this potential.

A: Your argument is the same one that's always been used to justify these programs: If preschoolers can learn to read, they should learn to read. This position is based on a limited understanding of literacy, as well as limited definitions of learning and achievement.

It's true that reasonably intelligent children as young as three can be taught basic word-recognition skills. However, saying that that justifies teaching preschool children to read is like saying the fact that thirteen-year-olds can be taught to drive justifies giving them the opportunity to obtain driver's licenses.

Indeed, preschool children do have a great capacity for learning. Parents and educators share responsibility for responding appropriately to that potential. The question then becomes, "What kinds of learning experiences are appropriate for preschoolers?"

We know that a preschool child's understanding of the world is earthbound. In other words, it is fairly limited to the universe of concrete, tangible things. Reading involves the intervention of an abstract symbol system—the printed word—to describe tangible and intangible aspects of the universe. Piaget's research tends to indicate that for most children, the critical period for introducing symbol systems of this sort is around age six. In European schools, where this rule of thumb is generally practiced, there are few reading problems, compared to the epidemic of them that plagues our educational system. In Russia, formal education doesn't begin until children are seven, yet Russian children seem none the worse for it.

Just exactly what does it mean to be able to read? Literacy is traditionally defined in terms of an individual's ability to correctly recognize and comprehend words and word passages. If one adheres to this limited definition, then it is possible to induce literacy in preschool children. But any definition of literacy is incomplete unless it also includes the ability to enjoy reading. After all, it matters not that children can read if they fail to do so for lack of enjoyment. When this third standard is applied to the issue of teaching reading to preschoolers, the complete bankruptcy of the idea is revealed.

In *The Hurried Child*, psychologist David Elkind cited studies showing that the earlier children are taught to read, the less they enjoy reading and the less they read. Every public school first-grade teacher I've ever discussed this issue with has told me that it is not at all necessary that children come to first grade with more than a basic knowledge of the alphabet. Their only hope is that their young students come to them with a desire to read that's been instilled and reinforced at home.

The trick in helping a child become literate in the complete sense of the term is no trick at all. Starting as young as six months, read to the child on a regular basis for at least thirty minutes a day. There's no better way than this to prepare a child for later reading instruction.

Q: I've put our eight-month-old son in a playpen for short periods during the day ever since he was three months old. Until recently, he would occupy himself quietly until I was able to return. Lately, as soon as I put him in the playpen, he begins screaming bloody murder and doesn't stop until I pick him up. I can't possibly be with him every minute of the day, nor can I let him be free to roam about the house.

The playpen seems like the most sensible and convenient way of solving these problems. On the other hand, he hates it. What can I do?

A: Before we go any further, understand that playpens aren't for play, not in the real sense of the term. Boredom is about all that's possible in a fenced-in area no larger than sixteen square feet. The more stuff a parent heaps in there to occupy the child, the more cluttered the pen becomes, further restricting the child's ability to interact creatively with his environment (play).

Before they begin crawling, most children will endure the relative isolation of a playpen for brief periods during the day. Crawling, however, stimulates an infant's desire to explore the world. Once your son discovers what excitement there is to be had by moving from one place to another and then another, getting his hands in the stuff of what's happenin', he's not likely to sit quietly in a playpen. Add to his curiosity the fact that a toddler between eight and twelve months isn't quite sure how much closeness he wants with his mother. This business of getting around on his own is more fun than a barrel of monkeys, but it also takes him farther away from the one he depends upon the most.

So your child is caught in his own dilemma. He wants to be with you, and he wants to be away from you, doing his own thing. He feels a bit better if he's in control of how much distance there is between you when the separation occurs. If you walk away, he yells, but if he crawls off, it's good-bye. Just to make sure you haven't vaporized while he wasn't looking, he checks on you every few minutes. When you put him in a playpen, his anxiety level goes up. He isn't controlling the separation, and he can't get to you when he needs to.

Let's take the example of the ducks. Several days after they hatch, a brood of ducklings will line up behind their mother and follow wherever she goes. This is called imprinting. After a few weeks of parading about in this fashion, they break away and begin fending for themselves.

Dutch ethologist Nikolaas Tinbergen wanted to see what would happen if he tampered with the imprinting process. He placed small barriers around a circular track where mother ducks walked. As their babies followed, they had to scramble over the barriers to keep up. The result? These frustrated ducklings persisted in following their mothers long after the time that ducklings usually move off on their own.

The child who begins making motions of independence must know beyond the shadow of a doubt that Mother will be easily accessible in time of need. Playpens frustrate the newly mobile child the same way Tinbergen's barriers frustrated the ducklings. As was the case with the ducklings, frustration makes your child more determined to keep his mother close. So by using a playpen to contain a child who has started moving about under his own steam, you increase the likelihood that he will cling to you long after most children have become more self-sufficient.

Once he begins crawling, one of the nicest gifts you can give your son is a childproofed living area where he can crawl and putter and get into safe, unbreakable things to his heart's content while you relax, knowing he's all right. He'll experience the same insecurities as other crawlers, but instead of getting stuck, he'll go right through them.

Q: Our sixteen-month-old daughter has recently started climbing and getting into lots of things that are off-limits. We have tried popping her hand whenever she picks up something we don't want her to handle, but that doesn't

seem to faze her and often makes her even more determined. How would you suggest we go about keeping her
out of mischief?

A: The most effective way of keeping your daughter out of mischief is to remove the potential for mischief by childproofing.
Childproofing a home protects the child from danger and valu-
ables from breakage while at the same time providing the child
with an open, stimulating environment in which to explore to her
heart's content.

Take a room-by-room inventory of things dangerous or valuable that are within your daughter's reach. Put childproof latches
on lower cabinets and childproof covers on electrical outlets, and
place gates across staircases. Bring down to your daughter's level
things she can touch. Give her a low cabinet of her own in the
kitchen and stock it with things like wooden spoons, pots, large
spools, boxes, flexible straws, and anything else that might fascinate her and help stimulate creative behavior. If you do a good job,
you should be able to let your daughter roam around the house
with much less supervision than you've previously provided.

When she's about thirty months of age, you can begin slowly
restoring your home to its previous state. Introduce one valuable
at a time, first letting your daughter see and feel the item, then putting it where it belongs and letting her know it's not a plaything.
The discrimination between "can touch" and "can't touch" is easily
made at this age, as long as parents don't introduce too many interesting things at any one time.

Here's a tip for parents of toddlers when the youngster picks up
something fragile, like a piece of valuable crystal: The child is
almost certain to drop and break the item if an adult puts on a hor-
rified expression, says, "Give me that!" and moves rapidly toward

the child with arms outstretched and hands open like claws. Panic breeds panic. Instead, control your fears, stay in one spot, squat down so you're at eye level with the child, put a smile on your face, extend your hand palm up, and say, "Ooooh, how pretty! Will you put it in my hand so I can see, too?"

If you've done a good acting job, the child will smile in return and place the item gently in your palm. Let her know this wasn't a trick by putting her on your lap and examining the object together for a minute or so before getting up and saying, "I'm going to put this up here so we can both look at it. Isn't it pretty?" This procedure satisfies the child's curiosity, saves money, and helps build a cooperative parent–child relationship, rather than an antagonistic one.

Q: Our three-year-old daughter has recently invented and is spending lots of time with an imaginary playmate she calls Cindy. Her obsession with Cindy is beginning to go a bit far. She wants me to set a place for her at the dinner table and invite her along whenever we leave the house. When I suggest that Cindy doesn't really exist, my daughter becomes extremely angry and upset. Do I have reason to be concerned, or is this just a passing phase?

A: Your daughter's fascination with her imaginary friend is just a passing phase, but an important one. Rather than being worried, you should be glad.

Fantasy thinking emerges around age three. Like any other mental attribute, imagination must be exercised in order to strengthen and grow. Cindy is your daughter's way of doing just that. She's taking a very important step toward the eventual mastery of abstract thinking. Also, since an active imagination is essential to reading comprehension, Cindy is actually helping your daughter to eventually become a successful reader.

Trying to debate the issue of Cindy's existence with your daughter is a lost cause. To a three-year-old, if something can be imagined, that something truly exists. In your daughter's eyes and mind, Cindy is as real as you are. Three-year-olds invest a considerable amount of security in their imaginary playmates. They need them. No wonder your daughter became upset when you tried to reason away Cindy's existence. Just as your adult mind cannot comprehend your daughter's obsession with Cindy, her child's mind can't understand your failure to accept Cindy's existence. Call it a draw and stop worrying.

At this stage of her life, your daughter is starting to form relationships with other children. Cindy enables her to practice social skills in a safe, nonthreatening context and thus strengthens her ability to interact successfully with other children. When your daughter and another child play together with Cindy, they're practicing small-group social skills.

The more your daughter plays with Cindy, the fewer demands she makes on your time and energy. Instead of relying on you for occupation, she's relying on Cindy, which effectively means she is relying on herself, and self-reliance is a good thing.

Any way you look at it, Cindy is probably one of the best things that's ever happened to your daughter. Her invisible friend is contributing to almost every aspect of her growth and development. Instead of worrying about Cindy, relax and count your blessings.

Q: Much to our chagrin, our six-year-old son, Robbie, has always preferred to play with dolls and other "girl" things.

He also prefers playing with girls because boys, he says, play too rough. We saw a therapist who wanted Robbie to be present at the first appointment. I felt this was unnecessary, even humiliating, so we went by ourselves. The therapist accused us not only of being resistant, but also of enabling Robbie by, among other things, letting him play with dolls. At that point, my husband and I walked out, but now I'm worried that perhaps the therapist was right. How serious is this sort of problem, and do you think we're enabling?

A: Let me answer the first half of your question by asking, "If Robbie were a little girl named Roberta who preferred playing with boys and doing 'boy' things, would you be worried?" I'll bet your answer is, "Of course not!" You'd just shrug your shoulders and say, with a smile, that Roberta was a tomboy. My point is, your anxiety over Robbie's play preference reflects a knee-jerk cultural bias. Unfortunately for boys, it's generally regarded as okay—even admirable—for females to do traditionally masculine things, even wear masculine clothes, but a male who prefers stereotypical feminine things is generally looked upon with suspicion, to say the least.

You neatly avoided any mention of your real worry, which is that Robbie's preference for girl things presages adult homosexuality. The fact is, masculine play preferences for boys do not guarantee heterosexuality any more than feminine play preferences foreshadow homosexuality, and that's equally but oppositely true for girls. I can't guarantee that Robbie won't, as a young adult, announce that he's gay, but I can assure you that whether he plays with dolls or toy guns at this age will have nothing to do with his later choice of sexual partners.

Are you enabling Robbie's preference for girl things? My dictionary defines *enable* as "to make possible," so in the strictest sense of the term the answer is "Yes, you are definitely enabling, but so what?" If Robbie were my son, and he wanted to play with dolls, I, too, would make it possible for him to do it. However, if the therapist was using *enable* in the pejorative psychological sense, to mean you are aiding and abetting improper behavior, then my answer is "Hogwash!" In the first place, Robbie's play preferences are not improper, much less pathological. In the second, it would be highly improper if you forced Robbie to play with things he didn't enjoy.

In answer to "How serious is this sort of problem?" I don't see that it is a problem at all, outside of the fact that his parents think Robbie might have one. If he hasn't already, Robbie will eventually pick up on your anxiety, which will cause him to feel self-conscious about something that is really quite innocent. In this regard, I approve of your decision to leave Robbie out of the appointment with the therapist. Stop worrying and enjoy being Robbie's parent. You'll only get one shot at it, you know.

When all is said and done, this is a matter of his personality. You didn't cause it, and you can't change it. You can make him feel as if there's something wrong with who he is, in which case Robbie may never become the person God intended him to become. And I suspect God doesn't like us messing with His creations.

POINT SIX

Television, Computers, and Video Games— More Than Meets the Eye

I n January 1979, Willie and I sat down for what was probably our sixth conference with Eric's third-grade teacher, Mrs. Stewart, who informed us that Eric stood absolutely no chance of being promoted to the fourth grade. She had decided to give us plenty of time to digest this news, she said, rather than surprise us with it at the end of the school year. Eric was reading more than a year behind grade level. Furthermore, Mrs. Stewart described him as easily distracted, inattentive, and slow to finish his work. He rarely finished an assignment in class and therefore ended up with double the homework assigned to a typical classmate, none of which Eric would have done had it not been for constant pushing and prodding by Willie and me. According to the diagnostic guidelines published in the most recent edition of the *Diagnostic and Statistical Manual,* Eric had a fairly serious case of attention deficit disorder.

When we got home, Willie and I sat down for what turned out to be a turning-point conversation. It was time, she said, to stop what we were doing—the sort of parenting promoted by my own profession—and do things differently.

"What are you talking about?" I responded, more than slightly defensive. After all, I was a psychologist and, compounding the irony, I was already writing my nationally syndicated newspaper column. I knew everything there was to know about children and how to parent them properly. Or so I thought.

"When we had Eric," she said, "we made a conscious decision not to raise him the way we had been raised. The truth is, we didn't turn out so bad. Our parents weren't perfect, but neither of us had the sort of problems Eric is having. I think we need to start being the kind of parents our parents were."

Three months later, Mrs. Stewart began our next meeting by saying, "If someone told me back in January that I would be telling you what I have to say now, I'd have thought he was crazy. To come straight to the point, assuming that Eric progresses the way he has over the past three months, I will promote him to the fourth grade. Quite frankly, this has been remarkable. Mr. and Mrs. Rosemond, I don't know exactly what you are doing, but keep on doing it."

Eric did pass the third grade. By the end of grade four, he was an A student. In grade seven, he was inducted into the National Beta Club honor society, and apart from some occasional minor lapses, typical of any highly gregarious, risk-taking youngster, Eric did very well throughout the rest of his academic career, including college. Now in his mid-thirties, he is a successful corporate pilot, a successful husband, and a successful father to three young boys.

What did Willie and I do between January and April? First, this is what we did not do: We did *not* provide Eric with a tutor, and we all but completely stopped helping him with his homework or even prodding him to do it. We did *not* put him on medication, although by today's standards he qualified for a diagnosis of attention deficit disorder (ADD), not to mention oppositional defiant disorder (ODD), and a learning disability (LD)—all the big D's. We asked Mrs. Stewart for no special consideration, such as lowering her academic standards where Eric was concerned. What we did was simply realize that postmodern psychological parenting had not worked. If we were going to get our family on track, we had to begin raising our children pretty much the way our parents had raised us—the old-fashioned, prepsychological way.

Nearly overnight, Willie and I became *our* parents. We created a benevolent dictatorship, the antithesis of the parenting that was popular at the time. We began telling Eric and Amy what we wanted them to do instead of asking, pleading, bargaining, bribing, reasoning, and explaining—i.e., wishing. We embraced a zero-tolerance policy concerning disobedience. If one of them disobeyed, we punished instead of talked. The kids came home from school one day and were told that from that day forth they were going to do most of the housework: vacuum, dust, clean bathrooms, mop floors, and so on. As Willie had suggested, we turned the parenting clock in the Rosemond family back some twenty years.

Coincidentally, around this same time, someone had given me a book by journalist Marie Winn entitled *The Plug-In Drug* (recently republished in a greatly expanded twenty-fifth anniversary edition). As the name implies, it was about the evils of letting children watch television. Reading Winn's description of the problems she attributed largely to TV-watching—not an excessive dose, but a "normal" amount—I realized Winn was describing Eric to a tee and convinced Willie to try an experiment: Cut the kids off, cold turkey, from their obvious addiction to watching television.

The next day, Eric and Amy came home from school to discover that we'd gone completely over the edge—we'd given the television to charity. Naturally, they were devastated. "How could you do such a thing?" they asked incredulously. "Everyone has a television!"

"No," I pointed out, "not everyone. We don't."

For the next week or so, the children whined constantly about our decision, but the end result was nothing short of remarkable.

The children began playing more creatively, paying better attention to us, and acting generally more calm. The level of sibling conflict—much of which had swirled around the issue of what TV shows to watch—diminished considerably. Undoubtedly, some of the improvement was due to the other changes we were making, but I'm convinced that the single most critical variable in Eric's rehabilitation was the sudden and complete absence of television in his life.

Later that year, I wrote a feature-length article for the *Charlotte Observer* that they subsequently shared with more than two hundred newspapers around the country. I laid out what I'd discovered, through both personal experience and research, concerning the effects of watching television on young children. I'd come to the inescapable conclusion that the constantly flickering image on a television screen actually disables the young brain's ability to develop a long attention span. Since a long attention span is essential to impulse control, I further concluded that TV-watching encumbered the development of good self-control, leading to behavior problems that in all likelihood would not have otherwise existed. Other psychologists were infuriated! I was accused of misinforming the public and promoting hysteria, and I later learned that a group of psychologists in my home state of North Carolina even met to discuss the possibility of convincing our licensing authority to strip me of my professional credentials. By this stage of my life, however, I had learned the hard way that a point of view capable of causing general outrage and uproar is either completely misguided or right on target. Having witnessed firsthand the results of breaking Eric's television addiction, I was convinced I was right on target.

Subsequent experience and research have led me to the conclusion that television-watching during the formative years actually obstructs proper brain development and is a significant factor in the epidemic rise of learning disabilities that has taken place since the 1960s. Keep in mind that the typical American child has watched close to five thousand hours of television, including videos pumped through a television screen, before entering the first grade! I'm also convinced that television-watching is unhealthy for the family as a unit, that when a family spends significant discretionary time watching television, a certain family culture or atmosphere develops that breeds disobedience, disrespect, irresponsibility, whining, depression, sibling conflict, laziness, low impulse control, boredom, and—last but certainly not least—communication problems between family members.

Since our experience with Eric and Amy, I've taken my turn-off-the-TV spiel to every corner of the United States through public presentations, a syndicated newspaper column, and several of my books. Hundreds of people have since shared turn-off-the-TV testimonies with me, people who have removed television from their children's lives, if not from the home altogether. Every parent has said it was the very best decision they ever made for their children and family. Take Lulu's parents, for example.

When her parents decided to turn off the television, mostly for the benefit of their three older children, Lulu was just a year old. As Lulu began growing into her terrible twos, her mom noticed that she was absolutely mesmerized—read *pacified*—by the television set at a friend's house. Lulu's mom later wrote me this letter:

So I started letting her watch shows here and there, rationalizing that occasional TV really wasn't harmful. It felt like that was the only way I could get anything done or have any peace! She was hyper and wired all the time. She threw tantrums constantly and was referred to as the rotten egg by her sisters. I assumed that she was just higher maintenance than my other children, and that this stage would soon pass.

I took her in for her routine check-up a couple of days after her second birthday. She screamed through the entire exam. I told the doctor that this was her personality all day long. I told him of her inability to entertain herself and constant crankiness. He felt that while whininess, tantrums, *et cetera*, were certainly *part* of being two, they shouldn't be part of every waking hour. He referred me to a developmental specialist.

I came home that day and started searching through the archives at *www.rosemond.com*, trying to figure out what on earth could be wrong with my child. One thing kept cropping up: Children, even toddlers, watch too much TV. I sat down and honestly assessed how much time she spent in front of the TV and discovered she was watching around six hours a day. I just didn't realize how TV time adds up, and I'd convinced myself TV was just helping me get through a temporarily difficult time. In other words, she and I were both addicted—her to watching TV and me to allowing her to watch TV.

I spoke to my husband that night. I told him that I hadn't realized how much we were relying on TV. We decided to stop it altogether. The next morning, we refused to turn it on, and she cried a bit. She was a little cranky that morning, but by the end of the day she was playing blocks, running around the house with her sisters, and laughing. We noticed a difference in her personality just that first day. By the end of the second day, we felt we'd witnessed a miracle. Her personality was truly transformed. She was happy, occupying herself a lot, and actually pleasant. She was so much calmer, so much more agreeable, that it was almost spooky.

She's still two, mind you—she dumped all the salt out of the salt shaker this morning and was so pleased with herself she clapped when I came into the room. But the constant crankiness and hyperactivity are completely gone. I should also mention that she is a year behind verbally, but has almost doubled her vocabulary in the past two weeks.

Interestingly enough, I previously discussed her personality with several people who have kids the same age as Lulu, and the ones who "do TV" all thought her past behavior was completely normal for a two-year-old. That's pretty scary, huh?

Yes, it's certainly scary to realize that most American's don't know what normal child behavior is anymore, regardless of the age in question. For example, most parents think tantrums are normal for children four and five. They aren't. Most parents think sullen moodiness is normal for teenagers. It isn't. The list goes on. Technology and postmodern psychological parenting have changed children in dramatic ways, and not a single one of the changes is desirable. Today's parents are dealing with problems that a mother of fifty years ago would not have been able to even imagine.

If one testimony doesn't convince you—and it shouldn't, actually—then allow me to share another, received from the mother of a five-year-old boy who at age three was disobedient, "mouthy," and often belligerent. He was also an enthusiastic television watcher. One morning, at their wits' end concerning their child's misbehavior, she and her husband pulled the plug on the television. She writes:

What happened in the ensuing days was amazing. The misbehavior, most of which I'd put down as being an age thing, went away completely, and the creativity that television had siphoned off emerged with a vengeance. Suddenly, tents began appearing in the playroom, which became his operations center. He became a chief for a while, then an explorer, then a scientist. We began the habit of reading the newspaper together every morning, a ritual that continues to this day. The most amazing change that occurred was in his overall attitude. He went from surly and belligerent to cheery and cooperative almost overnight.

I hadn't realized how much his behavior had been adversely affected by television, even the small amount that we had previously allowed. Our television has been "broken" now for more than two years. He occasionally watches something at someone else's house but here, in our home, we have completely replaced it with other things too numerous to mention, including blessed silence. Today, my former rebel without a cause is a highly energetic, creative five-year-old who occasionally misbehaves. This experiment had and continues to have a happy ending!

For those of you who are inclined to use television as a babysitter, here's yet another testimonial from the mother of children who were, when she wrote her letter, ages one, three, four, and six.

I stay at home and my oldest goes to school. We recently eliminated television completely from our children's lives, and we have had nothing but positive results. At first the children whined and complained of having nothing to do, but they quickly learned that if they told me they were bored, I would put them to work, so that stopped. It only took a week for them to completely turn around! They stopped asking me to find things for them to do and began entertaining themselves like never before. I think it is so sad that today's children, because they rely so much on television, video games, and the computer to occupy themselves, are not learning to entertain themselves. My husband and I un-plugged the television because of your advice, John, and we are very grateful. We have been television-free for seven months now, and we will never go back!

I've said it before many times, but I'll say it again: Television is not your parenting friend. While your children are watching television, they are developing a dependency that they transfer to *you* as soon as the television is off or no longer interests them. This is when the whining and complaining begins. At this point, parents tend to think that turning the television back on is the way to solve the whining and complaining. Not so; turning the television back on only makes matters worse. What do you think moms and dads did in the pretelevision days when families were bigger? The answer is they didn't have to do much at all because when a child's creative spirit is not dampened by addictions to various electronic drugs, he will find creative ways to entertain himself, and—read the next six words slowly, savoring their meaning—he will leave his parents alone (for the most part).

How *Not* to Raise a Gifted Child

Between birthdays two and six, the average American preschool child watches some twenty-five hours of television a week. This isn't a number I pulled out of thin air, but one that's been confirmed by one Nielsen survey after another since the early 1970s. At one time, in fact, the number was closer to thirty hours a week! The higher the educational level of any individual child's parents, however, the more likely it is that the child is watching less than the national average. Since the average reader of parenting books is fairly well educated, I'm going to adjust the above figure downward to fourteen hours a week, or an average of two hours a day.

Multiply 14 hours a week by 52 weeks, and the preschool child of the typical adult reader of parenting books is probably watching 728 hours of television a year. That's the equivalent of eighteen 40-hour workweeks, and tallies to a grand total of 2,912 hours between birthdays two and six. Based on a 12-hour day, with 2 hours taken up with meals, baths, getting dressed, and other mandatory activities, this means that preschool children spend roughly one-fifth of their daily discretionary time sitting in front of a TV set.

You're probably saying, "That's not my child! My child watches no more than seven hours of television a week!" That's a perfectly understandable reaction, but I'm going to burst your bubble. Studies have also shown that most parents tend to underestimate their children's television-viewing time by approximately 50 percent. They also tend not to count time their children spend watching videos. So if you think your child is watching 7 hours a week, the actual number is probably much higher, perhaps even as high as my original figure of 14. On the other hand, if you insist, let's say your preschooler watches an average of only 7 hours a week. That means he will have watched 1,456 hours by age six. Does that make you feel more comfortable?

In order to appreciate fully what these numbers mean, you must understand that your child's preschool years are among the most important of all. Developmental psychologists and educators refer to them as the formative years. They are called formative because they comprise that period during which the young child is discovering, developing, and strengthening the skills he will need to become a creative and competent adult.

Nearly every human being is born already programmed for achievement in nearly every conceivable area: intellectual, artistic, musical, athletic, interpersonal, and spiritual. During the formative years, these programs are activated by exposing the young child to environments and experiences that push the right genetic buttons, so to speak.

In other words, releasing the richness of each child's developmental birthright requires that the child have sufficient opportunities for exploration, discovery, and imaginative play. Environments and experiences that stimulate and exercise the young child's emerging skills are, therefore, compatible with his developmental needs. On the other hand, environments that fail to offer these important opportunities are incompatible. Time is of the essence. Developmental research has consistently demonstrated that a child has approximately six years in which to get in touch with the many basic skills that comprise competency and creativity. The formative years are the window of opportunity for giftedness. A child of six who, for lack of opportunity, is deficient with respect to one or more aspects of giftedness will probably always have problems in those areas.

When a child sits and becomes absorbed in watching television, that television becomes his audiovisual environment. Since the average American child spends more time watching television than doing any other single thing during their formative years, we must conclude that television has become a primary environment for our children and will therefore influence their development in significant, far-reaching ways.

The question becomes: "Does television create or constitute a healthy or unhealthy environment for children?"

For the past forty years or more, social scientists have been attempting to answer that very question. Their research has focused almost exclusively on the effects of television's content—whether a program is violent or nonviolent, sexy or not—on the social behavior of children. This has had unfortunate consequences, because the average American parent has been led to believe that television's only danger to children is a matter of theme. If a child is watching a nature documentary or a family sitcom, we tend to think there's no harm. On the other hand, if the child is watching a program that contains themes of sex or violence or both, we're probably going to turn the television off, change the channel, or send the child from the room. Because of this tendency to judge television by its content, American parents are largely unaware of the more insidious and far more damaging influence of TV-watching as a process independent of the content of the programs.

In order to see firsthand what I'm talking about, the next time your child is watching television, look at the child instead of the program. One picture is worth more than a thousand words. Not a pretty sight, is it? Ask yourself, "What is that child doing?" The answer is "Nothing." Not one competency skill, not one gift, is being exercised.

Regardless of the program, therefore, watching television inhibits the development of initiative, curiosity, resourcefulness, creativity, motivation, imagination, reasoning and problem-solving abilities, communication skills, social skills, fine and gross motor skills, and eye-hand coordination. Shall I go on? Because television causes the child to stare at, rather than scan, the environment, it's safe to add that visual tracking skills are not being strengthened either.

Furthermore, watching television interferes significantly with development of the attention span. Many people mistakenly believe that if children can sit mesmerized in front of a television set for two or three hours at a stretch, they must have—or at least be developing—a long attention span. That's a misconception. The "steady" picture on a television screen is an optical illusion, changing, on average, every three to four seconds. Because of this constant perceptual shift, or flicker, the TV-watching child isn't attending to any one thing for longer than a few seconds. As a result, watching television is a strangely paradoxical situation for the young child. The more time spent watching television, the shorter the attention span becomes.

Finally, because the action on a TV set shifts constantly and capriciously backward, forward, and laterally in time (not to mention from subject matter to subject matter), television fails to promote the logical sequential thinking that is essential to an understanding of cause-and-effect relationships. This causes difficulties both in following directions and in anticipating consequences.

Once again, these failings are the same regardless of whether the child is watching a documentary, a fast-paced drama, or a movie on DVD. In each case, the child is watching in the same passive manner. This means that for the preschool child, program content is a largely irrelevant issue as far as that child's development is concerned.

As I said earlier, the preschool child's competency skills emerge and begin developing through exercise. During the formative years, play is the natural form this exercise takes, but children watching television are not playing. In fact, they aren't doing anything competent at all. Therefore, every hour that a preschool child spends watching television is an hour of that child's potential being wasted.

One is forced to conclude that watching television is a deprivational experience for young children. It deprives them of the opportunity to discover and take delight in developing their natural potential for giftedness. The sad fact is that once that window of opportunity closes, it can never again be fully opened.

But don't just take my word for it. As with everything else, the proof is in the pudding. I'm saying that the child who spends a significant amount of time during the formative years parked in front of a television set is likely to be much less competent than he would otherwise have been. If watching television diminishes a child's potential for competency, there ought to be evidence that our TV-generation children are less competent than children of previous generations. Does such evidence exist? Indeed it does.

Television Disabilities

Since 1955, when American children began watching significant amounts of television, scholastic-achievement test scores have steadily declined. As a nation, our literacy level has declined as well. Today, nearly one of every five seventeen-year-olds in this country is functionally illiterate, meaning he cannot read with comprehension at a fifth-grade level. The functionally illiterate individual cannot read a newspaper, a recipe, or a manual for operating a power tool. Both trends become even more alarming when one considers that academic standards are lower today than they were in 1955. Today's fifth-grade reader, for instance, is comparable to a third-grade reader from 1955.

To top it off, since 1955, learning disabilities have become nearly epidemic in our schools. Learning-disabled children are children who can't seem to acquire the basic academic skills of reading and writing. Some researchers estimate that as many as three out of ten children in our schools today are learning-disabled to one degree or another. Interestingly enough, the symptoms that characterize a population of learning-disabled children and the list of developmental deficiencies inherent to the TV-watching experience are one and the same.

Learning-disabled children often have visual scanning problems. Their eyes fail to scan a line of print smoothly from left to right. They tend to exhibit problems with eye-hand coordination and fine and gross motor skills. Often they are not proficient at tasks requiring active problem-solving (reading, for example). They are frequently deficient with respect to active listening and communication skills. They often display social adjustment difficulties. Their teachers typically report that these children have difficulty following a sequence of directions or the steps involved in solving a problem and frequently describe them as passive and easily frustrated by challenges. They tend to be unimaginative, and imagination is essential to reading comprehension. Last but not least, almost all learning-disabled children have short attention spans.

Thus, an almost perfect parallel exists between the list of competency skills that television fails to exercise and the symptoms characteristic of a population of learning-disabled children. Learning disabilities are just the tip of the iceberg. Again and again, veteran teachers—those who are in the best position to have seen the steady decline in competency skills since 1955—tell me that today's children are less resourceful, less imaginative, and not nearly as motivated as the children they once knew and taught. They also tell me that the average child's attention span seems to have shortened significantly.

I know a woman who taught second grade in public schools for forty-four years, from 1934 to 1978. In her early years, she would bring her students back from lunch and read them stories from books that had few, if any, pictures. Up through the 1940s and early 1950s, her story time lasted one hour. In the late 1950s, however, she began noticing that most of her children were no longer able to sit still and pay attention for that length of time. So she cut her story hour to thirty minutes. By the mid-1960s, even though she was now reading from books that had pictures on every page, she again cut story time in half to fifteen minutes. In 1972, because her students were unable to sit and pay attention for longer than three to five minutes, she eliminated story time altogether.

I've heard stories like this one from nearly every veteran teacher with whom I've talked, and I'm not at all surprised. You take a child whose formative years have been dominated by television—a child whose abilities are weak because television has pacified nearly every aspect of the inborn potential for competency—and you put him in a classroom where learning demands resourcefulness, initiative, curiosity, motivation, imagination, eye-hand coordination, active listening, adequate communication skills, functional reasoning and problem-solving skills, and a long attention span, and it is likely that child will have problems with learning and performance in school.

It would be a gross oversimplification to imply that television alone is responsible for the plague of learning, behavior, and motivation problems in our schools. It also would be naive to ignore the connection between television-watching and the deficiencies that characterize not only the learning-disabled child but also several generations of television-overdosed children. Keep in mind also that no other single influence has more dramatically altered the nature of childhood in the last fifty years than the TV set.

The Plug-In Drug

The addictive quality of television is equally frightening. The more children watch it, the more they want to watch. If they are prevented from watching, they often go through a period of emotional withdrawal that's stressful to them and to their parents. They become sullen, moody, and irritable. They are obsessed with television and make repeated attempts to connect with it. They become aggressive, unruly, and anxious. Frustration and anxiety build, choking off their ability to engage in constructive behavior.

When addicted children aren't plugged into the TV set, they will probably plug themselves into one or both of their parents, hassling, whining, and bored. After reaching the limits of tolerance, parents are likely to put them back in front of the TV set, hoping to buy a moment's peace. The parents don't realize that their children's inability to occupy themselves is partly a result of the time they spend glued to the tube. Television drains them of initiative, motivation, and autonomy and weakens their tolerance for stress.

Why is television addictive while radio is not? It's a matter of different technologies. Typically, live or filmed television productions are shot using several cameras, each watching the action from a different angle. The networks have found that viewers will watch the screen longer when the scene shifts from one camera to the next. So shift it does, usually at three-second intervals.

This is why small children will sit for long periods, transfixed by programs they cannot possibly comprehend. The incessant shifting of the reference point overrides the need for understanding. It does not interest children—it mesmerizes them.

Paradoxically, a child who sits staring at a television screen for several hours is adapting to an attention span of a few seconds and thus learning how not to pay attention. After over a thousand hours of this insidious training, the child arrives in a classroom, where the teacher discovers that the child cannot concentrate. Since television has never required anything of its watchers, these children don't finish anything they start. They don't know why they can't sit still, can't pay attention, and can't finish their work—they just know they can't. And so "I can't" becomes more and more a part of their self-image.

Veteran teachers have remarked to me that, as a group, children today are far less imaginative and resourceful than children were a generation ago, when childhood TV-viewing was less than half what it is today. This observation is hardly surprising. The explicit nature of the television experience leaves little to a child's imagination. In fact, it subtly discourages children from exercising their creative resources.

Over the past thirty years, we have allowed television networks to create their own myths; among them are the terms *children's program, family program,* and *educational program.* Presumably, shows like *Sesame Street* are children's programs, but watching television is not an appropriate pastime for any children, preschoolers in particular. Television is a handicap to childhood, not a help. There really are no children's programs. They exist and thrive because of parents, not children. These shows keep children occupied, but contrary to what their producers would have parents believe, they offer nothing of value. There are no programs for families either. The terms *family* and *program* are incompatible, because the moment a family sits down to watch television, the family process stops.

The terms *watch* and *together* are also incompatible. You don't watch television together. You watch alone. Regardless of how many people are in the same room watching the same show, each has retired into a solitary audiovisual tunnel. Television may not actually be spawning communication problems, but it certainly becomes an excuse for maintaining them. The more that members of a family drift apart, the more the watching of television becomes a convenient means of dutifully enduring one another's presence while simultaneously avoiding acknowledgment of it—all under the pretense that watching television is a family affair.

"All television is educational," said Nicholas Johnson, former member of the Federal Communications Commission. "The question is, What's being learned?"

On the surface, a child watching a Saturday morning cartoon and a child watching a nature show are viewing entirely different kinds of programs; one is pure entertainment, the other supposedly educational. But no one program earns the right to the term *educational* more than any other. A child watching a cartoon and a child watching a documentary on elephants are both exposed to the same educational message: You can get something—entertainment—for nothing. Children are impressionable little people. They have no way to evaluate television's insidious message and thereby resist it. They need parents who will provide the resistance for them, which leads me into my next point about the seductive effect of television commercials.

Big Brother Doesn't Have to Be Watching What Your Kids Are Watching

The American Psychological Association (APA) claims there is unequivocal evidence that young children don't realize commercials are biased attempts to sell products. Well, duh!

Psychologist Dale Kunkel of the University of California–Santa Barbara says that most television ads aimed at children are "like shooting fish in a barrel." He wants the government to ban commercials that target kids younger than nine. In light of the epidemic of childhood obesity, one of Kunkel's concerns is the influence of ads that promote junk food.

Betsy Taylor of the Center for a New American Dream was quoted in a *USA Today* article (February 24, 2004) as saying, "Where is the public policy on this? Lots of parents work two jobs, many work long hours. We can't micromanage every moment of our kids' days." (The Center's mission statement, posted on their official Web site, reads: "The Center for a New American Dream helps Americans consume responsibly to protect the environment, enhance quality of life, and promote social justice." I'll translate: "We are a bunch of meddling, Big Government–loving liberals who voted for Al Gore and worship Hillary Clinton.") Ms. Taylor obviously thinks that a second income is more important than providing children with necessary supervision.

Psychologist Allen Kanner, a consumer behavior expert, thinks parents, even those who want to, *can't* provide adequate supervision: "You've got a multibillion-dollar industry trying to do an end run around parents because you can't keep kids away from all these ads," says Kanner.

Of course you can! Willie and I did, and so can any parent who is willing to take a stand, stand tall, and stand firm. The problem is that most of today's parents are not willing to take any stand that causes their children to be different, much less one that causes their children to be upset with them. The spine is lacking in American parenthood, the very spine needed to stand tall and firm.

A mother once complained to me that her children want all the junk food and junk toys that are advertised during the commercial breaks in children's programs. She said, "I don't understand why the government doesn't do something about this brainwashing of America's kids."

In my very conservative estimation, parents *should not* want the government solving this problem for them and should resist any attempt on the part of the government to do so. Besides, "government help" is nothing but a euphemism for *government interference,* and the only parents who want the government to solve this problem for them are parents without backbones.

The APA report says children see forty thousand TV commercials a year. Really? Whose fault is that? Family spending for children has grown tenfold in the last twenty years and more than doubled in the last seven. Whose fault is that? Let's face it, folks— parents without backbones aren't going to stand up straight because the government bans free speech (in this case, the free speech of television commercials). If anything, relying on the government to do the job is going to make a parent even lazier, even more spineless.

Are junk ads on junk television a problem? Absolutely. Both junk ads and junk television either are or lead to unhealthy child behavior. The solution is stand-up parents who can say no and mean it; and as it turns out, parents should be saying no to more than just television.

Video "Games"

The March 3, 1990, issue of *TV Guide* carried an article on video games that quoted Patricia Marks Greenfield, professor of psychology at UCLA and author of *Mind and Media: The Effects of Television, Video Games, and Computers,* as saying, "Video games develop a whole bunch of intellectual abilities, like problem-solving and visual/spatial skills." Greenfield also pooh-poohed the notion that children can become addicted to video games. Commenting on the observation that some children seem to become obsessed with them, she said, "Of course, kids are going to want to play till they've mastered a game, but I would call that mastery motivation rather than addiction."

Professor Greenfield should come down from her ivory tower and talk to people like Ken and Kathy Kelly of Charlotte, North Carolina. After determining that they would never purchase a video game unit for their five-year-old son, Kenny, they finally relented and bought him a Nintendo system. Here's what the Kellys had to say about their decision.

We had two rules: Kenny was to share with his sister, and they could play for forty minutes a day. After just a few days, we began seeing changes in Kenny's behavior. He became irritable and bossy. He would get very upset—crying, stomping his feet—when he couldn't get to the next level in Super Mario. He constantly tried to sneak additional time, and there were several nights when we awakened at three o'clock in the morning to find him playing Nintendo.

Kenny also began to balk at going to school. When we dropped him off, he would start crying and screaming. On several occasions, his teachers had to help peel him out of the car. He also started fighting with his classmates and sassing his teachers. He was belligerent with us and our babysitter.

We couldn't figure out what was the matter. We were almost at the end of our rope when I read about a situation in your book that was very similar to our own, so we removed the Nintendo from the house and told Kenny it was broken. Within a few days, Kenny was back. No more tantrums, no more belligerent, sassy behavior, and he started happily going to school. Needless to say, the unit will never be "fixed," and we'll happily go back to being the only house in the neighborhood without one.

The Kellys' experience could be dismissed if it was an isolated case, but it isn't. Over the past few years, several hundred parents (no exaggeration) have written me concerning similar video-game–related horror stories. These tales don't sound like mastery motivation to me. I've been around enough addicts and enough highly motivated people to know the difference.

Video games are not really games at all. They provoke high levels of stress and are, indeed, addictive in the sense that many children become obsessed with constantly increasing their scores, or skill levels, as they are deceptively termed. Compared to the harm they cause, the contention that video games improve certain problem-solving and visual/perceptual skills rates a big "So what?" Unfortunately, it's what many parents want to hear.

Willie and I refused to purchase a Nintendo game for our children. The children didn't like that. It could be said that they even conjured up some hate for us on that account. On one occasion, the president of Nintendo USA sent us a state-of-the-art Nintendo game system. It was the most expensive, elaborate version on the market at the time. He had read my newspaper column slamming video games as addictive and noncreative. Eric and Amy were overjoyed, but their delight was short-lived because we put the unopened box in the attic, where it stayed for more than twenty years. A year ago, I gave it to my son-in-law, who'd told me vintage game systems were the rage, but not before making him promise not to let my grandchildren play with it. He'll keep his promise because he knows I'll make his life miserable if he doesn't. I am the Clint Eastwood of grandparenting.

When we told Eric and Amy that they would never have a Nintendo, our only television was already locked in a closet in the master bedroom, for adults only. Our kids grew up watching very little TV (mostly what they watched before ages ten and six), never playing a video game in our home, and having very few toys. They grew up to be fine, responsible, honest, ethical, moral, hard-working, compassionate, creative adults. While they are reasonably intelligent, neither of them is brilliant. I am the only parent in America, I think, who has never had a gifted child. That means nothing to me, actually. Character, not IQ, is what counts in this life.

Computer Illiteracy

A growing number of experts are recommending that young children not be allowed on computers for any reason at all. These people are not technophobes, but rather psychologists and educators who have taken a cold, hard look at the issue of kids and computers and found potential problems in the mix.

Psychologist and author Jane Healy spent several years researching the issue. She began with a favorable attitude toward educational computing but came reluctantly to the conclusion that computers stifle learning and creativity and may cause damage to both vision and posture. She has even speculated that early introduction to computer learning may also interfere with proper brain development. Her research led to a book, *Failure to Connect: How Computers Affect Our Children's Minds—and What We Can Do About It.*

"We have no evidence that stands up under scrutiny," Healy says, "that computer education is helpful for learning in children under the fourth grade."

Douglas Sloan, professor of history and education at Columbia University's Teachers College, feels likewise. He charges that companies like Intel that are providing free computers to schools have no appreciation for child development or a proper educational process. The motive behind their philanthropy, Sloan says, is money.

Healy would not introduce computers until the fourth or fifth grade. Theodore Roszak, a history professor and author of *The Cult of Information,* would wait until high school. Computers download information, he says. They do not teach children to think.

"The Internet," Roszak recently told the *Dallas Morning News*, "offers electronic graffiti. The idea that they should be swimming in a sea of information is idiotic. The essence of thinking is mastering ideas."

Said another way, computer education may be imparting technical skills, but it is not imparting knowledge. Clifford Stoll, the author of *High-Tech Heretic: Why Computers Don't Belong in the Classroom and Other Reflections by a Computer Contrarian*, says that the instant gratification involved in downloading information off the Internet—to which 94 percent of America's public schools are now connected—"discourages study, reflection, and observation."

Teachers and administrators on education's front line are seemingly in thrall of the new technology. This is unfortunate, because as has been the case with every other fad embraced by public education over the last forty years, research into computer education and its effect on child development or the learning process is, at best, lacking. In fact, much of the existing research raises lots of red flags.

Unfortunately, America's parents are also sold on the benefits of computers. If booming sales of academic programs for preschoolers are any indication, parents seem to think the sooner a child gets his hand on a mouse, the better. As a result, it has become difficult for schools, and preschools, to market themselves if they don't have computers in every classroom.

There are schools bucking the trend. The Calvert School in Baltimore is one such low-tech bastion. Calvert's students are required to write daily compositions. During a visit in the fall of 1999, I was impressed by the level of literacy reflected in compositions by children as young as first grade. Headmaster Merrill Hall told me computers are not introduced until the fifth grade, and parents of children in grades K–4 are even encouraged not to let their children use computers at home.

If what I saw at Calvert is any indication, Healy, Roszak, and Stoll are right. Computers and the Internet are certainly more impressive than libraries, pens, and paper, but education is not about impressive technology. It's about acquiring knowledge and learning to think, in which case libraries, pens, and paper are the clear winners, hands down.

Questions?

Q: What guidelines do you recommend to help parents decide how much television to let children watch?

A: I don't believe there's any justification for letting a preschool child watch any television at all. In fact, I think it makes sense to keep a child completely away from television until he has learned to read, reads fairly well, and enjoys reading. For most children, that point will be reached between the third and fifth grades. Once literacy has been fairly well established, I see no problem with letting a child watch programs that represent life in a realistic manner and broaden his understanding of the world, his relationship to it, and how it works. Nature specials, documentaries, historically based movies, sports, and cultural events all fit these criteria. Such programs open up the child's view of the world and stimulate visits to the library to find out more about the subject, be it whales, baseball, or the Civil War. Regardless of the quality of the programs chosen, however, I strongly recommend that parents not allow children to watch any more than five hours of television a week.

Q: Television may not be doing anything wonderful for my two small children, but it certainly helps me get some time

to myself during the day. Besides, I still fail to see how a few hours a day spent watching programs like *Sesame Street* can harm a child's mind. Have you ever tried to keep small children entertained all day every day?

A: You are sadly mistaken if you think television is doing you or your children any favors. The more a young child watches television, the more that child will eventually come to depend on it as a primary source of occupation and entertainment. Every dependency encumbers the growth of self-reliance. When the set is off, young children who become dependent on television will seek to satisfy that dependency in other ways. Predictably, they transfer it to the next most available or receptive object or person, and Mom is usually right up there at the top of the list.

A vicious circle quickly develops. The more children watch television, the more television pacifies their initiative, resourcefulness, imagination, and creativity. When the set is off, instead of finding something else to do, they look for Mom to take over where the television left off. They complain of being bored; they whine for Mom to find something to entertain them; they demand that she become a playmate. Partly out of fear that her child will interpret any denial as rejection, Mom is at first likely to cooperate with these complaints and demands. When it becomes obvious that the child can't get enough of her, Mom looks for an excuse to turn on the TV set again, and just about any excuse will do.

There you have it. The child becomes increasingly addicted to watching television, and the mother becomes increasingly addicted to permitting it. Little does she realize that this strategy is slowly eroding the only thing that will ever give her and her child the independence they need from each other, and that is her child's ability to be self-sufficient.

What did children do before television? They entertained themselves, that's what! Weather permitting, they went outside to play. They made mud pies, built forts out of tree branches, skipped stones across ponds, played "It" and "Mother, may I?" and pretended to be all sorts of heroes and heroines and damsels in distress. They rarely complained of having nothing to do. Remember? This is the television-generation child's complaint. When are we going to wake up and realize it isn't a coincidence?

Q: **My husband and I are seeing a psychologist because of discipline problems with our six-year-old son. Chuck has also had problems in school this year, in concentrating and in finishing work. The psychologist recently told us that part of Chuck's problem is attention deficit disorder. He said Chuck's short attention span is causing most of the problems at school and is contributing to many of the problems we are having with him at home. We agree that Chuck is impulsive and very difficult to control but are somewhat confused about the attention-span thing. If, as the psychologist said, Chuck can't control his attention span, then why is he able to sit quietly and watch television for two or three hours at a stretch? In fact, television is just about the only thing that will keep him quiet. The psychologist had no explanation for that. Do you?**

A: The fact that your son can watch television for two to three hours doesn't contradict a diagnosis of attention deficit disorder. Television holds Chuck's interest in a way the everyday world doesn't because the picture on a TV screen changes every few seconds.

Not only is television's flicker highly stimulating, it also has a mesmerizing, or hypnotic, effect upon the viewer. This hook is created through the use of anywhere from three to five cameras in the production studio. Some people seem better able to resist the bait than others, but children are especially susceptible. Furthermore, television's constantly shifting perspective is perfectly suited to a child with attention deficit disorder.

Although you find that television keeps Chuck quiet, it's actually making his attention-span problems worse rather than better. He can watch television for three hours and not have to watch any one thing for longer than about ten seconds, three seconds being the norm. In other words, television is actually reinforcing Chuck's short attention span. The longer he watches, the more his short attention span becomes habit.

Where else in the real world does the scene in front of you flicker every few seconds? Nowhere. So the perceptual habits Chuck develops while watching television will be worthless, even harmful, in other environments, particularly school.

In my experience, the most effective treatment plan for children with moderate to severe cases of attention deficit disorder involves a combination of behavioral interventions along with a medication such as Ritalin to assist in impulse control and the development of a longer attention span. In addition, I always recommend that these kids be allowed to watch no more than three hours of television a week—preferably shows like nature documentaries, where content rather than production technique is the hook.

Q: Our eight-year-old son has a learning disability that handicaps his ability to pay attention, follow directions, and

correctly decipher the printed word. He's already more than a year behind in reading skills. We recently watched a talk show featuring a specialist in learning disabilities who said most, if not all, learning disabilities are inherited. Is there a way of finding out for sure whether Greg's disability is inherited?

A: The fact is, learning disabilities come in many varieties, and no one knows for certain what causes any given one. Some may be inherited, or at least related in some way to genetic factors. Even if there were a way of making this determination, I don't think bad genes would be found to account for more than a small minority.

Since the early 1960s, learning disabilities have become epidemic among school-age children in America. Many say the sharp increase is due to better identification procedures. That argument doesn't make a lot of sense. Better identification procedures don't cause epidemics; they come about as a result of them. I think we've had to put more effort into research and identification because of the increase in the incidence of these disorders.

It's interesting to note that learning disabilities are not nearly as much of a problem in European school-age populations as they are in the United States. Since we share much of the same gene pool, this would seem to minimize a genetic explanation and suggest that the reason for this country's epidemic may be largely environmental.

The question then becomes: "What are the most typical differences in upbringing between European and American children?"

There are many, but one of the most striking has to do with television. By and large, European children watch less than five hours of television a week, and American children watch between twenty-five and thirty. Can large amounts of television cause learning disabilities? Developmental theory strongly suggests it can.

A vast array of skills and talents is contained within the human genetic code. In order to activate this program, the preschool child must be exposed to environments and experiences that promote the exercise of those talents. In other words, the more creatively active the child is during his formative preschool years, the more talented he will eventually be.

Watching television is a "passivity," not an activity. It does not properly engage human potential, whether it be motor, intellectual, creative, social, sensory, verbal, or emotional. Therefore, by its very nature and regardless of the program, television is a deprivational experience for the preschool child.

Reading is not one skill, but a collection of skills. In order to learn to read well, a child must come to the task with the complete collection. If pieces of the puzzle are missing or damaged, learning to read will be that much more frustrating.

Remember that the average American child has watched four-thousand-plus hours of television before entering first grade. Think of it. Can we truly expect a puzzle to endure that amount of developmental deprivation and survive intact? Let us not forget that learning-disabled children are only the tip of the "Why Can't Johnny Read?" iceberg. Since the early 1950s, scholastic-achievement measures have slipped steadily downhill, and illiteracy among seventeen-year-olds has risen to 25 percent.

Could our love affair with television be lurking behind our national reading crisis? We may never know for sure. The question is: Is it worth the risk?

Q: Is there any truth to the idea that watching violence on television can make children more violent?

A: In the mid-sixties, a growing number of people became concerned about television's preoccupation with murder and mayhem. The question was asked, "What possible adverse effects could a daily dose of video violence have on the impressionable minds of America's children?"

Television and Growing Up: The Impact of Televised Violence, Report to the Surgeon General, U.S. Public Health Service, published in 1972, verified that children can and often do act on the suggestion, inherent in the themes of many TV programs, that violence is an acceptable way of handling conflict and other problem situations. The idea that violence on television can stimulate violence on the playground has since become generally accepted, but the so-called smoking gun, the tie that could forever bind TV violence to aggressive behavior in children, has yet to be found.

No matter. After all, the public has a scapegoat on which to hang the growing threat of juvenile aggression, and consumer advocacy groups like Action for Children's Television have a drum to beat. The networks can demonstrate their sensitivity to social issues by reducing violence on television. In the final analysis, all this brouhaha costs the networks nothing.

There's definitely reason to suspect a link between television and aggressive behavior among children. Since the mid-1950s, when television first moved into our homes, the number of violent crimes attributed to juveniles has increased more than tenfold. Over the same period, big-city public schools have become a battleground, where students fight not only among themselves, but also with their teachers. Even without a final answer from the scientific establishment, the anecdotal evidence strongly suggests that the television generation is also a more violent generation.

Efforts to prove or disprove this theory, however, might be exercises in barking up the wrong tree. The relationship between television and aggressive behavior in children may have more to do with process than content, more to do with the watching than with what's being watched.

Animal behaviorist Harry Harlow of the University of Wisconsin isolated juvenile chimpanzees in environments that offered no opportunities for play. He observed unusually violent behavior in these chimps when he reunited them with normally reared peers.

Psychologist Jerome Singer of Yale University found evidence that children who engage in frequent fantasy play are less likely to be aggressive and hostile and better able to tolerate frustration than children who do not engage in make-believe games.

Joseph Chilton Pearce, author of *Magical Child,* writes that play is the most important of all childhood activities. It is through active, imaginative play, Pearce says, that children develop creative competence, or mastery of their environment.

In his book *Bond of Power,* Pearce adds that children who are not allowed extensive playtime or whose play is restricted to forms prescribed by adults (store-bought toys, adult-supervised activities) develop feelings of isolation and come to perceive the world as a threat instead of a challenge. Anxiety causes them either to withdraw or to attempt to control the world by force. In this regard, it's interesting to note that the incidence of depression, long regarded by psychiatrists and psychologists as violence turned inward, is also on the rise among our nation's children.

While sitting and staring at thirty hours of television a week, the average American child is not playing in any sense of the term. Watching is hardly doing anything at all. If play, especially fantasy play, is as essential to the formation of a healthy personality as Harlow, Singer, and Pearce indicate, television is fundamentally unhealthy for children regardless of the program being watched.

It is distinctly and disturbingly possible that television can so isolate a child from the world (while seeming to bring the world closer) that rage or retreat is, his only option.

Q: Our board of education has just approved the installation of computers in the schools. Several questions remain, one of which is whether to make computer-assisted education available to children at all levels of instruction. As you might expect, there is no consensus on this issue. The progressives are in favor of computers at every grade level; the purists argue for a traditional education during the elementary years (K–6). We would like to know where you stand on this issue.

A: I stand slightly left of purist and considerably right of progressive. Computer-assisted education at the early elementary level (K–3) isn't sensible, necessary, or practical.

Like any other set of abilities, intellectual skills unfold according to an immutable maturation sequence. Each stage of growth develops on previous stages and forms the framework for succeeding ones. Furthermore, each stage is compatible with and nurtured by certain forms of learning. Harm can be done either by failure to provide appropriate forms or by imposing inappropriate ones.

Computers present an inappropriate instructional format for early elementary children because for the most part, a child's cognitive abilities are not mature enough before fourth grade for either the level of learning technology represented by a computer or the level of abstraction inherent to the computer-learning process.

It may not make developmental sense to put computers in early elementary classrooms, but I'm not surprised at the general eagerness to do so. It is typically American to try to pull the maturational horse behind a cart full of technological hardware.

I notice that several computer companies are pushing software for children as young as two or three, along with the insinuation that the child who isn't computer literate by the time he enters school will forever be a cultural cripple. This is the latest farce from Madison Avenue, the same bunch that brings you soaps that keep your hands looking younger longer and other equally delirious nonsense. Need I tell you that people who write advertising copy aren't interested in your child?

At a seminar sponsored by several big corporations, the question was raised, "How important is it that elementary children become familiar with computers?" The consensus: Not important. The technology is changing so rapidly that whatever children learn now will have to be unlearned when they enter the marketplace. The fact is, our public schools simply don't have the resources to keep up with the innovations. Furthermore, programming and design are the only two really marketable computer skills. Depending on the software package involved, virtually anyone can be taught to operate a computer in anywhere from three hours to three days. Computers definitely are here to stay, and schools have a responsibility to familiarize children with them, but they should not act as if lives and livelihoods depend on it.

In the history of our species, written and print communication evolved before computers. It seems logical to require that a youngster attain a certain level of proficiency in reading, writing, and arithmetic before graduating to computer learning. For instance, if we set fourth-grade achievement as the standard, some children would be ready in second grade, others not until much later.

In his landmark book *The Disappearance of Childhood*, Neil Postman makes the point that mastery of traditional literacy skills is essential to maintaining a vital distinction between adulthood and childhood. Television and other electric media, Postman says, erase this distinction and render it meaningless.

No doubt computers represent a quantum leap in human tool-making, with benefits limited only by our vision. Unless that vision incorporates and is tempered by an appreciation for what childhood is all about, we risk doing more harm than good to our children— and therefore ourselves—with this new technology. With this in mind, a few words from early-twentieth-century education philosopher John Dewey seem appropriate: "If we identify our-selves with the real instincts and needs of childhood, and [require] only [their] fullest assertion and growth . . . discipline and culture of adult life shall all come in their due season."

Q: **We recently bought a popular and expensive video game unit for our eight-year-old son. Actually, he earned it by making good grades in school. We're beginning to think we made a mistake, however, because all he wants to do is use it. We've also seen some disturbing personality changes—a lower tolerance for frustration, temper tantrums, more conflict with his younger brother, talking back to us—and wonder if they could be related to his obsession with the video games. Unfortunately, we don't see how we can take it away or even put limits on it with-out seeming to break our promise. Any suggestions?**

A: You're not alone. I've heard the same story of regret from lots of parents. I said it in 1982, when the first wave of the video game craze hit, and I'll say it again: At the very least, these devices are worthless. At most, they are dangerous. The younger the child, the greater the potential for danger. Before I go any further, I must distinguish between the video games that are included in educational software and those that are noneducational. My remarks pertain exclusively to the latter.

In the first place, video games are not toys. By definition, a toy is something that provides opportunity for creative, imaginative play as well as constructive learning. Not only are video games noncreative and nonconstructive, they're also stressful. I've watched lots of children, including my own, play video games. They don't look like they're having fun. Typically, the body is tense, the facial expression strained. Then there's the howl of protest or temper tantrum when the "Game Over!" sign flashes. If this is fun, things have certainly changed since I was a kid. I'd call this type A behavior.

In the second place, video games lead to addiction, and the "high" is a high score. The problem is, no score is ever high enough. As in a drug addiction, where the addict must constantly increase the dose in order to feel satisfied, the video-game–addicted child becomes obsessed with constantly increasing the score.

A situation of this sort can lead to exactly the kinds of behavior and personality changes you describe. Put a child—or any human being for that matter—in a stress-producing environment for long periods of time, and you're going to see negative behavior changes. Prolonged stress lowers an individual's tolerance for frustration and increases the likelihood of conflict in relationships as well as other acting-out behaviors. Eventually, the individual's coping skills break down completely. Keep in mind also that children are far more vulnerable than adults to the effects of stress.

In conclusion, I don't think you should have bought your son a video game unit in the first place, but you've raised a good point: Since you promised you would, what can you do now?

You can limit his game time to, for instance, thirty minutes a day on non-school days only. Better yet, you can tell him, "We made a mistake," and take it away completely. Perhaps he'd agree to let you sell it and replace it with something of equal dollar value but greater play value, like a new bike. Believe me, the additional expense would be worth it.

Q: Didn't your kids feel out of it when their friends talked about television programs?

A: If they did, they never told us. I suspect it was somewhat frustrating for a while, but I'm sure they got lots of sympathy from their friends. In the final analysis, losing the TV set gave them more time to socialize, and they developed not only more friendships but much better social skills. I'm sure the TV industry would like us all to believe that children who don't watch television can't relate to their peers, but it simply isn't so. Over the years, I've talked to many other parents who've had the courage to remove television from their children's lives. They all say basically the same thing: The children become more imaginative, resourceful, self-sufficient, conversational, interesting, and outgoing. I have never heard anything negative.

Q: When you reintroduced television into Eric's and Amy's lives, how did you control it?

A: Four years after taking it away, we bought the smallest color portable then available and set it on a bookshelf in the den. Every Sunday, the children went through the television listings and selected five hours' worth of programs, at least two of which had to be educational. The children listed the programs they wanted to watch and turned that list in to us. If we approved, those became the only shows they could watch that week. Substitutions were allowed but had to be cleared in advance. In other words, if they missed one of the programs they had selected, they were not allowed to make up the time later in the week. This method works because it hands responsibility for enforcement over to the child or children. Because children would rather police themselves than be policed, they cooperated.

Q: If you had it to do over, what if anything would you and Willie do differently?

A: We would not let the television-watching habit get started in the first place. An ounce of prevention is always better than a pound of cure.

301

POINT SEVEN

In Closing . . .
Love 'em enough
to do the first six.

Rosemond's Bill of Rights for Children

Article One: Because it is the most character-building word in the English language, children have the right to hear their parents say no at least three times a day, every day.

Article Two: Children have the right to find out early in their lives that their parents exist not to make them happy, but to offer them the opportunity to learn the skills the children need to eventually make themselves happy.

Article Three: Children have a right to scream all they want over the decisions their parents make, albeit their parents have the right to confine said screaming to certain isolated areas of their homes.

Article Four: Children have the right to find out early that their parents care deeply for them but don't give a hoot what their children think about them at any given moment in time.

Article Five: Because it is the truth, the whole truth, and nothing but the truth, children have the right to hear their parents say "Because I said so" on a regular and frequent basis.

Article Six: Because it is the most character-building activity a child can engage in within the four walls of the home, children have the right to share significantly in the doing of household chores.

Article Seven: Every child has the right to discover early in life that he isn't the center of the universe, and that in the overall scheme of things and in strictly earthly terms, he isn't very important at all—no one is. This will prevent him from becoming an insufferable brat.

Article Eight: Children have the right to learn to be grateful for what they receive. Therefore, they have the right to receive all of what they truly need and very little of what they simply want.

Article Nine: Children have the right to learn early in their lives that obedience to legitimate authority is not optional, that there are consequences for disobedience, and that said consequences are memorable and therefore persuasive.

Article Ten: Every child has the right to parents who love him enough to make sure he enjoys all of the above rights.

Postscript: Convinced it was my duty as a patriot, I have suggested to the Office of Homeland Security that children whose parents deny them one or more of the above rights can reasonably be classified as explosive devices and should not be allowed in airports or other public buildings. Brat screeners—"Sorry, ma'am, but we're going to have to confiscate that child"—what a concept!

About John Rosemond

John is a family psychologist licensed by the state of North Carolina, but he doesn't believe in psychology. He has long since realized that psychology is a secular religion that one believes in by faith, and he's lost his. He works hard at helping his readers and audiences lose theirs.

John's weekly parenting column has been syndicated since 1978 and currently appears in some two hundred USA newspapers.

This is his twelfth book for Andrews McMeel.

John is the busiest and most popular public speaker in his field. In an average year, he gives more than two hundred presentations across the United States. He's also spoken in Europe and the Middle East.

His real qualifications are that he's been married to Willie since 1968. They have two adult children, Eric and Amy, each of whom is married with three children. Willie and John, the children, their spouses, and the grandchildren presently live in Gastonia, North Carolina.

John relaxes by listening to good music, mostly rock 'n' roll, and mostly from the 1950s and 1960s. He thinks the Dave Matthews Band is the most overrated band of all time and that Hootie and the

Blowfish are a comedy act. Some of his favorite musicians/bands are the Rolling Stones (of old), the Beatles, Led Zeppelin, Jimi Hendrix, Steve Miller, and Van Morrison (of old). He thinks Eric Clapton is good but overrated and . . . doesn't hold a candle to Eric Gale. In April 2006, the CDs most in play in John's car player were Robinella's *Solace for the Lonely* and Dion's *Bronx in Blue.*

For more information on John, see his two Web sites at www.rosemond.com and www.parentingbythebook.com.